Night Whispers
'Contextual Tilting'
Volume 01-Q2

April-May-June

Edition 01-Revision 06

Victor Robert Farrell

Night Whispers
All current
Contact & Sales Information
Can be found at
www.NightWhispers.com

Night Whispers
'Contextual Tilting'
Volume 01–Q2

April-May-June

Copyright © Rev. Victor Robert Farrell

2019

All Rights Reserved

No part of this book may be reproduced in any form, by photocopying or by any electronic or mechanical means, including information storage or retrieval systems, without permission in writing from both the copyright owner and the publisher of this book.

ISBN Number 978-1-910686-02-7

First published in this format
March 2015 by WhisperingWord

All current contact and sales information can be found at

www.NightWhispers.com

Printed in The United Kingdom

for

WhisperingWord Ltd.

Night Whispers
'Contextual Tilting'
Volume 01–Q2

April-May-June

Dedication

This book is dedicated, very simply,

To the now four most important people

In the whole wide world to me.

My daughter Gemma,

My son Jonathan,

My grandaughter Ellie May,

And of course,

My wife

Bridget.

PREFACE

I am Pastor, Rev. Victor Robert Farrell, and these everyday Bible insights called 'NightWhispers' have long since been a global endeavor to communicate the God of the WHOLE Bible in very raw terms to very real people. This is my passion and the reason why I founded The 66 Books Ministry, who, through our 66 Cities project, over the course of the next 25 years, by the grace of God and according to His will and favor, shall be preaching consecutively from each of the 66 Books of the Holy Bible, the Gospel of the Lord Jesus Christ in 16,500 of the most influential cities of the world on an annual and ongoing basis! In this regard, these NightWhispers accompany our endeavors by providing Every Day Insights into the whole Bible.

These NightWhispers are presented in such a way as to be read each day. They are produced on a regular basis, and the 366 daily readings for each year are presented with a unique volume number. That 'Volume' year is then divided into four Quarters. For example:

> Year 01= Volume 01-Q1 | January-February-March
> Year 01= Volume 01-Q2 | April-May-June
> Year 01= Volume 01-Q3 | July-August-September
> Year 01= Volume 01-Q4 | October-November-December
> Year 02= Volume 02-Q1 | January-February-March
> **Followed by Volume 3, 4, 5, 6 etc., and the associate four Quarters for the consecutive years. I am sure you get the picture!**

The point is, that you can start any volume of NightWhispers IN ANY YEAR you wish, and AT ANY TIME you choose, because whilst these Everyday Bible Insights are fresh and relevant to each day, they are not interconnected in a way which means you have to read one volume before another. Indeed, NightWhispers are produced as stand-alone products rather than connected volumes. Therefore, if you wish, you can also consecutively read any Quarter from any Volume you choose! For example: Volume 02-Q3 might easily be followed by Volume 05-Q4, because each book is a standalone product. Got it? Excellent! So, now that I have most thoroughly confused you, may I say that along with the team at The 66 Books Ministry and Whispering Word, I do hope and pray that these particular *NightWhispers,* will be an enormous blessing to you in *revealing just a little more to you of the God of the WHOLE BIBLE.*

Rev. Victor Robert Farrell, June 2019

INTRODUCTION TO NIGHTWHISPERS

VOL 01-Q2-'Contextual Tilting'

This is our second standalone quarterly volume of NightWhispers and we hope that these particularly, and we think, very provocative readings will 'Tilt' you so much that your 'Game-over' bells start ringing loudly!

The rate and depth of change within our cultural and political context in which the church now operates means that we need both to change the way we think and also to change the way we do things, and in to do so in such sweeping terms, that nothing else will do but the 'transplanting' of our thinking into a completely different operating context. Let me use yet another metaphor here as well, for there is no available upgrade for our present system of understanding my friends. No, we need a complete new operating system installed that our thinking can run upon.. Thankfully, the Bible is always relevant, and may I say, it is become even more relevant within the new context of the coming together of multiple singularities within which the church must now begin to operate. Multiple singularities! Now then, how's that for a paradoxical statement!

To that end, these NightWhispers will continue to present the God of the Bible in very raw and very real terms and also challenge you to think very differently about the coming years on planet earth. Therefore, as you find us pursuing and applying Biblically correct truth to our current cultural and geo-political and technocratic context, you will find that not only are we not politically correct, but some of the things I might suggest for your immediate consideration, well, you might find to be just a little 'out there.' However, your children of now, and the up and coming 'Alpha' generation (those born from AD 2010 onwards) will find them to be the norm. Remember, I am a Bible believing Christian, and thus part of the biggest and most solid 'conspiracy theory' ever revealed to man, and if you are a Christian, so are you! It is your responsibility to know the unfolding of the times and seasons according to God's Holy Word for never has morality been engulfed by the selfish application of the sciences like they are today. This, is being done with purpose by the great enemy of our souls both to destroy the image of God and set up his anti-God kingdom upon this earth. 'Contextual Tilting' will attempt to address just a few of those 'inroads of our enemy.' That we might be prepared to protect the image of God and rightly proclaim the Name and claims of His so Great Son, Jesus Christ our Lord.

As usual, all we earnestly desire is that you especially check the Scriptures to see if these things are so, and also to do your own digging both there in particular and elsewhere in general. May God the Holy Spirit truly guide you in this.

Some global historical acknowledgements

Now then, I have been writing these Bible Insights for many years and I have gleaned in a multitude of fine meadows and otherwise. For me to give credit where credit is due then, would not only increase the size of this quarterly volume many, many times, but I would undoubtedly miss many more people out of that massive list of those which I tried to give credit to. It is Solomon who said that *"there is nothing new under the sun"* and I believe it! Therefore, please then take it for granted that when someone like myself, who almost sees 'cut and paste' as an unspoken gift of the Holy Spirit, says he might have gleaned from another person's work, in someplace, somewhere, and at some point in time without giving appropriate credit where credit is due, that I probably have! If this is the case, it was not my intention to rob you of any glory, but if I have, then please inform me of the same and the necessary changes and/or credits will be made. Remember, I have borrowed from everywhere, I have taken from everyone. 'Everywhere' and 'everyone;' there you go, that should have you covered!

US, UK or elsewhere-or, "How do you spell that?"

To be British, is to be somewhat like 'the last of the Mohicans.' The Britain, that is, the United Kingdom I grew up in is breaking apart. No, sadly, it is broken and never to be repaired. Even so, I am of Irish & Scottish great-grandparents, grandparents and parents, and I was also born in England. Therefore, I am British and a Celt at that. In addition to this, I love North America and the South in particular, so much so, that I feel like a British Red-Neck. Does this make me a Yankophile, or loving the South in particular (and its battle flag) does it make me more especially a Dixiophile? Alternatively, maybe I could be an Americophile or a Canameriphile? Who knows? Suffice to say, that as our nations were once only divided by a common 'English' language, (America still being the residence of the majority of our English readers,) I have tried to adopt the spelling and grammar of the Americas. In this, I have no doubt failed, and in the so doing, both mixed and matched the UK and US spelling and English grammatical styles. In doing this, I confess that I am a double-minded man, and unstable in all my editorial ways. The purists, either side of the pond, I am sure will never forgive me. The rest do not care. Either way, I need your help. So, if you spot any 'howlers,' do let me know. Email me your corrections on,

getyouracttogetherman@whisperingword.com

BIBLE VERSIONS

Ah, the Bible. The true meta-narrative of the real world and therefore all things meta-physical. Well, preferring the 'Textus Receptus' or the 'Majority Text,' I have tried to use the New Separatist Bible (NSB), which is a confluence Bible based on the 1560 Geneva Bible and the 1611 Authorized version, (Pure Cambridge Edition) when I have referenced the Bible, though where necessary, for mere contemporary clarity of course, when I have I have deviated from this norm, at that time I have clearly indicated which other Bible Version has been referenced.

NIGHTWHISPERS ARE WRITTEN FOR……..

There is so much 'devotional' material available nowadays for the Christian that a great part of me says that no more should be written. Yet I do believe that we are moving speedily to the time of the end. What devotionals are written to truly address the needs of Christians living in the approach to this period, or in this period? In my opinion, there are none. NightWhispers then, are written for those people of this darkening time in particular. Therefore, you will find that NightWhispers are battle rations that demand your time, attention, study and consideration. If you need a little ear tickler folks, a quick little cuddle before you go to bed at night, a sleeping pill even, indeed, if you have sold out the truth, your calling and your very self for ten shekels and a shirt, then these Bible Insights are NOT for you. They demand your thoughtful consideration and further investigation and ardent application. They need your time! NightWhispers are written for those seekers who are looking for the God of the whole Bible. They are written for those who hate the color grey but love black and white. They are written for those who want to know the truth, even if it is unpalatable to them. They are written for the awakened; that is, for those people who know that the darkness is alive and like a black incoming tide, is infiltrating every area of present life. They are written for those people who know that a Night is coming when no man can work. They are written for those people who refuse to be spoon-fed. They are written for Bible hungry people. They are written for those who are done with distractions. They are written for those people who have not sold out to cultural compromise and refuse to sell themselves to social niceness and religious self-righteousness. They are written for those who want to cease being unpaid social workers for the unthankful and want to love and arm the saints. They are therefore written for fighters, even that growing band of brothers who are no ragged or rag-tag remnant, but rather, are the released people of 'The Revolution,' that back to the Bible, boots on the ground, present movement of God, who are done with everything that has silenced the one true church and with the removal of its voice, have killed our nations. They are written for the sold out the followers of Christ who have at last found their proclamation voice. They are written for the rooted, fruited and flowering stump. Therefore, to all you great and holy people then, who, even in this darkness might just turn the world right ways up once more, I say then this to you this very night: ***"Welcome to NightWhispers, Volume 01-Q2-'Contextual Tilting!' "Be strong and keep looking up for your salvation draweth nigh."***

JUST A HUCKSTER

Some young preacher will study until he has to get thick glasses to take care of his failing eyesight because he has an idea he wants to become a famous preacher. HE'S JUST A HUCKSTER buying selling and getting gain. They will ordain him and he will be known as Reverend and if he writes a book, they will make him a doctor. And he will be known as Doctor; but he's still a huckster buying and selling and getting gain.

And when the Lord comes back, HE will drive him out of the temple along with the other cattle.

A.W. Tozer

(from 'Tozer on Christian Leadership,' compiled by Ron Eggert)

John 3:30 **He must increase** but I must decrease.

STILL LOOKING

Wise men speak of trees
From the Cedar to the Hyssop
Springing from the wall
From the Aspen to the Alder
Beside the water fall

Wise men speak of animals of creeping things and fish
Of birds and bees and smooth black cats
That lap the dainty dish

Wise men sing of love and capture moments in a jar
Wise men suck the juice of days
Wise men shop at Spar!

Wise men count the fallen ticks
Of old clocks running down
Wise men number muscles
That help create the frown

Wise men follow after
Wise men follow far
Wise men seek the Savior still
Beneath the wandering star

1 Kings 4:33 Also he spoke of trees, from the cedar tree of Lebanon even to the hyssop that springs out of the wall; he spoke also of animals, of birds, of creeping things, and of fish. (NKJV)

The Old 100th!

All people that on earth do dwell,
Sing to the Lord with cheerful voice.
Him serve with fear, His praise forth tell;
Come ye before Him and rejoice.

The Lord, ye know, is God indeed;
Without our aid He did us make;
We are His folk, He doth us feed,
And for His sheep He doth us take.

O enter then His gates with praise;
Approach with joy His courts unto;
Praise, laud, and bless His name always,
For it is seemly so to do.

For why? the Lord our God is good;
His mercy is for ever sure;
His truth at all times firmly stood,
And shall from age to age endure.

To Father, Son and Holy Ghost,
The God whom Heaven and earth adore,
From men and from the angel host
Be praise and glory evermore.

From 'Fourscore and Seven Psalms of David'
(Geneva, Switzerland: 1561); attributed to William Kethe

CONTENTS

Dedication vii

PREFACE ix

INTRODUCTION TO NIGHTWHISPERS xi
VOL 01-Q2-'Contextual Tilting' xi
Some global historical acknowledgements xii
US, UK or elsewhere-or, "How do you spell that?" xiii

NIGHTWHISPERS ARE WRITTEN FOR............................... xv

JUST A HUCKSTER xvii
STILL LOOKING xix
The Old 100th! xxi

| Vol 01 | Q2 | NW00092 | April 01st | 1
    NIGHT-WHISPER | **CHANGE** 1
Contextual Tilting! 1
    Jeremiah 39:2-7 1

| Vol 01 | Q2 | NW00093 | April 02nd | 5
    NIGHT-WHISPER | **COURAGE** 5
"Pearls of great price" – setting Europe ablaze once more 5
    Judges 4:8-10 5

| Vol 01 | Q2 | NW00094 | April 03rd | 8
    NIGHT-WHISPER | **FIGHT** 8
Operational Necessity-V-Politically Correct Idiocy. Or, the 'Sexodus' and the making of Muslim men 8
    Deuteronomy 3:19-20 8

| Vol 01 | Q2 | NW00095 | April 04th | 12
    NIGHT-WHISPER | **CONSIDER** 12
The bones of the elephant man 12
    Galatians 2:9-10 12

| Vol 01 | Q2 | NW00096 | April 05th | 16
    NIGHT-WHISPER | **JUDGE** 16
A day of silence 16
    Amos 5:20-27 .... *16*

| Vol 01 | Q2 | NW00097 | April 06th | 20
    NIGHT-WHISPER | **FEAR** 20
Goodness from the bones of the deranged man 20
    1 Samuel 31:11-13 .... *20*

| Vol 01 | Q2 | NW00098 | April 07th | 23
    NIGHT-WHISPER | **ACTION** 23
Dystopian devilishness 23
    Revelation 7:2-4 .... *23*

| Vol 01 | Q2 | NW00099 | April 08th | 27
    NIGHT-WHISPER | **CHANGE** 27
Smelling the flowers of fear 27
    Isaiah 28:1b-4b *27*

| Vol 01 | Q2 | NW00100 | April 09th | 30
    NIGHT-WHISPER | **COURAGE** 30
'Call the Mid-wife,' or, 'Buying your own ticket to Auschwitz' 30
    Exodus 1:15-16 .... *30*

| Vol 01 | Q2 | NW00101 | April 10th | 34
    NIGHT-WHISPER | **FAITH** 34
Germs and Jesus and the P.C.C 34
    Hebrews 11:27 .... *34*

| Vol 01 | Q2 | NW00102 | April 11th | 37
    NIGHT-WHISPER | **PROSPER** 37
How to turn a cabbage into a King 37
    2 Samuel 23:15-17 .... *37*

| Vol 01 | Q2 | NW00103 | April 12th | 39
    NIGHT-WHISPER | **FOCUS** 39

Germs or Jesus? What should be our focus? 39
 Mark 7:2-3 .... *39*

| Vol 01 | Q2 | NW00104 | April 13ᵗʰ | 43
 NIGHT-WHISPER | **PREPARE** 43
When the 'Mitochondriacs' crossed the 'germ-line' 43
 2 Thessalonians 1:7,8 .... *43*

| Vol 01 | Q2 | NW00105 | April 14ᵗʰ | 47
 NIGHT-WHISPER | **GOODNESS** 47
Free direction, free correction and free blessing 47
 2 Samuel 7:1-3 .... *47*

| Vol 01 | Q2 | NW00106 | April 15ᵗʰ | 50
 NIGHT-WHISPER | **HAPPY** 50
Job's Jemima and the trail of tears 50
 Ezra 3:11-13 .... *50*

| Vol 01 | Q2 | NW00107 | April 16ᵗʰ | 53
 NIGHT-WHISPER | **STRENGTH** 53
Served with sago 53
 Deuteronomy 23:1 .... *53*

| Vol 01 | Q2 | NW00108 | April 17ᵗʰ | 56
 NIGHT-WHISPER | **CHANGE** 56
The un-hooding of God the Holy Spirit 56
 Ezekiel 1:10 .... *56*

| Vol 01 | Q2 | NW00109 | April 18ᵗʰ | 59
 NIGHT-WHISPER | **COST** 59
Of obstinate heretics and tri-fold fetters 59
 Acts 23:1-2 .... *59*

| Vol 01 | Q2 | NW00110 | April 19ᵗʰ | 62
 NIGHT-WHISPER | **ACTION** 62
My Robot 62

Romans 6:19 .... *62*

| Vol 01 | Q2 | NW00111 | April 20th | **66**
NIGHT-WHISPER | **PAIN** 66
Broken hallelujahs 66
2 Samuel 19:7 .... *66*

| Vol 01 | Q2 | NW00112 | April 21st | **68**
NIGHT-WHISPER | **MERCY** 68
Beware of your own doomsday book! 68
2 Samuel 24:14 .... *68*

| Vol 01 | Q2 | NW00113 | April 22nd | **71**
NIGHT-WHISPER | **INTEGRITY** 71
Of preaching and pulpit monkeys 71
1 Corinthians 1:21-24 .... *71*

| Vol 01 | Q2 | NW00114 | April 23rd | **74**
NIGHT-WHISPER | **DARE** 74
A Game of Thrones. 74
Judges 9:48 .... *74*

| Vol 01 | Q2 | NW00115 | April 24th | **78**
NIGHT-WHISPER | **REPENT** 78
Find me a wriggling maggot and get me a pierced worm! 78
1 Kings 2:36-39 .... *78*

| Vol 01 | Q2 | NW00116 | April 25th | **82**
NIGHT-WHISPER | **FOCUS** 82
Words of a different kind and work of a different kind 82
Acts 20:24a,b *82*

| Vol 01 | Q2 | NW00117 | April 26th | **84**
NIGHT-WHISPER | **CONFIDENCE** 84
The pro-video vintage of God in the places of dark providences 84
1 Timothy 5:23 .... *84*

| Vol 01 | Q2 | NW00118 | April 27th | **88**

NIGHT-WHISPER | **HOPE** 88
The Solomonian solution 88
   1 Kings 11:4 .... *88*

| Vol 01 | Q2 | NW00119 | April 28th | 92
NIGHT-WHISPER | **HAPPY** 92
Of soul food, tables and smelly, story telling 92
   John 12:1-3 .... *92*

| Vol 01 | Q2 | NW00120 | April 29th | 94
NIGHT-WHISPER | **STRENGTH** 94
The orator little pleader and the enemy of the state 94
   Acts 24:1-9 .... *94*

| Vol 01 | Q2 | NW00121 | April 30th | 97
NIGHT-WHISPER | **CONTINUE** 97
Meat is murder! And other mad hyperbole 97
   1 Corinthians 8:13 .... *97*

PAUSE FOR PRAYER | 66CITIES 101

| Vol 01 | Q2 | NW00122 | May 01st | 103
NIGHT-WHISPER | **PROSPER** 103
Six quid and six silver spoons 103
   Luke 18:22-23 .... *103*

| Vol 01 | Q2 | NW00123 | May 02nd | 106
NIGHT-WHISPER | **CONTINUE** 106
Sinister sinners and shining sons 106
   1 Thessalonians 2:11 .... *106*

| Vol 01 | Q2 | NW00124 | May 03rd | 109
NIGHT-WHISPER | **HAPPY** 109
The garage of the joy wagon 109
   1 Chronicles 16:26,27 .... *109*

| Vol 01 | Q2 | NW00125 | May 04th | 112

NIGHT-WHISPER | **SEE** 112
The clang of symbols **112**
    Revelation 17:3-6 .... *112*

| Vol 01 | Q2 | NW00126 | May 05th | **115**
NIGHT-WHISPER | **RESCUE** 115
The real resurrectionists **115**
    Hebrews 13:20-21 .... *115*

| Vol 01 | Q2 | NW00127 | May 06th | **117**
NIGHT-WHISPER | **HAPPY** 117
The whirling dervish of Sunny Delight **117**
    James 1:2-3 .... *117*

| Vol 01 | Q2 | NW00128 | May 07th | **120**
NIGHT-WHISPER | **FEAR** 120
God the gravedigger **120**
    Nahum 1:14 .... *120*

| Vol 01 | Q2 | NW00129 | May 08th | **122**
NIGHT-WHISPER | **REAL** 122
A stir of echoes **122**
    Genesis 27:22 .... *122*

| Vol 01 | Q2 | NW00130 | May 09th | **124**
NIGHT-WHISPER | **BE** 124
The cotillion of smelly corpses and cleaned up cadavers **124**
    Numbers 9:6 .... *124*

| Vol 01 | Q2 | NW00131 | May 10th | **127**
NIGHT-WHISPER | **FIGHT** 127
Rightly using conception control, abortion and infanticide **127**
    James 1:15 .... *127*

| Vol 01 | Q2 | NW00132 | May 11th | **130**
NIGHT-WHISPER | **OBEY** 130
When your stomach feels dismal **130**

1 Peter 1:10-12 .... *130*

| Vol 01 | Q2 | NW00133 | May 12th | **132**
    Night-Whisper | **CONFIDENCE** 132
Building on a math's lesson for moles with memory problems **132**
    2 Peter 1:10 .... *132*

| Vol 01 | Q2 | NW00134 | May 13th | **135**
    Night-Whisper | **CONNECT** 135
Five bees from God's honey hive **135**
    1 John 4:1-2 .... *135*

| Vol 01 | Q2 | NW00135 | May 14th | **139**
    Night-Whisper | **SEE** 139
The double, double cure for gullibleitis **139**
    2 Timothy 3:6-9 .... *139*

| Vol 01 | Q2 | NW00136 | May 15th | **142**
    Night-Whisper | **RESCUE** 142
Do you have demons in your drawers? **142**
    Acts 10:38-39 .... *142*

| Vol 01 | Q2 | NW00137 | May 16th | **145**
    Night-Whisper | **CHANGE** 145
The smashing of serenity **145**
    Matthew 19:26 .... *145*

| Vol 01 | Q2 | NW00138 | May 17th | **148**
    Night-Whisper | **POWER** 148
The real prayers of watching angels. Or, 'Sons or serfs?' **148**
    Daniel 4:16-17 .... *148*

| Vol 01 | Q2 | NW00139 | May 18th | **151**
    Night-Whisper | **WORD** 151
Its' time to get out the Kevlar **151**

| Vol 01 | Q2 | NW00140 | May 19th | **154**

NIGHT-WHISPER | **PREPARE** 154
The purpose of 'portals of horror!' **154**
    1 Corinthians 15:54 .... *154*

| Vol 01 | Q2 | NW00141 | May 20th | **158**
NIGHT-WHISPER | **PREPARE** 158
Lesbians, the lie of savior siblings and the seconds left 'till midnight ... **158**
    Genesis 6:1-8 .... *158*

| Vol 01 | Q2 | NW00142 | May 21st | **162**
NIGHT-WHISPER | **ACTION** 162
Dirt and the Finger of God **162**
    John 8:3-5 .... *162*

| Vol 01 | Q2 | NW00143 | May 22nd | **165**
NIGHT-WHISPER | **JUDGE** 165
Keeping 'IT' in the family **165**
    1 Corinthians 6:3-8 .... *165*

| Vol 01 | Q2 | NW00144 | May 23rd | **170**
NIGHT-WHISPER | **CHANGE** 170
Cold chicken and gluten free bread **170**
    Isaiah 5:1 NKJV *170*

| Vol 01 | Q2 | NW00145 | May 24th | **175**
NIGHT-WHISPER | **COURAGE** 175
Bearing your buttocks to the church **175**
    Isaiah 22:12-14 .... *175*

| Vol 01 | Q2 | NW00146 | May 25th | **178**
NIGHT-WHISPER | **TRUST** 178
What snake told you that? **178**
    Matthew 16:24-27 .... *178*

| Vol 01 | Q2 | NW00147 | May 26th | **182**
NIGHT-WHISPER | **STRENGTH** 182
Rebekah, her daughters, and HADEC3 .... **182**

Genesis 24:60 .... *182*

| Vol 01 | Q2 | NW00148 | May 27th | **186**
NIGHT-WHISPER | **CHARACTER** 186
What a sight! **186**
Luke 21:16-19 .... *186*

| Vol 01 | Q2 | NW00149 | May 28th | **189**
NIGHT-WHISPER | **BECOME** 189
Of Righteousness and respectability and 'getting over' ourselves **189**
Matthew 5:20 .... *189*

| Vol 01 | Q2 | NW00150 | May 29th | **192**
NIGHT-WHISPER | **ACTION** 192
The soon coming 'Wonders of The Lord' **192**
Job 14:7-9 NKJV *192*

| Vol 01 | Q2 | NW00151 | May 30th | **195**
NIGHT-WHISPER | **WORD** 195
How to approach God 'All-Matey' **195**
Isaiah 6:1-5 .... *195*

| Vol 01 | Q2 | NW00152 | May 31st | **198**
NIGHT-WHISPER | **INTEGRITY** 198
The sentiment of the slashing sword **198**
Acts 2:37 .... *198*

IT'S TIME TO ORDER YOUR NEXT QUARTER OF.... .... **201**

| Vol 01 | Q2 | NW00153 | June 01st | **203**
NIGHT-WHISPER | **CONSIDER** 203
The problem of Prometheus and the preparation for death **203**
Ecclesiastes 7:2 .... *203*

| Vol 01 | Q2 | NW00154 | June 02nd | **206**
NIGHT-WHISPER | **SEE** 206
From the beak of the eagle **206**

Psalms 141:2 .... *206*

| Vol 01 | Q2 | NW00155 | June 03rd | **209**
NIGHT-WHISPER | **DANGER** 209
The prophets and the profiteers **209**
Nehemiah 5:1-7 .... *209*

| Vol 01 | Q2 | NW00156 | June 04th | **212**
NIGHT-WHISPER | **CHANGE** 212
Mystery slappers **212**
Acts 23:1-3 .... *212*

| Vol 01 | Q2 | NW00157 | June 05th | **215**
NIGHT-WHISPER | **CONSIDER** 215
What's your monument? **215**
Jude 9   215

| Vol 01 | Q2 | NW00158 | June 06th | **217**
NIGHT-WHISPER | **PREPARE** 217
Getting rid of your secret prayer language **217**
Luke 18:1 .... *217*

| Vol 01 | Q2 | NW00159 | June 07th | **220**
NIGHT-WHISPER | **CHOOSE** 220
Another woman – another well **220**
2 Samuel 17:17-20 .... *220*

| Vol 01 | Q2 | NW00160 | June 08th | **222**
NIGHT-WHISPER | **RESCUE** 222
Below bastards – the position of the pariah people **222**
Joshua 9:22-27 .... *222*

| Vol 01 | Q2 | NW00161 | June 09th | **225**
NIGHT-WHISPER | **CHANGE** 225
Rizpah and the hanging of red meat **225**
2 Samuel 21:11-14 .... *225*

| Vol 01 | Q2 | NW00162 | June 10th | **228**

NIGHT-WHISPER | **INTEGRITY** 228
Baby got Babylon **228**
    Revelation 17:1-2 ....*228*

| Vol 01 | Q2 | NW00163 | June 11th | **231**
NIGHT-WHISPER | **CARE** 231
The "physog's" of three women at a window **231**
    2 Samuel 6:16 ....*231*

| Vol 01 | Q2 | NW00164 | June 12th | **233**
NIGHT-WHISPER | **BELIEVE** 233
Frankly, she was wrong **233**
    Romans 7:18-19 ....*233*

| Vol 01 | Q2 | NW00165 | June 13th | **235**
NIGHT-WHISPER | **PREPARE** 235
Wonder down the wire **235**
    Matthew 6:6 ....*235*

| Vol 01 | Q2 | NW00166 | June 14th | **238**
NIGHT-WHISPER | **RESPECT** 238
'Oh Aberystwyth! Bring back the old, old thing 'or, 'the singing of meat' **238**
    Jeremiah 6:16 ....*238*

| Vol 01 | Q2 | NW00167 | June 15th | **241**
NIGHT-WHISPER | **OBEY** 241
The correct use of cotton buds and spiritual direction **241**
    James 3:1-2 ....*241*

| Vol 01 | Q2 | NW00168 | June 16th | **244**
NIGHT-WHISPER | **COST** 244
Of Betty Crocker brioche and tired sweaty bakers **244**
    Nehemiah 9:15 ....*244*

| Vol 01 | Q2 | NW00169 | June 17th | **246**

NIGHT-WHISPER | **OBEY** 246
The newer colossus of true love amidst a lost liberty **246**
    Deuteronomy 28:15 & 43 .... *246*

| Vol 01 | Q2 | NW00170 | June 18th | **249**
NIGHT-WHISPER | **GOODNESS** 249
Holy helicopters! Or, slipping the snares of surrounding sorrows **249**
    2 Samuel 22:5-7 .... *249*

| Vol 01 | Q2 | NW00171 | June 19th | **251**
NIGHT-WHISPER | **COST** 251
An open heart, an open house and an open wallet **251**
    Nehemiah 5:14,15 .... *251*

| Vol 01 | Q2 | NW00172 | June 20th | **254**
NIGHT-WHISPER | **CONFIDENCE** 254
The mark of the lion **254**
    1 Thessalonians 2:4 .... *254*

| Vol 01 | Q2 | NW00173 | June 21st | **256**
NIGHT-WHISPER | **DANGER** 256
Dealing with the seven dwarfs of a much diminished Christianity **256**
    Matthew 24:23-25 .... *256*

| Vol 01 | Q2 | NW00174 | June 22nd | **259**
NIGHT-WHISPER | **PREPARE** 259
Chiseled **259**
    1 Kings 6:7 .... *259*

| Vol 01 | Q2 | NW00175 | June 23rd | **262**
NIGHT-WHISPER | **RESCUE** 262
Removing the leper's squint **262**
    Luke 5:12-15 .... *262*

| Vol 01 | Q2 | NW00176 | June 24th | **266**
NIGHT-WHISPER | **CONSIDER** 266
Sticking around to taste the vintage **266**

Song of Solomon 4:10 .... *266*

| Vol 01 | Q2 | NW00177 | June 25ᵗʰ | **268**
Night-Whisper | **HOPE** 268
Dealing with "Die Falscher" **268**
3 John 4 268

| Vol 01 | Q2 | NW00178 | June 26ᵗʰ | **271**
Night-Whisper | **PREPARE** 271
Jecholia of Jerusalem **271**
2 Kings 15:1, 2 .... *271*

| Vol 01 | Q2 | NW00179 | June 27ᵗʰ | **274**
Night-Whisper | **DANGER** 274
The pantomimic caricatures of the wonderful word of God **274**
Proverbs 6:22 .... *274*

| Vol 01 | Q2 | NW00180 | June 28ᵗʰ | **277**
Night-Whisper | **CONSIDER** 277
The monosodium glutamate of the mind **277**
Joel 3:18a *277*

| Vol 01 | Q2 | NW00181 | June 29ᵗʰ | **281**
Night-Whisper | **SEE** 281
Reflective donkeys **281**
John 12:14-15 .... *281*

| Vol 01 | Q2 | NW00182 | June 30ᵗʰ | **283**
Night-Whisper | **INTEGRITY** 283
Let the juice----loose! Serve it like sushi **283**
Mark 12:37b *283*

DID YOU REMEMBER? **289**
DON'T FORGET TO ORDER YOUR NEXT QUARTER OF NIGHT WHISPERS **289**

THE MISSION STATEMENT OF THE 66 BOOKS MINISTRY **291**

MORE ABOUT 'THE 66 BOOKS MINISTRY'	293
AUTHOR BIO | PURPLE ROBERT	295
JOIN THE FELLOWSHIP OF THE BOOK	296
ANOTHER BOOK BY THE AUTHOR, VR	299
Habakkuk A Prophecy For Our Time	299
ANOTHER BOOK BY THE AUTHOR, VR	301
The 66-Minute Bible	301
AN INTRODUCTION TO 'PURPLE ROBERT'	303
Some Dangerously Different Devotionals!	303

| Vol 01 | Q2 | NW00092 | April 01ˢᵗ |

Night-Whisper | **CHANGE**

Contextual Tilting!

The increasing speed of the rate of cultural change continues to shock me. The country I was born in, together with its cultural and common history is, to all intents and purposes, gone. Open border immigration, forced multi-cultural integration, the plotted dumbing down of society, the encouraged rise of individualism without a common cultural context, accepted selfish hedonism together with the destruction of Biblical moral absolutes will mean that by 2030, in the West, we shall live in a Biblically ignorant, antagonistic and overtly anti-Christian society. The God of the Bible shall have been thoroughly disremembered, and that by design. If the Alpha generation is everyone born from 2010, then God help the Alpha generation and God help those who have to live with them!

Jeremiah 39:2-7

In the eleventh year of Zedekiah, in the fourth month, on the ninth day of the month, the city was penetrated. Then all the princes of the king of Babylon came in and sat in the Middle Gate: ...Then the king of Babylon killed the sons of Zedekiah before his eyes in Riblah; the king of Babylon also killed all the nobles of Judah. Moreover he put out Zedekiah's eyes, and bound him with bronze fetters to carry him off to Babylon.

Presently, the church is not ready for what is to come upon it. It is as blind as old King Zedekiah, who, after not too long a siege, witnessed the breaching of his capital city walls and stood bowed before the enemy now sitting in the 'middle gate.' I tell you that even now, the sons of Zedekiah and the princes of our own land are being killed before his face and his already blind eyes shall soon be popped out of his head before being clothed in bronze fetters, in which he shall be dragged and beaten into Babylon, where we shall see him no more and the land he ruled shall be left desolate. Presently, the church is not ready for what is to come upon it. "Hush! The babies are sleeping now."

The old mechanical pinball machines, both pre-flippers and with flippers, allowed the gamer to 'nudge' the whole unit to help keep the stainless steel ball in play. As a teenager, I remember seeing these machines violently nudged and even lifted and slammed to the ground by over excited youths. When the nudge became so violent that it could have damaged the machine, the front player-facing gaming board would ring erratically and white flashing lights would light up one solitary word for all the world to see, 'TILT!' It was 'Game over.' I tell you now, for the old church in the old West, regarding its present expression, the word on the board is, 'TILT.' It is 'GAME OVER.'

The church is made up of individual members, and the truth is, if we want to keep the stainless steel ball in play, then it is the members of the body of Christ who need to violently nudge their own minds. Look you now, the context of Christianity has changed speedily, rapidly, irrevocably, and none of our previous gimmicks (for that is what they all were) will work anymore. Only one thing will work, and that is a return to Apostolic New Testament Christianity.

We must first heed the voice of the true prophetic and that means it is time to wake up and realize we have been living in a fantasy land of our making and liking.

I am not talking about remnant survival in the hope of a revival here. No, this has been our defeatist fantasy and we cannot, we should not, we dare not put our trust in this anymore! No, I am talking about a remnant revolution, I am talking about thriving Bible churches and victorious Christians, I am talking about sacrificial Gospel witness, I am taking about the grass roots, boots on the ground, five-fold ministries advancing of the Kingdom of God which we need to see in our lands. For this to happen, however, the Church of Jesus Christ needs to be violently nudged and tilted herself, such that the bells start ringing and a new game begins. The old has gone friends, let us prayerfully bring in the new.

How does this tilting begin? How can we successfully start over? How can we start again before Nebuchadnezzar comes and pops our own eyes out? Well, we must first heed the voice of the true prophetic and that means it is time to wake up and realize we have been living in a fantasyland of our making and liking.

I believe that God the Holy Spirit has been 'nudging' His people for some time; however, it is obvious that the people of God have been lied to by their leadership. Sometimes, we have been lied to by well-meaning and hopeful people. Sometimes, we have been lied to by people simply wanting to keep their religious jobs, but in either event, we have been lied to. Look! God is not simply waiting for an invitation to bless us and neither is there any silver bullet revival fix for this terrible mess that we are in. It is therefore time for each individual Christian now to hear the ringing bells and see the word 'TILT!' light up on their own play board. It is game over. We need to start again.

This means that each one of you needs to truly see and understand the continually changing context in which you now are living. This is your responsibility and the greater responsibility still is that you get into the Word of God and ask God to show you 'great and mighty things' which thus far you have not been aware of. You see, God's plans need to be unfolded to us, revealed to us, yes, only God can unlock the secrets of the present and of the immediate future. Therefore, you must continually call to God in prayer and He will share with you those hidden and fortified things, which are thus far hidden from you! This must happen, this TILTING must occur in you for a deep contextual shifting is the only answer to the call of the true prophetic and it is the only beginning of any hope for remnant thriving and Kingdom coming expansion!

In our Western lands, a generation of Biblical treasure and common Biblical cultural connectivity will soon be gone. Everything has changed my friend, and you need God to reveal to you the reality, which lies beyond your present blindness. As you get into the Word of God, ask Him to do so. Test the spirits. Examine the Scriptures. Fast and pray, for the contextual shifting required of you is enormous. However, if you do not engage in this, then in fifteen years, it is your eyes, which will be popped out of your heads as you are carried off to Babylon in fetters of bronze.

> *A generation of Biblical treasure and common Biblical cultural connectivity will soon be gone.*

Listen: *'Call to Me, and I will answer you, and show you great and mighty things, which you do not know.' (Jeremiah 33:3 NKJV)*

Pray: O Lord, stay Your hand and bring us health and healing. O Lord, empower and revive Your remnant that we would become a mighty and effective army. Let all peoples of the knowing past, of the seeing present and of the hopeful future, not have to pass our nations and hiss and recall Your righteous judgment, which has befallen us. Rather Lord, let them be amazed at the vast goodness, which You have shown toward us through Jesus Christ our Lord, such that, we shall become a name of joy, and of praise, and even an honor before all the nations of the earth. Lord, let the earth hear all the good that You do to us that they might fear and tremble for all the goodness and all the prosperity that You have provide for us through the blood bought mercies of Jesus Christ. Stay your hand O Lord and turn us Your church around, amen, and let it be so.

Night-Whisper | **COURAGE**

"Pearls of great price" – setting Europe ablaze once more

Founded in 1940, the Special Operations Executive (SOE) was ordered by Winston Churchill to "set Europe ablaze" with the fires of resistance. Women volunteers for the SOE were initially used as couriers, on the grounds that they were: "less likely than men to be suspected of illicit activities."

Judges 4:8-10

"And Barak said to her, 'If you will go with me, then I will go; but if you will not go with me, I will not go!' So she said, 'I will surely go with you; nevertheless there will be no glory for you in the journey you are taking, for the Lord will sell Sisera into the hand of a woman.' Then Deborah arose and went with Barak to Kedesh. And Barak called Zebulun and Naphtali to Kedesh; he went up with ten thousand men under his command, and Deborah went up with him." NKJV

It was into the SOE's 'F' Section, which then covered France, that 'Pearl Cornioley, nee Witherington,' recruited herself in August 1943. Aged just 29 years, and after just 7 weeks of 'resistance' training, she was dropped by parachute from just 300 feet out of an RAF Halifax bomber, losing her equipment in the waters of a nearby lake!

Cornioley, cool and brave of character, was nevertheless previously determined by her seniors to not have the temperament and abilities to qualify as leadership material. However, after the capture of the then leader of the Maquis (the French resistance) to which she had been assigned, London, nevertheless, divided the remaining force into two units, placing Pearl at the head of the one they code named 'Wrestler.'

Wrestler, numbering some 1,500 resistance fighters which later swelled to some 3,000 or more, was the group which became responsible for the death of over 1,000 combat Nazis and also boasted at the capture of some 18,000 others! Wrestler also engaged in the disruption of command and communication channels to the D Day Landings and later, they also disrupted the German retreat from France. Indeed, Pearl's leadership of Wrestler was so "ineffective" that this 'Pearl of great price' had a reward of 1 million French Francs put on her head by the Gestapo!

This woman would after the war, marry her wartime fiancé and together they would settle in France. He too was a former resistance fighter, and later worked as a chemist while she spent the rest of her life as a secretary. They each retired to an old people's home and in 2008, Pearl Cornioly herself, CBE, Légion d'honneur, Croix de Guerre, departed this life, her earthly destiny fulfilled.

> *Pearl's leadership of 'Wrestler' was so "ineffective" that this 'Pearl of great price' had a reward of 1 million French Francs put on her head by the Gestapo!*

Interestingly enough, Pearl was initially refused receipt of her Operational Parachute Wings and had to wait 63 years for them to be granted! Remarkably, she even turned down a civil MBE, which had been offered to her in place of the Military Cross which she had been already recommend for but then not qualified to take as she was a woman! Though somewhat rejected by organized religion, Pearl is reported to have had a great "sense of destiny" and a private and personal belief in God. Pearl, when asked why she insisted in joining the SOE and placing herself in such remarkable peril, replied very simply that, "There was a job to be done."

As the whole of Europe now dangles its scabby knees over the wall of that which will undoubtedly be the last dark age, for those who will hear, the call goes out again for women who will set Europe ablaze once more and resist this so quickly rising tide of darkness. Make no mistake about it, there is a job to be done and the sacrifices once required of brave women like Pearl, will also be required by you and so much more besides! However, unlike Pearl, all honor, glories, rights and rewards shall also speedily be yours through Jesus Christ the Lord.

I wonder how many Pearls of great price are sat behind a desk right now, just waiting for an opportunity to fulfil their gifts and calling and live out their destinies? I am no unbiblical egalitarian here for the Bible is clearly complementary in terms of male leadership in both the church and home, but even so dear sisters, we male leaders of the church of Jesus Christ, shall not stop you fulfilling your God approved destinies, but rather, shall be very pleased to give you all possible aid and training to do just that, and I know you Godly women will aid us men in doing the same. Indeed, speaking as a man, it shall be our honor to fight alongside you in the 'wars of the Lord,' shoulder to shoulder in the years to come and also to honor you, just as you shall be honored by Christ Himself.

I have said this before and I shall say it again, that it is my firm belief that in the Kingdom of God, the future and final iteration of God's order shall reflect the first iteration of it, in that a man shall sit enthroned at the right hand of Christ and a woman shall sit at His left. Let us all then, whether male or female, make sure we go to glory with an enemy price on our head. How many millions are you worth to the great enemy of our souls?

Listen: *"Far from the noise of the archers, among the watering places, there they shall recount the righteous acts of the Lord, the righteous acts for His villagers in Israel; then the people of the Lord shall go down to the gates. 'Awake, awake, Deborah! Awake, awake, sing a song! Arise, Barak, and lead your captives away, O son of Abinoam!'" (Judges 5:11-12 NKJV)*

Pray: Lord, set us Your people on fire again, that we might set the world ablaze once more with Your glory and Your love! In Your great name we ask it, amen and let it be so.

Night-Whisper | **FIGHT**

Operational Necessity-V-Politically Correct Idiocy. Or, the 'Sexodus' and the making of Muslim men

Do women have a killer instinct? You're kidding me right? Some of you who think otherwise need to get up to Glasgow on a Saturday night. Good grief, think about it, a woman who can murder the child in her own womb and then 'go out on the Shandy' a few nights later is capable of anything.

Deuteronomy 3:19-20

But your wives, your little ones, and your livestock (I know that you have much livestock) shall stay in your cities which I have given you, until the Lord has given rest to your brethren as to you, and they also possess the land which the Lord your God is giving them beyond the Jordan. Then each of you may return to his possession which I have given you.' NKJV

It would appear the British army is about to allow women into combat infantry units. Gender discrimination laws means they will have to. The soccer, rugby leagues, boxing and every other sport will have to eventually provide the same level playing field of male/female involvement and mutual participation. The madness of Political Correctness and the need for gender equality will drive this forward faster than you think. The criteria will be, even for the Infantry 'person,' "can they compete on the same level as a man?" There is no doubt that even without enhancement, this is possible for some women. Though as one retired US General put it, "There are a few women who can carry a pack and fight like a man but I certainly would not like to be married to them."

Soon, the infantry solder shall dress like a Knight of old. Battle armor, enhanced exoskeletons, some of which will no doubt be integrated into their body, will all be the norm for the infantry 'person' in the next 100 years. Why shouldn't women then be part of this new thoroughly integrated fighting force? Hasn't every film from 'Tomb-raider' to 'Star-Trek' been promoting and preparing us for the same? The Killer instinct of women is beyond question, but it will be further genetic enhancement, drug use, behaving like men, eating, living and training like men, that will make some women march in the infantry, shoot in the artillery and ride in the cavalry.

Yesterday's Night-Whisper was about a brave women leader of the French resistance. Indeed, just this last Sunday I had tea with Jesse, an old Scottish women whose proudest achievement was shooting down a Nazzi bomber with her 'Ack-Ack' gun. She even got a medal for it! Women can fight. Women have the pioneer spirit and leadership qualities required to do so. Indeed, it is true that men in the Christian church have been shamed in times past by women leading the way to and on the mission field. My point is this: sometimes operational necessity, the absence of men through unavailability, cowardice, or wrong choices, especially in total war, makes gender-marring a necessity. When women are put on the front line and in 'harm's way' it is nothing but gender marring.

> *Society has been manipulated to destroy the order of God and in the so doing, the image of God, and in the so doing, man and woman as distinct Biblical gender entities.*

Egalitarians will not read these NightWhispers, nor will any other person who has already closed their mind to what the Holy Bible is saying regarding gender roles, for they will have already brought to the canvas the covering paints of 'ancient,' 'outdated,' 'abusive,' 'misogynistic,' 'ingrained sexism,' and a few hundred more words besides. So, what I am about to say is not for them. No, the next few wee paragraphs are for you men and women who have not changed the Word of God to suit you or this present ungodly culture. Four things then, just or your consideration tonight.

First, be aware, that society has been manipulated to destroy the order of God and in the so doing, the image of God, and in the so doing, man and woman as distinct Biblical gender entities. From Lara Croft to Ripley, from Trinity to Katniss, from Aeon Flux to Buffy the Vampire slayer, those and a few hundred more powerful, superhuman and sexy women action heroes have been splashed over our screens, and splashed with purpose. Men, on the other hand, have been portrayed thousands of times in hundreds of commercials put out every seven minutes on our TV sets as the bumbling idiots at home. I could talk about estrogen in the water supply, and much more about the cultural feminization of men for a long, long time, but suffice to say, you must be aware that society has been devilishly and politically engineered to destroy Biblical gender roles. The nominal church, that sold out to the devil apostate body full of heretics, for its own preservation has not only gone along with this but embraced it and caressed it, even fostered and prospered it and in the so doing has filled its belfry with every black winged bat that has managed to scamper and crawl through the snotty grid over the sewer pipe of hell. And some of you are still mixed up with it! Shame on you.

Second, be aware that The Bible clearly states that men should be men and women should be women. They should retain their Biblical distinctives in style, dress, adornment, position and leadership.

Thirdly be aware that the problem we must deal with is the problem of the Bible. The more a man reads and takes in the word of God, the more he will be a man. Let me ask you then, can such a Biblical man have his little sister go a fighting for him? Would such a Biblical man see His mother going to the front lines? Could such men look each other in the eyes? Listen up now, just in case you are reading this in the future and have lost even the whiff of what a man is and how they act with one another. In my day, even when the gender war was lost, when a woman took a man to an industrial tribunal for calling her 'Darling,' men mourned for her. Should a man have ever taken a woman to an industrial tribunal for calling him 'Sweetie,' then they would have called him a 'puff' (see ancient texts for that meaning) and metaphorically speaking, kicked his backside up and down the street while laughing at him without pity.

> *Can such a Biblical man have his little sister go a fighting for him? Would such a Biblical man see His mother going to the front lines? Could such men look each other in the eyes?*

Finally, at the beginning of the 21st Century please not that some bodies are reporting of a 'SEXODUS,' even of an entire generation of young men who are literally "abandoning female company, relinquishing relationships and retreating into a virtual reality world of pornography, video games, lad culture and chemical addictions." Why? Because radical feminism, to which I say the nominal church has fully signed up, is destroying masculinity. Listen up now and listen closely: Muslim converts in the West at the beginning of the 21st century are most recently women. Women who are looking for a man. I am seriously considering that in the next twenty years, most Muslim converts might just be men and be so because they are looking for a woman!

The real church must separate itself from this compromised nominal mess of a feminized church, even if some of it does fly under an Evangelical banner. The real men who are left within the church, and there are that frightened few, must now band together and be men in every sense of the word, and I don't mean by eating greasy breakfasts and calling each other blokes! Men need to band together in acts of provision, protection and power. Forsake this present age, for I tell you, this society cannot be reclaimed and eventually it will be destroyed by God. However, people from this society can be saved and they must be saved into the Kingdom of God where men and women live and work in accordance with Biblical distinctive roles. It is time to leave apostasy. It is time to leave the world. It is time to set up our own Biblical society, even a Kingdom within a State, and what a bloody State it is in.

> *It is time to set up our own Biblical society, even a Kingdom within a State, and what a bloody State it is in.*

Consider this; Is there not something so very pitiable in the maiming of men in battle? But is there not something so devilishly abhorrent, in the maiming of women in the same? Man, be a man. Lead, provide and protect and let the Christian women in this present age, know and delight in the plan and place which God in His best order has put you. In the order of God, we men stand shoulder to shoulder with you.

Listen: *"Take a census of all the congregation of the children of Israel, by their families, by their fathers' houses, according to the number of names, every male individually, from twenty years old and above — all who are able to go to war in Israel. You and Aaron shall number them by their armies. And with you there shall be a man from every tribe, each one the head of his father's house. "These are the names of the men who shall stand with you:............" (Numbers 1:2-5 NKJV)*

Pray: Father, have mercy on manhood. Father, help us to rise above the depth of depravity of all that is culturally anti-Christ. Amen and let it be so.

Night-Whisper | **CONSIDER**

The bones of the elephant man

Someone commented regarding God, that "The invisible God is sat on a cloud somewhere, looking at people who break His ten commandments and then on their sad demise, will throw these law breakers into a molten and ever burning hell forever and forever for doing so! But He loves you! Yes He loves you and He needs your money. He always needs your money! He is all-powerful and all-perfect and all-knowing and all-wise, but somehow, He can't handle money! Religion takes in billions of dollars every year and they pay no taxes and yet, they always need a little more money."

Galatians 2:9-10

"And when James, Cephas, and John, who seemed to be pillars, perceived the grace that had been given to me, they gave me and Barnabas the right hand of fellowship, that we should go to the Gentiles and they to the circumcised. They desired only that we should remember the poor, the very thing which I also was eager to do." NKJV

I do not want to deal with the gross contextual inaccuracies of the first part of that statement, as it simply points out the two glaring facts of the twentieth century, those being, that postmodern man does not know the God of the Bible and most Christians find the full revelation of God in the Bible to be rather troubling, and so much so, most Christians don't really like Him either and much prefer the watered down version presented by pale and pink, silky slick preachers, sliding those slippery-elm like words down their throat, from behind some not so pure Perspex pulpits. No, it is the latter part of that opening statement that I would like to look at tonight, which says that, "God needs money."

Religion has always been a multi-million dollar industry and even when the leaders are not stealing all the cream, then churches of this day always present their folks with a 'vision budget,' and the top three line items, reflecting the Old Testament Temple requirements (and in this order usually) are always monies for 'personnel,' monies for 'premises' and monies for 'programs.' Local churches meeting in buildings with paid staff and programs to get and keep the pew punters in there, will always be asking for money. So, what does a leader riding a money eating machine of the churches own making have to do? Well, they have to ask! And I say, "Ask away!" Lay out your plans and get the funding in. Ask! But please my friend, in all your asking, OH God please! Stop telling people it is God that needs their money! That's just male bovine manure. It's your personnel, your premises and your programs that need the money mate, not God!

> *OH God please! Stop telling people it is God that needs their money! That's just male bovine manure*

I have been to too many vision casting meetings, building drive meetings, dream casting meetings, end of year, beginning of year, mid-year emergency meetings, all of which in the end have focused on money, and frankly I have to tell you friends that the most important item, of local and foreign missions and money for them, have NEVER been on the top three line items. Mission giving is there mind you, yes it makes an appearance, kind of, maybe, sometimes, but hey, charity begins at home and most of us have very costly local home churches, programs and well pad staff to take care of. Missions, I say MISSIONS, rarely get a look in.

Today I returned from the residing place of the bones of the elephant man, the Royal London Hospital. A light set in the continued dark area of the Whitechapel area of continual immigrant turn over. Throughout the years it has seen French Huguenots, Irish and then Jewish immigrants and now Bengali Muslims. Indeed, the 4000 seated East London Mosque also now resides in this Muslim area. It was once a former church built by a Christian company called Laing. There is no connection to what I am about to say, but even Jack the ripper did his dirty work around these once prostitute ridden and continually Gospel darkened streets. I was visiting my brother who has a ministry right there amongst the sick of every kind. As I walked out of the hospital with him, it seemed that every can carrying junkie with the saddest story in the world to tell you, seemed to know him and to respect him. One of his many friends was an old Jamaican Christian lady, who, armed only with an old collapsible table upon which she laid out her old second hand Bibles, for several years now had been preaching the word to the Muslims in that area. She has had her table over turned many times and had indeed, feared for her life on more than one occasion. Still, she continues right there in London's Yashmacaddam streets. Welcome to England, welcome to London, whose majority population is now non-indigenous peoples.

The only monies these two particular ministries have, that is my brother's and the old Jamaican lady's, are what these two good servants bring to it. They ask for no money, but simply, in the most spiritually hardest and darkest places of this old girl of a city, they spread what goodness and light they can with the resources they bring themselves. Frankly, I am not sure you could pay me enough to do either ministry! Yet, these two ministries are more intriguing than even the bones of the elephant man, which are still kept in the Royal London Hospital, who, by the way, died when the great size of his head crushed and closed his own wind pipe when he laid himself down to a suicidal sleep aged just twenty eight years.

As long as the church continues to serve itself, and finance those top three line items of premises, programs and personnel, and in doing so perpetually prattle on about money, money, money, in both the name and the need of God, it shall always lay itself open to such terrible criticisms like those contained in my opening paragraph. However, as long as my brother, my black warrior sister and people of their like shall walk the streets of Whitechapel in both simple truth and unpaid goodness, such criticism will always be confounded!

> *Those churches of vast premises, expensive programs and enormous salaries which fail in financing the great commission do all need to die. And they will. Like Laing, I wonder if they shall in the end be sold off for a £1.00?*

I have no idea of specific times, but friends, the grotesque largess of the churches' Laodicean, elephant man sized church diseased head, all laced with the grey lice of all creeping compromise, shall be finally laid down on the bed of doomed destiny. Unless we are revived, (and frankly I do not think there is anything left to revive) then I reckon we too have but 28 years before our crushed windpipe shall remove the Christian life totally from the lungs of our lost land. Those churches of vast premises, expensive programs and enormous salaries which fail in financing the great commission do all need to die. And they will. Like Laing, I wonder if they shall in the end be sold off for a £1.00?

I am never the less, optimistic for the future. For once all the Laodicean limbs have been lopped off by the Lord and the trunk of compromise has been removed from the Church, I think we can then all look for a holy stump, even the stump of the Lord which shall root and fruit and flower in triumph. I suppose my two challenging questions for tonight are these: "How big is your head and how much can you give without being asked!"

Listen: *"If My people who are called by My name will humble themselves, and pray and seek My face, and turn from their wicked ways, then I will hear from heaven, and will forgive their sin and heal their land." (2 Chronicles 7:14-15 NKJV)*

Pray: Lord forgive us for acting as Your bankers and so using Your name in vain. Lord for Your many people, just doing what they can where they can, please encourage their hearts and give them enough faith and enough stuff to get the job done. Now O Lord, what can we say to You concerning our nation except that our fathers, we ourselves and our children have sinned against You. Please turn Your face to us once more, and send the Holy Spirit across this land to do as You said, that is, to convict us of sin, of righteousness and of judgment to come, and then please remove the rot from us and if possible, then revive us again once more, for the weight of our large and rotted, most arrogant of heads has just about finished us of Lord. Root, fruit and flower Your Holy stump O Lord. Root fruit and flower. Amen and let it be so.

| Vol 01 | Q2 | NW00096 | April 05th |

Night-Whisper | **JUDGE**

A day of silence

I have been to Atlanta's Ebenezer Baptist Church and to the King Centre located nearby. Here homage is made to the man and to the actions of one of America's best known citizens, Dr. Martin Luther

Amos 5:20-27

"At God's coming we face hard reality, not fantasy - a black cloud with no silver lining. "I can't stand your religious meetings. I'm fed up with your conferences and conventions. I want nothing to do with your religion projects, your pretentious slogans and goals. I'm sick of your fund-raising schemes, your public relations and image making. I've had all I can take of your noisy ego-music. When was the last time you sang to me? Do you know what I want? I want justice - oceans of it. I want fairness - rivers of it. That's what I want. That's all I want. 'Didn't you, dear family of Israel, worship me faithfully for forty years in the wilderness, bringing the sacrifices and offerings I commanded? How is it you've stooped to dragging gimcrack statues of your so-called rulers around, hauling the cheap images of all your star-gods here and there? Since you like them so much, you can take them with you when I drive you into exile beyond Damascus.' God's Message, God-of-the-Angel-Armies. (from The Message: The Bible in Contemporary Language © 2002 by Eugene H. Peterson. All rights reserved.).

King Jr, who was assassinated in Memphis today in 1968. King, a man with feet of clay, was nevertheless, a brave man, a man of great passion and a man of great courage, probably doing more for the destruction of atrocious racial laws and advancing the cause of civil rights than anyone else in America either before or since. I speak of course, merely as a little white man from Derbyshire.

It is of no surprise that the King's Centre lists racism as one of the triple evils of vicious and cyclical violence. Interestingly though, underneath the general heading of racism they list 'homophobia' along with other actions, similar they say to racism, as a subset of one of the triple evils, so much so, that if the explanatory paragraph for racism has the word homophobia 'understood' into it, it just might read as follows, "Homophobia is a philosophy based on a contempt for life. It is the arrogant assertion that male and female are the centers of value and object of devotion, before which gays and lesbians, bi-and transsexual persons, must kneel in submission. It is the absurd dogma that male and female gender practices and roles, are responsible for all the progress of history and alone can assure the progress of the future. Homophobia is total estrangement. It separates not only bodies, but minds and spirits. Inevitably it descends to inflicting spiritual and physical homicide upon the out-group."

Darkness is very clever, in that to survive, no, even to proliferate itself, it will hitch its wagon to any good thing and then Chameleon like, will try and cloth itself with goodness, affability and acceptability, whilst Salami slicing away the true essence of what once was a good thing.

Later this month of April, school children will be encouraged to engage in a day of silence in schools to highlight bullying and harassment against these so called alternative lifestyles. Hundreds of thousands are expected to participate and the number is growing. In the last four weeks, where I have first seen a woman, having previously undergone gender reassignment surgery yet electing to keep her reproductive organs, now, despite looking like a spotty, ugly, hairy chinned geezer, pose naked, whilst being full and fat with pregnancy and secondly seen a glove puppet being investigated by the Northamptonshire Police hate crimes unit in Britain for a remark that "gypsies sold heather and clothes pegs," I can only say that the time is shortly coming when you shall visit me in prison! (By the way, my wife has gypsy blood running through her beautiful veins and when I was kid, gypsies did come to our door selling heather and clothes pegs, which my mother always bought because she was frightened of being cursed by them! A different world maybe, but factual nevertheless.)

Darkness is very clever, in that to survive, no, even to proliferate itself, it will hitch its wagon to any good thing and then Chameleon like, will try and cloth itself with goodness, affability and acceptability, whilst Salami slicing away the true essence of what once was a good thing. God might be mocked in this respect but He is not deceived and though we humans even go contrary to nature and all creation, which in itself always forces that separation between night and day, darkness and light, sinfulness and holiness, it is God Himself who will step in soon to sort out these crimes against nature. Yes, what we see is contrary to nature and the universe itself will eventually eject it from its bowels, never mind the soon and coming intervention from a very angry God. Meanwhile, encouraged by the misleading mass media and marching folk touched at some point with all the madness of these abominations, the percentage of people practicing these sins increases every year. The big question for praying and loving Christians is this, how should we then live among them, with them, even for them?

> *It is God Himself who will step in soon to sort out these crimes against nature.*

First may I say that we need to note that in the Bible, light never accommodates the darkness. It is always separate from it. So then Christian, separate yourselves from such darkness. Do not live with among them.

Secondly, we must remember that we have been delivered from such darkness and indeed, many of us are still in that daily process of deliverance. Yes, such were some of us but we have been washed and we have been made clean, no longer to live in these sinful ways. So don't judge yourselves better! But rather as forgiven, washed and delivered. So then Christian, separate yourselves from such darkness. Do not live with them.

Lastly I must tell you to prepare yourselves, for darkness is an active force, which will always seek to extinguish the light. It does this, because it cannot stand to be seen for what it truly is. Evil. Such evil never comes to the light but always tries to extinguish it. If you want to test the truth of this statement, then let your true light shine before these folks and see what happens. Nevertheless, our response to these things is in the truth trident of proclamation, separation and reclamation. We must proclaim the truth of the Scriptures. We must then be a people of separation, as we cannot afford to be found to be associated with such sins that are bringing calamity upon our nations. We must however at all costs, through the power of the Gospel and repentance and faith in Jesus Christ, offer the divine possibility of both redemption and reclamation from these most pernicious evils. I tell you now though, not many people want such redemption. Therefore, do not live for them.

Darkness will always seek the silence of such Biblical proclamation, separation and reclamation. Yes, darkness will always seek to choke the light, even if it is with a bullet through the throat. Proclaim the truth in love. However, be careful who you are found to be among.

Listen: *"The earth was without form, and void; and darkness was on the face of the deep. And the Spirit of God was hovering over the face of the waters. Then God said, 'Let there be light;' and there was light. And God saw the light, that it was good; and God divided the light from the darkness. God called the light day, and the darkness He called night. So the evening and the morning were the first day." Genesis 1:2-5 NKJV*

Pray: Lord, as the earth once again moves towards a formless, dark and swirling void, once more O Lord, cry "Let there be light!" Then O Lord, may the darkness flee away and Your glory, Your grace and Your truth be clearly seen. In Jesus name we pray, amen.

Night-Whisper | **FEAR**

Goodness from the bones of the deranged man

In 1st Samuel 11, we read how Nahash the Ammonite came up and camped against Jabesh Gilead. The men of Jabesh were not up for a fight that day, for they knew they were greatly outnumbered and also believed that they could not overcome their enemies. Therefore as already defeated men, having obviously lost their will, their strength and their courage to even engage in conflict, they therefore sued for peace, humbly approaching Nahash and asking for terms of surrender. Nahash speedily returned his price by saying to them, *"On this condition I will make a covenant with you, that I may put out all your right eyes, and bring reproach on all Israel."* 1 Samuel 11:2 NKJV Nice man. You know, sometimes the enemy would rather blind us than kill us. Look at Samson. Remember that.

1 Samuel 31:11-13

"Now when the inhabitants of Jabesh Gilead heard what the Philistines had done to Saul, all the valiant men arose and travelled all night, and took the body of Saul and the bodies of his sons from the wall of Beth Shan; and they came to Jabesh and burned them there. Then they took their bones and buried them under the tamarisk tree at Jabesh, and fasted seven days." NKJV

It was King Saul who eventually heard of their plight, rallied Israel, rode to save them and delivered them from so great a calamity and the men of Jabesh, who by now had miraculously found their courage revived that day, regained their strong dignity and found their lost respect and mislaid manhood. So, according to our text tonight who else should have the thankful impetus to ride so valiantly that night well behind enemy lines to retrieve the mortal remains of their lately deranged but once so magnificent a deliverer? Of course, none else but the once delivered and extremely thankful, still two eyed and now 20/20 vision men of Jabesh Gilead.

This Christian journey we are on dear friends, is both glorious and dangerous at the same time, but this side of heaven, it is mostly dangerous. The wrong choices we can make whilst upon the journey can allow a foothold for the enemy, which then can, and indeed has for so many, wreck the later lives of those who once had begun to march so well. Yes, as we move on along our own coastal paths, we shall see upon our own very shaky horizons, the shipwrecked hulks of those who once were God's bright sail!

I have seen too many wrecks. Like the surrounded, sad and threatened men of Jabesh Gilead they can indeed be salvaged though, but if we would be men to them in their pitiful wrecks, if we would be valiant to come to their aid and re-float them off their rocks, then let us first take good care of ourselves by never forgetting the good which God did also do to us through maybe those same now sunken saints, who, when in their more saner and spiritually strong days, also delivered us from every big bad and very mad belligerent evil which, without their intervention, would have left us half blind and broken as well. So, as we look upon their broken wrecks of far too many of our brethren let us say, "Truly, there but for the grace of God go I." Listen, don't condemn and curse your fallen leaders, but rather, pity and rescue them, for no doubt they once did you great good in their so great a past. Do not forget this.

> *So, as we look upon their broken wrecks of far too many of our brethren let us say, "Truly, there but for the grace of God go I."*

The decayed flesh was burnt from the bones of Saul and his sons and those same charred bones were then with all honor and due rites, buried in the private heartlands of the land of Jabesh Gilead, in the land of their own redemption. Let us do the same for those fallen that cannot be reclaimed. Yes, let us remove the sin rotted flesh from what remains of our fallen heroes and keep their essential structure, even the very bones of all that was once good and righteous, and bury it under the trees of the heartland of our own redemption, so that now in their death, they might still succor the root system of our own and continued spiritual growth. He who has ears to hear, him hear, and he who still has two eyes, let him watch and be careful for his own soul!

Listen: *"And Moses took the bones of Joseph with him, for he had placed the children of Israel under solemn oath, saying, 'God will surely visit you, and you shall carry up my bones from here with you'." Exodus 13:19 NKJV*

Pray: Lord, we mourn for all our fallen comrades whose sin, for whatever reason, has this side of heaven made them unrecoverable. We shall redeem their bones and remember the former days of their glory and look to the full redemptive honor yet to come upon them. Yes, with both our saved eyes we look for them in Your redemption. Meanwhile great King, help us to watch and be aware and mark well on our own sailing charts both the place and manner of their destruction that we might avoid it. Amen and let it be so.

| Vol 01 | Q2 | NW00098 | April 07th |

Night-Whisper | **ACTION**

Dystopian devilishness

Google has financially backed innumerable kick-starter companies. One of these companies was California-based '23andMe,' the firm which offered US customers details of health risks based on the gene variants they carry. Though it was banned in 2013 by the FDA from touting its genomic snake oil, sorry, from marketing its services in the USA, in 2014/2015 it came to the United Kingdom. It shall be one of many to arrive and flourish on our Alpha generation shores.

Revelation 7:2-4

Then I saw another angel ascending from the east, having the seal of the living God. And he cried with a loud voice to the four angels to whom it was granted to harm the earth and the sea, saying, "Do not harm the earth, the sea, or the trees till we have sealed the servants of our God on their foreheads." And I heard the number of those who were sealed. One hundred and forty-four thousand of all the tribes of the children of Israel were sealed:
NKJV

The estranged wife of the founder of Google, and '23andMe' chief executive Anne Wojcicki said, "The UK is a world leader in genomics and we are very excited to offer a product specifically for UK customers." In response, the UK Department of Health said it was, "behind the idea of using gene tests to guide patient care within the NHS." Did you get that? Do you see the implications for designated and allocated resources for patient care that gene testing brings with it?

This '23andMe product' offers the user a kit to test for our own genetic propensity to develop a range of diseases. In other words, this product is a kit that will 'prophecy' our likely health future and thus give the kit user (and whoever else holds the data) an opportunity to plan and prepare for it. This is nothing but the 1997 dystopian movie, 'Gattaca,' being now birthed into the new millennium, and despite Biblically errant cultural legislation, 'Big Pharma,' backed by even larger corporate entities are shaping their 'product offerings' for the new Alpha 'markets' which they are being allowed to break into. There is nothing new here and the rise of genetic supremacy is once again among us, and the financing of such by corporate fascism is clearly seen once more. Yes, big German business backed Hitler and his Arian mob half a century ago, committed ethnic genocide along the same philosophical fault lines, without German big business financing he would never have come to power. (See William L Shirer's, 'The Rise & Fall of the Third Reich.') Make no mistake about it, knowing or unknowingly, the spirit driving the current mob is bringing the last world dictator to power.

Genetic manipulation, racial segregation and racial re-creation is not new. Satan has been involved in creating a Master race ever since his pride and jealousy got the better of him when the Word made man. Satan has always believed that he could 'improve' humanity and make it less like its original designer and more suited to his enslavement purposes, and make no mistake about it, this building block engineering is not new and its previous zenith resulted in the global judgment flood, and its continued practice to even the purging of the promised land in the wars of the Lord recorded in Joshua. A final purging is coming and this time it shall be with fire.

> *Satan has been involved in creating a master race ever since his pride and jealousy got the better of him when the Word made man.*

Meanwhile, I wonder if a time is coming when your Biometric data shall contain your genetic ID as well. I wonder if a time is coming when in some way, and by some means, you shall be forced to carry this information and even be marked by it. I wonder if a time is coming when such data shall entitle you to levels of service, areas of operation, functionality, relationship, society, jobs, food and goods. I wonder if a time is coming when you shall not only be designed by others, but defined by them as well. I wonder if that time has come and the implementation of that devilish dystopia has started.

What can the church of the living God do in such a rising dystopian darkness? I would also suggest that there are seven major practical things we must do immediately:

First and foremost, we must first attend to our own DNA building blocks. In other words, Christians now must be sure of God's Biblical design for humanity. One man, loving one woman to 'naturally' produce a human, a person created in God's image. Forgo fertility treatment. If you are barren, adopt.

Secondly, not only we must be the caretakers of both natural birth but also become, like never before, the active midwives of Gospel new birth. We must understand the operations of God the Holy Spirit and the birthing of the new man. We must see and know, like never before, what it means to be born again. We must be able to clearly identify those who bear the mark of God, that flower of the fruit of the Holy Spirit. Do you know how to spot the workings of the Holy Spirit in others?

Thirdly, local churches must all prepare to effectively function in this rising darkness, and the chief way to do this is to put boots on the ground, where the itinerant nature of the fivefold ministries must once again be the connection and supply lines of the people of God. Is your church compromised? Is it in cahoots with the devil? If so, get out now!

In conclusion then, I say this night both to the church to you. BE READY!

Fourthly, others of us must now, like Daniel of old, be educated in all the arts and sciences, then infiltrate all the high levels of madness and megalomania, and be salt and life in this most unsavory machine of darkness. Be salt and light! Even today, harvested organs of aborted babies are being grown in rats for commercial use. Where are the Christian voices against this? Have we become as silent as Nazis Scientists? Christ's Nuremburg is coming. How will you be judged?

Fifthly, we must put the people of God first. Charity must begin at home. This calls for new organization, active fund allocation, and the Biblical preparation of the people of God as effective spiritual fighting 'families,' that we might thrive and grow in this dystopian demonic age.

Sixthly, and most of all, everyone one us must now see the miracles of God among us once more, even at a genetic level. We must see the rise and practice of the real supernatural. All we have seen so far is smoke and mirror magic. Let us plead that God will release the truly supernatural.

Lastly, we must learn how to happily pay the price for being a Christian. What price do you put on your own skin? What price has the devil put on your head? Have you valued yourself and your impact recently?

In conclusion then, I say this night both to the church and to you as a church member in particular. BE READY! Christian, the future is here. TILT!

Listen: *In Him you also trusted, after you heard the word of truth, the gospel of your salvation; in whom also, having believed, you were sealed with the Holy Spirit of promise, who is the guarantee of our inheritance until the redemption of the purchased possession, to the praise of His glory. (Ephesians 1:13-14 NKJV)*

Pray: Father, give me the much needed gift of true spiritual discernment. Father, give your true church a wakeup call this night, and draw Your people together in provision, practicality and power like never before. In Jesus name I ask it, amen, and let it be so.

| Vol 01 | Q2 | NW00099 | April 08th |

Night-Whisper | **CHANGE**

Smelling the flowers of fear

I bade farewell to some friends this morning as they left for a few of well-earned days of relaxation in the Lake District and in particular, Ullswater, Windermere and Cockermouth. I returned home via an area of Brighton called "Poets Corner," driving past both Coleridge and Wordsworth Streets, both named after the founding poets of the English Romantic movement. Today of course, is Wordsworth's birthday, born 1790, in Cockermouth and who isn't familiar with his poem entitled 'Daffodils,' written no doubt from images he saw around Ullswater, whose first line also begins, "I wandered lonely as a cloud." Within the poem, the happy memories of the daffodils Wordsworth had seen had been so etched onto his spirit, that he was able to later call them forth in better times of fuller reflection, and the beauty and joy of that recall, would cause his soul to dance with joy. If he hadn't fathered five or six kids, I would have worried about Wordsworth!

As Wordsworth poetically called upon nature for the remembrance of joy, so Isaiah, that great poet prophet of old, takes the mind of the Hebrews to some flowers and verdant valleys of a very different kind. Where Wordsworth calls forth flowers of joy, Isaiah calls forth flowers of fear.

Isaiah 28:1b-4b

"Whose glorious beauty is a fading flower which is at the head of the verdant valleys, to those who are overcome with wine! Behold, the Lord has a mighty and strong one, like a tempest of hail and a destroying storm, like a flood of mighty waters overflowing, who will bring them down to the earth with His hand. The crown of pride, the drunkards of Ephraim, will be trampled underfoot; and the glorious beauty is a fading flower which is at the head of the verdant valley." NKJV

It was Omri, who had purchased a mountain from Shomeron and built the new capital city of his Northern Israelite Kingdom upon it, naming the city after the original holder, Shomeris (Samaria). This well heeled city was surrounded by garland hills and moated by fertile and verdant plains. The rebellious people of God lived here in comparative comfort and luxury, enjoying in particular, flower garland wine parties of wild wet drunkenness, whilst the dry drunkenness of pride and arrogance, disdain wealth and power, hardened both their arteries and their hearts!

God the poet Master, calls to mind these same 'pissed' up party petals and by book ending with the phrase, "the glorious beauty is a fading flower which is at the head of the verdant valley," portrays in picturesque and beautiful form, one of the most powerful descriptions of judgment the Bible has ever given! The Assyrians would soon grab Israel and like a strong and mighty, big and angry man, take the beautiful glass of Samaria, so full now of rich, red and sweet, teetering toppled wine, and smash it to pieces on the cold hard cobbled floor of judgment! Splattering its contents across her whitewashed walls for all the world to see. In our poetic text for tonight, God takes anger, tempest, hail and flood and binds them in a colorful party flower garland laid in the lap of the rich green grass of home. God in effect says "You wet and dry drunkards of forgetful and rebellious scorn, smell the fearful flowers now and behold their fragile petalled beauty, for I am coming to stomp them in the ground and grind them in the dirt." And so He did.

> *God the poet Master, calls to mind these same 'pissed' up party petals!*

We must be careful from what vine we drink and beware of its intoxicating nature, for the vine of vain glory and the flower of pride, has led to the downfall of many a gut-wet but heart-dry drunken nation.

It appears to me, in the spring of my writing, with binge drinking in the United Kingdom and alcohol consumption being the worst in the whole of Europe, that we need to remember what lies amidst these springing, swaying, yellow daffodils, especially as this physical manifestation of drunkenness is simply a metaphor for a national, spiritual organ failure! There are dark clouds on the horizon and hail in | April days. Summer's not looking good for ancient Albion, no, it's not looking good at all. Arrogant drunkenness, especially in young women is a clear sign that society is collapsing. Shall Islam bring dryness to our mouth and idolatrous hardness to our hearts?

Listen: *"In that day the Lord of hosts will be for a crown of glory and a diadem of beauty To the remnant of His people, for a spirit of justice to him who sits in judgment, and for strength to those who turn back the battle at the gate." Isaiah 28:5-6 NKJV*

Pray: Lord, have mercy upon our drunkenness both wet and dry and hold back Your wrath from our rebellious lands. Please Lord in Your anger, remember mercy, in Jesus name we pray, amen.

| Vol 01 | Q2 | NW00100 | April 09th |

Night-Whisper | **COURAGE**

'Call the Mid-wife,' or, 'Buying your own ticket to Auschwitz'

This Auschwitz guard never actually worked in the crematoriums. No, he never actually burned the one million human beings murdered there nor got involved with the corpses 'processed' through the crematorium. Let me say again that this same guard also never administered Zyklon B to the naked screaming women and children who were supposedly taking a delousing shower. No, and he never pulled the bloodied and broken fingernails out of the walls there either. No, this guard was merely an administrative assistant and sometime motor pool lackey. That's all. Out of the 7,000 guards involved in Auschwitz, he really had little hands on in murder. He was just part of the murder machine. That's all.

Exodus 1:15-16

Then the king of Egypt spoke to the Hebrew midwives, of whom the name of one was Shiphrah and the name of the other Puah; and he said, "When you do the duties of a midwife for the Hebrew women, and see them on the birthstools, if it is a son, then you shall kill him; but if it is a daughter, then she shall live."
NKJV

In Britain, the National Health Service is a murder machine for those who want abortions. Yes, the murdered babies little offal corpses are not only used in the incinerators to help heat the rest of the hospital, but now formerly 'Live birth Labor wards' are also utilized to both murder many babies as well as deliver those babies the mother wants to keep. Human babies, that is, baby human beings, are designed or disposed of at the whim of the woman who is pregnant all aided now by the N.H.S. (The National health Service) and the British Pregnancy Advice Service, that S.S. of the sexual services division of the anti-God, anti-human movement. What babies they do not burn might will be harvested for organ donation.

It was two Scottish Roman Catholic mid-wives, who, finding that abortions were now being brought to the labor wards of their hospital in Glasgow, wanted to go beyond the present 'protection' by law of forced participation in the murder, to going further and even getting legal protection from being involved in the murder machine itself by being a lackey in the motor pool and administration departments of the murder machinery. In 2015, the British pregnancy S.S. and the N.H.S. are rejoicing today however, for the British High Court has now ruled that these Mid-Wives in Scotland should have to support staff and the whole after care murder machine for those women who have recently had their babies sacrificed to selfishness. These Scottish Mid-Wives are saddened today and have already left their posts for they know that even though your hands are not popping in the Zyklon B or burning thousands of murdered corpses every 24 hours, you are still a guard in Auschwitz. You are still part of the murder machine. You are stull accountable.

> *Whether your hands are popping in the Zyklon B or burning thousands of murdered corpses every 24 hours, you are still a guard in Auschwitz. You are still part of the murder machine.*

Now tell me, how can a Christian be part of a machine that murders babies, euthanizes the old and the depressed and distressed and infanticides the unwanted children of our land? I ask this question now for the time is almost upon us when this will be the norm. Therefore, I wonder if a time is not too far away, when Christians will have to set up their own health care system, financial system, and defense department. The time is long past when we Christians say NO to these things.

Two things then for your prayerful consideration this dark night:

First, consider this, that once a male prostitute becomes a Christian, should they continue on a whoring? Can they do so providing that they do so in the precious name of Jesus whilst loving their client more and glorifying God in all they do? To many of you the very idea of this would be preposterous! Yet to some of you, however, I dread to say that because your mind and heart has been so infiltrated by the world, you are already considering the justifying of the same by trying to construct an affirmative consideration of the same.

Now secondly, consider this, that once an abortionist becomes a Christian, should they continue aborting babies? Of course not! Now then, once a Mid-Wife becomes a Christian, should they take care of the murderers in the precious name of Jesus showing them love and kindness for the glory of God? Should they at the very least for the sake of their colleagues and compassion for the former mother, and for the glory of God the most, work and facilitate the operation of the murder machine? Of course not! It is preposterous even to suggest it. However, what is a person to do without a job? The murder machine you see, has now reached into non-consenting lives.

The Real followers of Christ have a handful of options before them:

The first is to not only board the train but to buy our own ticket to Auschwitz. This, unfortunately, are what many of us are quietly already doing.

The second is the respectable middle class option of choice, which is to become salt and light in our nation once again. Yes, salt and light to all sources of power and authority to win them back for Jesus. This seems like a great idea, however, I personally believe that we are passed the tipping point of redemption here and besides, I see no one willing to speak up and speak out for Biblical Christianity and pay the price of the wrath and angst of the self-righteous and outraged, political correct for so doing. No, it would appear that we love our reputation and respectability far too much to cease to be anything other than quietly circumspect about our beliefs regarding this mass murder of babies. We Christians have marginalized ourselves and now I wonder if it is far too late to get back in the game.

Whether your hands are popping in the Zyklon B or burning thousands of murdered corpses every 24 hours, you are still a guard in Auschwitz. You are still part of the murder machine.

The third is to get out of the God judged country. Ah, but where are the New England's of today? It seems that even that once promised Christian land of America is also quickly being turned into a fascist nightmare. Maybe 'there's a land down under where women glow and the men still plunder?' Maybe?

The fourth is to rise up in armed rebellion against this ant-Christ takeover destruction of our nations. In Britain, however, we presently have neither the inclination, money, materials, manpower nor balls to do this. Our cousins across the pond, however, might well be more inclined and prepared to do so. It seems the government in that land, in militarizing the local police force and training their National guard against so called 'Christian Terrorism' are somewhat prepared for this possibility. I am advocating violence? No. I am however stating it as an option, an option we need to reject. After all, it is only a hundred million babies. Who cares?

The fifth of this little handful of options, is for Christians to withdraw from all that is unholy in our lands and set up a holy Kingdom within an unholy State. I am not talking here about a ghetto, but a broad representation of the Kingdom of God on earth where true believers take care of other true believers. Whatever happens, this needs to be put in place immediately.

Though there is a need right now for another new rebellion and a Glorious Revolution, the church in Europe is in no place to bring it. In addition to this, in my opinion, waiting for God to fire His 'Custard Pie Revival Cannon' from the surface of the moon in the hope that is just might land on us, somehow, somewhere, sometime, is deceptive and disobedient to the commands of Christ, is a 'cop out option' if ever there was one! No, we need to obey the commands of Christ and become a pure and holy church, separate from sinners and anti-Christ states, loving one another in truth and practicality, and obeying the commands of Christ to go into all the world and preach the Gospel no matter what.

Let me ask you tonight then dear Christian friend: have you already bought your own ticket to Auschwitz? Let me ask you tonight, are you part of an uprising, a rebellion against the darkness? If not, you are on that long dark train.

Listen: *But the midwives feared God, and did not do as the king of Egypt commanded them, but saved the male children alive. So the king of Egypt called for the midwives and said to them, "Why have you done this thing, and saved the male children alive?" And the midwives said to Pharaoh, "Because the Hebrew women are not like the Egyptian women; for they are lively and give birth before the midwives come to them." Therefore God dealt well with the midwives, and the people multiplied and grew very mighty. And so it was, because the midwives feared God, that He provided households for them. (Exodus 1:17-21 NKJV)*

Pray: "Father, we shall have nothing to do with this murder machine." Let this be the prayer of Christian Mid-Wives. Then, O Lord, provide houses for these Your servants. As for the rest of us Father, help us to walk honorably and courageously, separately and with great holiness and honor toward You and You alone. Amen and let it be so.

Night-Whisper | **FAITH**

Germs and Jesus and the P.C.C.

The mother again looks at her grubby son just before mealtime and says, "Have you washed your hands?" With unbelievable disdain, the five year old replies, "But mum, they are clean!" Then holds them out to her to prove it. The mother, exasperated, tilts her head and says, "Now darling we have had this conversation a thousand times! Just because they look clean does not mean they are. Germs are invisible and so you need to go and wash your hands before you eat. Immediately!" Throwing down his wee toy, the boy stamps to his feet and trudges to the bathroom rolling up his sleeves as he goes and muttering, "Germs and Jesus. Germs and Jesus! It's all I ever hear in this house and I have never seen either of them!"

Hebrews 11:27

By faith he forsook Egypt, not fearing the wrath of the king; for he endured as seeing Him who is invisible. NKJV

For not a few years, I was part of a team receiving questions from around the world regarding Christianity, spirituality, and a person's personal walk with Jesus. From this often, heart-wrenching bulk of questions it became evident that most people did not know how to walk 'as seeing Him who is invisible.' In other words, they did not know how to utilize the Scriptures in their walk of faith.

We have not seen Jesus with our eyes. Though I remember when one Pastor stated this, an older member of his congregation replied that he had in fact seen the Lord and reported that, "He was a fine big strapping lad." Fair enough, but the vast majority of us have not seen Jesus in the flesh and we have not met Him yet, eyeball to eyeball. His person remains to our eyes both unseen and therefore invisible. Like germs.

However, faith believes and therefore sees, and for the Post-Cannon Christian (The P.C.C.) we see Jesus brought into focus through the Word of God, the Holy Bible. Am I saying that without the Holy Bible we cannot see, we cannot perceive Jesus by faith? By no means. However, that kind if Bible separate perception is unusual and it is not the norm, and this 'invisible' Jesus we now see by faith has in all probability been brought into focus by the spoken Word of God from a proclaimer's lips anyway. Sure, the glory of God is clearly seen in creation. However, Jesus is only seen in His word.

As an aside, the latest testimony on many a person's lips is of how Muslims are coming to faith in Christ through dream encounters with Him. I do not discount this. However, I have yet to meet one of these dream believers and such regenerations are not the norm and seem to run contrary to the commands of the Gospel to His disciples. Should we ever start to truly get behind such dream evangelism then we should pray "Lord, send the angels or go Yourself on this Your great commission, for we can't be bothered, are busy doing other things, and are frightened as well, and besides these three, Your success rate will undoubtedly be 100%" No, I do not discount it, I just don't necessarily believe it. Interestingly, Muslims are reporting Christians becoming Muslims through such dream encounters as well.

> *Romans 10:17*
>
> *So then faith comes by hearing, and hearing by the word of God.*

Spurgeon says that until we are regenerate, until we are 'born again' until we have life, that we cannot participate in the Kingdom of God. I agree, and from this he goes on to say that, *"the life which grace confers upon the saints at the moment of their quickening is none other than the life of Christ, which, like the sap from the stem, runs into us, the branches, and establishes a living connection between our souls and Jesus. Faith is the grace which perceives this union, having proceeded from it as its first fruit."* So then, to see Jesus and participate in the Kingdom, we must receive the Word of God, believe the Word of God, be born again by the Word of God, and through the Word of God receive faith to first perceive our union with Christ and then to exercise that same faith in acting on all the benefits and promises of that union.

I put it to you tonight then, that if you would see Jesus and have faith in Him, that you must receive the Word of God, you must read the Word of God, you must have the Word of God proclaimed to you, preached to you, fed to you, placed in you, recited to you, indeed, whatever way you can get it, YOU MUST GET THE WORD OF GOD IN YOU TO SEE JESUS BY FAITH, TO WALK WITH JESUS BY FAITH, AND TO PARTICIPATE IN THE KINGDOM WITH FAITH! If you do not get into the Word of God and get the Word of God into you and act then upon it, then you shall be nothing but a mumbling little five year old, running to the bathroom and muttering, "Germs and Jesus. Germs and Jesus! It's all I hear in this house and I have never seen either the one."

Remember tonight then, that above all, faith believes when it does not see because it perceives that which is written and proclaimed to be the truth. All of us must lay hold of Jesus for ourselves, by faith and by faith alone. You are members of the P.C.C. and therefore there is NO EXCUSE for not having faith. Get into the Word of God.

Listen: *But without faith it is impossible to please Him, for he who comes to God must believe that He is, and that He is a rewarder of those who diligently seek Him. (Hebrews 11:6 NKJV)*

Pray: Father, Your Words were found and I did eat them, and Your word became to me, the joy and the rejoicing of my heart. So then, help me to eat Your book that Your Word dwell in me richly in all wisdom, teaching and admonition, and give birth to psalms and hymns and other spiritual songs, so that I might sing with grace in my heart to You the invisible God, who has become my clear and visible strength and redeemer. Amen and let it be so.

Night-Whisper | **PROSPER**

How to turn a cabbage into a King

William Sydney Porter published his second collection of short stories today in 1906. *The Four Million*, is a collection of stories set in New York at the turn of the twentieth century, the title, reflecting both what Porter and the census man considered to be the number of really important people in that particular city! Porter wrote these stories under his pen name of, O Henry, mostly because at the time, he was serving five years in the Ohio State Penitentiary for embezzlement! Yes, O Henry's personal life is more full of sentiment, pathos, largess, twists and turns than any of his short stories! Sadly, he died of the effects of alcoholism in 1910 aged just 47 years. Like David of old, some drinks just need pouring out on the ground. Porter's popularity was obviously one of them.

One of O Henry's most well liked short stories is called "The Gift of the Magi." Here, a poor working couple in New York, take the two most precious possessions of their poor flat, a gold watch in the husbands case and in the wife's case, her beautiful hair which flowed past her knees and then, unbeknown to one another, they sell their personal preciousness so that they are then enabled to buy gifts for their beloved. The wife sells her hair to a wig maker and buys a gold chain for her husband's precious watch and the husband of course, sells his gold watch to buy beautiful combs for his wife's most lovely hair! O Henry's final paragraph reads, "And here I

2 Samuel 23:15-17

"Oh, that someone would give me a drink of the water from the well of Bethlehem, which is by the gate!" So the three mighty men broke through the camp of the Philistines, drew water from the well of Bethlehem that was by the gate, and took it and brought it to David. Nevertheless he would not drink it, but poured it out to the Lord. And he said, "Far be it from me, O Lord, that I should do this! Is this not the blood of the men who went in jeopardy of their lives?" Therefore he would not drink it. NKJV

have lamely related to you the uneventful chronicle of two foolish children in a flat who most unwisely sacrificed for each other the greatest treasures of their house. But in a last word to the wise of these days let it be said that of all who give gifts these two were the wisest. Of all who give and receive gifts, such as they are wisest. Everywhere they are wisest. They are the magi." "In other words," says O. Henry, "Such thoughtful and sacrificial love made these two married folks, both Kings and Queens to one another, yes, in terms of giving, they gave Royally and that in turn, made them into Royalty!"

> *...in terms of giving, they gave Royally and that in turn, made them into Royalty!*

Our text for tonight paints a most similar picture for us, for out of love, these fierce warriors present such a present to their King, that the weight of it embarrasses David, yes, the magnitude of it so humbles him, that he publicly counts himself unworthy to receive it from such giants of gift giving, from such legends of largess, that now stood in love before him. Thus, he pours the precious gift upon the dry and thirsty ground.

This dangerous exploit into Bethlehem by the troops who loved David was not made under orders remember, but rather, was made under love. May I say tonight, that duty is a fine, fine thing, ah but love, love will set duty ablaze with the fireworks of beloved devotion and turn cabbages into Kings!

I know what kind of gift I would like to receive and I reckon I know the kind of gift Jesus would like to receive as well. What Kind of Royal gifts might you give to your King tomorrow? Remember, duty is great, but love is better still, for it always pushes the boundaries of expectation and takes the recipient into the land of astonishment!

Listen: *"Many waters cannot quench love, nor can the floods drown it. If a man would give for love all the wealth of his house, it would be utterly despised." Song of Solomon 8:7 NKJV*

Pray: Lord, when it comes to loving You, my love is like stewed cabbage. Holy Spirit, come and help me turn my love for my Savior into a crisp and gold leafed salad. Amen and let it be so!

Night-Whisper | **FOCUS**

Germs or Jesus? What should be our focus?

I remember that my wife and two children had finished off the little we had and now there was no food in the cupboard. The last jar of applesauce was consumed the previous day and so I had returned to the after lunch Missionary Training Camp 'work detail' hungry. Even today, in slow motion footage, I can picture one of my portly fellow Missionary training students titling back his big fat head, the afternoon sun, like a holy halo, highlighting his fat tubby cheeks hanging around his enormous bonce as he chomped into a big fat chocolate bar after already filling his gigantic face in his apartment with lots of lovely food. "Even on the mission field," said the foreign Missions instructor, "You will find first-world missionaries and third-world missionaries all working together, their support channels separate and consequently their standard of living together being of great disparity. Get used to it." Was God trying to teach me a lesson here?

Mark 7:2-3

Now when they saw some of His disciples eat bread with defiled, that is, with unwashed hands, they found fault. For the Pharisees and all the Jews do not eat unless they wash their hands in a special way, holding the tradition of the elders. NKJV

I later remember visiting a church in London which long time back had been the daughter church of a richer Evangelical Anglican church. It was built to ensure that the lower class Christians had somewhere they could go and be together rather than mix with the upper class intellectual elite of the same Parish. In parts of that same city today, poorer Christians get their lunch from food banks, whilst the richer London Christians holiday in Lanzarote. It would appear that the early church's first attempt at a Biblical commonality of goods and family, failed abysmally before the allure of mammon, prestige and family prosperity. Meanwhile, a Christian on the African continent has had his daughter stolen into sexual slavery by Muslim extremists, whilst at the same time a middle class Christian in 'somewhere suburbia' is selling his own daughter into the

Private boarding school system to ensure she receives the best education, to get a great paying job, good position in society and a rich understanding, significant other.

It is atheist activist Richard Cevantis Carrier, leading proponent of the present manifestation of 'The Jesus myth theory' (which is the proposition that Jesus of Nazareth never really existed, or if He did, He had virtually nothing to do with the founding of Christianity) that speaks about the fact Jesus never mentioned germs. No, more than that, says Carrier, Jesus even allowed His disciples to eat without washing their hands! Where simple hygiene could have saved millions of lives, Carriers points out that, "if Jesus was a loving deity, then He would have attended to simple hygiene." You cannot make this up can you.

> *"If Jesus was a loving deity, then He would have attended to simple hygiene."*

Even so, it's fair to say that Jesus never spoke about the sterilization of implements, or how to secure fresh water supplies. He never taught how to knit mosquitoes nets, produce anesthetics, nor gave lessons in flossing to maintain good dental hygiene. Jesus left no ingredient list for painkillers, nor gave advice on crop rotations. He set up no political party, never taught on the fairness of democracy, the extremities of selfish capitalism and the dangers of socialism gone wild. He gave no lessons on healthy eating, and frankly, had the worst and weirdest record on money management ever recorded, and His pension planning was not only non-existent, but it was a crime. Quite frankly, Jesus left undone a hundred thousand others things besides these, which, over the last two thousand years since Jesus walked the earth, man has discovered for himself and by his own perseverant grip has applied to humanities greater global good, and in the so doing has much decreased infant mortality rates whilst increasing cancer survival rates. (Though to be sure, man is global mortality rate is still 100% and by the way, that terrible and obvious fact is still worthy of note. All men still die.)

Let's face the fact that there us much of benefit to humanity which has yet to be discovered which God has never told us about, indeed, what we consider to be of enormous and obvious benefit to mankind, even in the simple alleviation of humanities suffering whilst on earth, Jesus never went near in His teaching and God's Word, the Bible, is totally silent about.

In addition to this, it seems that God does not apply His own ideas of social justice, that is for man to do, and in the meantime those who do not have money, suffer at the lack of its right application. God it seems, can live with cancer, hunger, murder, rape, abuse, greed, disparity, deprivation, drug abuse, downed aircraft, burning boats, crumpled blood filled car wrecks, and observe ten thousand other evils besides all this, and still sit back beholding and doing nothing. Yes, it would appear that Almighty God cares little for this sad little planet and the transient passing of this world of warts. So then, Carriers is correct in that Jesus never taught about simple hygiene, even though He knew germs existed.

Still, the historic Jesus is no myth. Germs exist and so does Jesus the Creator of all things. Christ's main focus, both then and now' was not to improve the health, bank accounts, social justice, nor the political landscapes of the nations of the world, but rather, it was to deal with the main cause of the whole calamitous infection of sin and its enormous eternal consequences.

> *Jesus is no myth. His main focus was to deal with the main cause of the whole calamitous infection of sin and its enormous eternal consequences.*

Our total being, this body of ours, this planet, our political institutions, even the true church militant, is all corrupted by sin. It is in a state of death and eternal death at that. It is winding down. Indeed, may I remind you that the widow's son in Nain, the Synagogue ruler's little girl, and even Christ's good friend Lazarus, who were all raised from the dead remember, still later died. Indeed, they had the privilege of dying twice, which, frankly, cannot have been that nice nor that much of a privilege.

Our political situations cannot be made perfect, we need an Almighty and all good, ruling Sovereign King to come and rule us. This body cannot be fixed, we need a new one. This planet cannot be fixed, we need a new one. This universe cannot be mended, we need a new one. Therefore, the focus of Jesus was on the one main thing. The removal of sin and all its calamitous consequences! On Calvary's cross, He died for our sins and dealt with the problem and consequences of sin once and for all. The process of that redemption, paid for and made on Calvary's cross, is well under way, BUT IT IS NOT TO IMPROVE OUR LOT HERE ON EARTH! No, it is not to put a plaster on an open bleeding tumor, but rather, it is to redeem the whole damned lot! (And I use that word advisedly.)

The comfort of Christians is for them to look for a new heaven and a new earth. The command to Christians is to preach the Gospel, which deals with the main thing, sin! All else, be it ever so laudable, is, in comparison, a side show, a simple washing of dirty and germ laden hands. Look friends, we live in a world of unfixable despair and disparity, this is fact! For despite our thousands of years of self-improvement the mortality rate of mankind is still 100%. For as in Adam, all die.

In my opinion and observation, it is the church who has been most active in alleviating human suffering of every kind and I am not suggesting this should cease. However, I am suggesting that this too has been our downfall for we have moved our focus from the most important thing of all, which is the preaching of the everlasting Gospel to save people from the consequences, penalty, power and presence of sin. I wonder then, that if it comes to either focusing on germs or Jesus, that the church needs to even more get back to Jesus.

Meanwhile some are fat and some are hungry. It really should not be that way, especially in the church, the family of God.

Listen: *But if there is no resurrection of the dead, then Christ is not risen. And if Christ is not risen, then our preaching is empty and your faith is also empty. Yes, and we are found false witnesses of God, because we have testified of God that He raised up Christ, whom He did not raise up — if in fact the dead do not rise. For if the dead do not rise, then Christ is not risen. And if Christ is not risen, your faith is futile; you are still in your sins! Then also those who have fallen asleep in Christ have perished. If in this life only we have hope in Christ, we are of all men the most pitiable. But now Christ is risen from the dead, and has become the first-fruits of those who have fallen asleep. For since by man came death, by Man also came the resurrection of the dead. For as in Adam all die, even so in Christ all shall be made alive. (1 Corinthians 15:13-22 NKJV)*

Pray: Lord, help us Your church to get back to the one main and most important thing. Give us a glimpse of eternity Oh God, that we might be tilted back in this primary direction of preaching the Gospel. Amen, and let it be so. Oh and meanwhile Lord, help us to rightyl take care of the family of God.

Night-Whisper | **PREPARE**

When the 'Mitochondriacs' crossed the 'germ-line'

You scientists must correct me if I am wrong, and in technicalities, I probably am, but the 'germ-line' is in fact 'cellular lineage,' where each descended or developed cell finds its 'distinctive' from earlier cells in the series. In other words, it is genetic code passed down from generation to generation and it is genetic code which cannot be changed and cannot be 'bred out.' Well, so what?

2 Thessalonians 1:7,8

....when the Lord Jesus is revealed from heaven with His mighty angels, in flaming fire taking vengeance on those who do not know God, and on those who do not obey the gospel of our Lord Jesus Christ. NKJV

If you have a blood transfusion then you will carry the donors DNA for a period until those cells die out. If you have an organ transplant then you will carry the Donors DNA in that organ until you die. If you have a bone marrow transplant then you will produce blood with the Donors DNA for the rest of your life. In any of these cases, however, the donor DNA will NOT mix with yours and you will NOT pass on the donor DNA to your next generation. In other words, you will not 'cross' that 'germ-line.'

In 1996, a United States IVF clinic utilized a procedure known as 'cytoplasmic transfer.' This procedure mixed the eggs of two women to produce the first three-parent children. Though the procedure was halted in 2002 after 'abnormalities' in some of the offspring, up to 30 children were born, some of which are alive today. In 2015, the British government has legislated to allow an 'oocyte modification' IVF procedure known as 'Mitochondrial Replacement therapy' or, 'MR,' which replaces the mitochondria in one women's egg with the mitochondria of another women. For the second time then I ask, "Well, so what?"

It has been said that the mitochondria, that fluid surrounding the nucleus of the egg, is simply the power pack of the cell and that replacing this is akin to putting just another set of batteries in a different camera. The problem here, however, is three fold: First, there does not appear to be a one size fits all power pack, for in fact, the mitochondria DOES contain the donors DNA. In other words, the results we get might not be those we expected! Second, it is only the mother who passes mitochondria DNA on to her children. This means that, though the Mitochondriacs are infecting, effecting and modifying the germ-line of the female line, complications seem to occur more often in males, because mitochondria are only passed down from mothers, never from fathers. The effect is that any negative effects of mitochondria on a male's DNA can, therefore, NEVER be removed by generational evolution. Third, we are creating three parent children, that is, genetically modified humans that can now pass on their 'new traits' to oncoming generations. In effect, the Mitochondriacs are creating modified humans, which will pass on those modifications and all the inherited and unknown product mixing, on to future generations. For the third time I ask then, "Well, so what?"

> *We are creating three parent children, that is, genetically modified humans which can now pass on their 'new traits' to oncoming generations.*

This purpose of this new MR-IVF procedure is to remove the chance of the baby expressing a range of inherited mitochondrial diseases. It is reported that each year one in 200 children in the UK are born with any such mitochondria mutation and one in 4000 develops a mitochondrial disease. My first question then is this, "Should the needs of the few sabotage the needs of the many?" I mean, shouldn't the best response to a woman with known propensity to mitochondrial mutation be quite simply, "Do not have any children?" My second question for some of you is this, "Why are you outraged at my first question?" My third question is, "Why are millions and millions of monies being spent on 'perfecting this procedure' at the expense of other human embryos being experimented on and murdered and the whole line of future humanity being altered for the worst in unknown ways?" My final question is this, "Why are governments legislating the furthering of a Eugenics program, mostly run by Universities, which are financed by commercial companies?" There is no doubt money in this madness, but I would suggest there is also another and hidden agenda. In short, my personal opinion is that we are indeed, reflecting the times of Noah. Politically and sociologically, Biblical gender roles have been removed and the God ordered society is in a tailspin. Under the guise of feeding the hungry, our food is being genetically modified. Under the guise of alleviating suffering, humanity is being genetically modified. Under the future guise of military necessity and even cosmetic demand, we shall quickly be moved into a trans-human society of flesh and robotic melding, and some would go further and say that even our planet is being geo-engineered under the guise of countering 'global warming.' The hidden agenda is to destroy humanity and make way for the more than human.

Now, either these conclusions are the mad ravings of a much misguided mild conspiracy theorist, (and God help me, they may be!) or they are the new landscape in which the Christian and the Gospel now has to function and now has to find its Biblical bearings in. I believe they are the latter. Again, I would suggest this new age we are entering is but an old Noahic age reborn in Microchipped Eugenics. Every Christian now has to reset their navigational compass. Therefore, I will finish this Night Whisper by stating just three further things:

First, unless the Christian of this age is rooted in the Scriptures and walking in the Spirit, they shall be swept away in the sins of the world, and made partakers of this rising madness. This is no time for stupid spirituality or lazy Christianity. Every tub must stand on its own bottom and it is your responsibility to educate yourself in where the battle between good and evil is currently raging. Wake up! You are being de-humanized.

> *This is no time for stupid spirituality or lazy Christianity.*

Second, separate yourself. Wherever Christians are, they should be salt and they should be light. However, the time for expecting to halt the rot by our presence, practice and prayers is over. This God rejecting generation is intent on becoming gods and in the so doing will make way for the anti-Christ. In my opinion, this momentum is now massive and its trajectory is certain. In other words, the world is accelerating into darkness; therefore separate yourself from it right now! Get off the bus.

Third, be ready. God is coming in judgment upon this wicked generation and this time the perversion of His creation shall be wiped away, not with water, but with fire. Be ready.

I say again, now is the time to establish the Kingdom within the State and may I say again, what a bloody State it is. How then do we establish a

Kingdom within a State? We preach the word. We live in Biblical order. We break bread together, fellowship and take care of one another. We prefer the brethren. We pray for, prepare for and proclaim the coming of the Lord, the day of His wrath, and safety in the Lamb. Let us remain human, reflecting God's glory.

Listen: *For from you the word of the Lord has sounded forth, not only in Macedonia and Achaia, but also in every place. Your faith toward God has gone out, so that we do not need to say anything. For they themselves declare concerning us what manner of entry we had to you, and how you turned to God from idols to serve the living and true God, and to wait for His Son from heaven, whom He raised from the dead, even Jesus who delivers us from the wrath to come. (1 Thessalonians 1:8-10 NKJV)*

Pray: Father, give us wisdom, compassion, courage, boldness and a large set of brass balls to stand against this awful flow, amen my God, amen, and please let it be so.

| Vol 01 | Q2 | NW00105 | April 14th |

Night-Whisper | **GOODNESS**

Free direction, free correction and free blessing

So, David has at last found some breathing space and with it all a vast amount of thankfulness. This is natural for we the Christian, in that when time allows for both observation and reflection, thankfulness should arise within us. In David's case this was an active thankfulness, not just politeness mind you, but a driving and seeking thankfulness which sought to please the giver. That kind of thankfulness is both rare and special and I reckon it is this kind of thankfulness that really tickles God's heart. When was the last time you said, "What special thing can I do today, just to show God my Father my thankfulness?"

2 Samuel 7:1-3

"Now it came to pass when the king was dwelling in his house, and the Lord had given him rest from all his enemies all around, that the king said to Nathan the prophet, 'See now, I dwell in a house of cedar, but the ark of God dwells inside tent curtains.' Then Nathan said to the king, 'Go, do all that is in your heart, for the Lord is with you.'" NKJV

So David, wanting to get the manner of this thanking just right, calls his personal chaplain, someone who is God's powerful and vocal representative. Nathan. Now, Nathan is a man close to God, and therefore familiar with both God and with David. Nathan is also a man who lives and walks in that same familiarity with God which produces both a receptive harts and a good discernment in all matters. That being the case, it is not unreasonable that Nathan should quickly speak what was on his heart, that he should speak out of his unfettered and uncluttered observation of both the material and spiritual realms. So a prophetic equation goes on in Nathan's head and heart. Here it is:

God is with David + there is nothing wrong with the motive or the plan = just do it!

It's great isn't it? This equation is very Tom Jones like, you know, "It's not Unusual!" Now, I want to put it to you that unless God had specific reasons, not made known to David or not yet made known to Nathan His prophet, then the conclusion of this equation would have been God's will, yes, this would have been God's plan and this would have been God's permitted direction. Do you see the freedom in this?

> *We do not have to go to God for permission to buy every bag of sugar!*

We do not have to go to God for permission to buy every bag of sugar. We just need to apply this very simple prophetic equation.

God is with me + there is nothing wrong with the motive or the plan = just do it!

This spiritual math is of course done in the wise context of a double or better still, a triple witness. So yes, go and seek out people of wisdom, power and prophetic insight to get advice from, but let's not get stupid about it all, for sometimes what comes forth from even a triune declaration is the simply the confirmation of simple spiritual mathematics, and there is nothing wrong with that and there is everything right about it!

Now wonder of wonders, it gets even better. For God later comes to Nathan and says, "Ahem, excuse me. Good words Nate me old mate, but there is a few things you don't know about this whole thing and neither does David, so, this is what I want you to go and do and say." I love that God Himself will instruct us when the right motives, intentions and practices of our hearts are contrary to His better will and plan for us. Isn't that magnificent? Simple spiritual math is Divinely correctable! Isn't that marvelous? Isn't that freeing! When we have sought His pleasure and His will, then it is God's responsibility to show us otherwise!

Now, if that wasn't fine enough, God puts some icing on the cake for us tonight, for in the rest of the passage God in effect says to David "Don't be upset about this change in plans, cause I am so 'cock a hoop' by your heart's desire, so blessed, so moved, that this is what I am going to do for you, right back at you Dave and a thousand times better! I'm 'gonna'' build you a house." So, there you have it. Free direction, free correction and free blessing. Does is get any better than that? Not really. So, stop freaking out so much about your choices! If your heart is right, then your choices, even if they are wrong, will be lovingly corrected and blessed by God!

Listen: *"Not that I have already attained, or am already perfected; but I press on, that I may lay hold of that for which Christ Jesus has also laid hold of me. Brethren, I do not count myself to have apprehended; but one thing I do, forgetting those things which are behind and reaching forward to those things which are ahead, I press toward the goal for the prize of the upward call of God in Christ Jesus. Therefore let us, as many as are mature, have this mind; and if in anything you think otherwise, God will reveal even this to you." Philippians 3:12-16 NKJV*

Pray: Lord, it might not be kosher but what a bacon sandwich of delight all packed with lettuce, mayo and ketchup all squeezed over the top. Thank You Lord for such decisional freedom, loving correction and gracious blessing, in Jesus name I thank You, amen!

Night-Whisper | **HAPPY**

Job's Jemima and the trail of tears

The remnant have returned, and the captives have recovered to build afresh the temple of the Lord, to then most wonderfully rediscover the lost and broken law of the Living God. Redemption from terrible places is both a great and wonderful thing. Redemption from terrible places that have been the result of the finding of long lost treasures, are however places of both wonderful and a very hard things to bear. Yes, though many things can be made better than before, many other things are seen to be lost forever and though their substitute may be wonderful and right, they are and can never be replacements for the wonders that have been lost. They were never intended to be! They might like Job's new daughter Jemima, be as beautiful as the day, but they shall never be as lovely as the days gone by, and so those who knew the lost temple of old, Solomon's most wise wonder, wept bitterly at the remembrance of that most tragic loss, whilst those who knew not the loss, most greatly rejoiced at the new wonder set before them.

The church of this day slowly lays its foundations and rejoices with wonder at what might be. The aged remnant among us however, looks to the mighty lost wonders of the past, even our most recent past, and weeps.

Ezra 3:11-13

"And they sang responsively, praising and giving thanks to the Lord: 'For He is good, For His mercy endures forever toward Israel.' Then all the people shouted with a great shout, when they praised the Lord, because the foundation of the house of the Lord was laid. But many of the priests and Levites and heads of the fathers' houses, old men who had seen the first temple, wept with a loud voice when the foundation of this temple was laid before their eyes. Yet many shouted aloud for joy, so that the people could not discern the noise of the shout of joy from the noise of the weeping of the people, for the people shouted with a loud shout, and the sound was heard afar off." NKJV

Those of the now, must investigate this trail of tears which runs down old creased and crinkled chops of aged Christians, that they might understand some sense of what has been done in the past, and therefore what might be done today and what will be done tomorrow! As an older man amongst the 'emergent,' whilst others smile and sway in heartfelt joy and praise, I find myself weeping at what has gone before and has been so terribly lost to us. The sunken church, whose masthead is even now slipping beneath the foaming waves, left much to be criticized but also much more maybe that should be praised. Think about that.

> *The sunken church, whose masthead is even now slipping beneath the foaming waves, left much to be criticized but also much more maybe that should be praised.*

In the same vein, during our personal journey of redemption, this side of heaven we shall find some lost things are restored to us and in many ways are better than they were before. There shall be, however, many things that can never be restored to us this side of heaven, and yes, maybe even never. Look now in the hope of reclaiming some lost things, though our God is so very great, be careful not to get your expectations to high. Selah.

So, at each new laying of fresh foundation then, the younger, and living parts of us rejoice but the older dying parts of us, weep in remembrance and wail in deep regret as this mixed cup of ours, bubbles in the effervescence of the continuing mixture of human tragedy and Divine grace. This is life under our present sun.

So, my I wish you well tonight. May I wish you both tears and praise and with them both, a deep, deep and strengthening joy. Let go of that which can never be recovered. Have faith but do not live in false hope.

Listen: *"Now the Lord blessed the latter days of Job more than his beginning; for he had fourteen thousand sheep, six thousand camels, one thousand yoke of oxen, and one thousand female donkeys. He also had seven sons and three daughters. And he called the name of the first Jemimah." Job 42:12-14a NKJV*

Pray: Lord, if I had known it was the last time that I would hold them, see them, touch them, pray and praise with them, rejoiced in them, lived in them, loved all those laws, all those precepts, all those promises, all those people and all those relationships, then I would never have let them go. Yet let them go we did. Have mercy then upon us O Lord our God and with tears and with rejoicing and with deep, deep strengthening joy, let us lay the foundations of that which is to come and in expectant hope, leave the restoration of all those former long lost things, in Your most gloriously good and most capable of hands. Amen.

Night-Whisper | **STRENGTH**

Served with sago

They disembarked the ship at "Risk Point" on the River Fly and were invited by the fierce Tribesmen into their longhouse for a meal. Little did they know that they were in fact the main ingredient of that meal. In just a few moments the stone clubs smashed into the back of their heads and then just as quickly, a bone dagger was thrust downwards into their gullets and their heads immediately sawn off their bodies with a bamboo knife. The headless corpses were then given to the women of the tribe, the flesh of which was removed and then cooked and mixed with sago, which in turn, was consumed with gladness that very day. It was via this most terrible route, that the younger missionary, Oliver Tomkins and the sixty-year-old walking legend of Rev James Chalmers (Tamate, the Great Heart of Papua New Guinea,) entered into heaven.

Deuteronomy 23:1

"He who is emasculated by crushing or mutilation shall not enter the assembly of the Lord."
NKJV

Chalmers was known as "Tamate," simply because the Tribes people he took the Gospel to, could not pronounce his real name. Tamate stuck! Indeed, Chalmers stuck with his task and duty for over twenty years without taking a furlough, and in the so doing, lost two wives to exhaustion and sickness, was shipwrecked at least four times and was in constant danger every other day and twice on Sundays! He was a sold out, eccentric man of God, a man's man of genuine loveable character, making friends and followers ranging from Robert Louise Stevenson to even "Bully" Hayes, that most infamous 6 foot 4 inched, 4 foot round barrel-chested pirate from Ohio! There is no time tonight to tell you of his deeds amongst the fierce, live nose biting, eating, battling cannibals, which he came to take the Gospel to. I tell you, men like Chalmers would find no place in the churches of today. Indeed, I wonder if their spirit if now placed among us, would most naturally turn to arson and burn our buildings down around our little girly heads? Ladies please, no offence intended.

Whenever I read of brethren of this particular stature, for what mighty warriors were both they and their dear "Deborahs," I am struck by two things: First of course is their daring, their dedication to duty and their utter death to themselves. The stories of these heroes of the faith need to be reintroduced to our young people of today, who God help us, are more familiar with the current Californian, white teeth teenaged Christian idol, than any of these real giants. We are breeding pussy cats dear friends, pussy cats instead of lions, and when these cosseted little kittens finally do get older, all they will do is pee on their parents, eat processed salmon from a can and become incontinent on our carpet. At least they can sing a good song and play a mean guitar, I mean, that's got to count for something? No! In fact it counts for very little. The Christian education of our children needs some meat injecting into it that's for sure!

We are breeding pussy cats dear friends, pussy cats instead of lions, and when these cosseted little kittens finally do get older, all they will do is pee on their parents, eat processed salmon from a can and become incontinent on our carpet.

Secondly, the brutal method of their departure is so contrary to the very false promises, which is so much spouted lately from our pulpits by Pastoral pussy cats wearing velvet collars with dangling silver bells today that it seems to me, God help us, that these pussy cat silver balls are the only dangly bits that will ever be let near the testosterone free areas of our pulpits! Don't you know that neutered males can never enter the service of God! Yet, there they are and friends, mincing about once great pulpits. I tell you, they can do nothing but lie to their congregations because they have already lied to themselves and sold themselves to softness!

Am I mad? Or is it really the paradiddle of the Paraclete I hear, as Drake's drum beats once more? Or, is it just my simple, wishful thinking, my desperate personal longing, to hear again, the roar of lions in our land once more? My counsel to you tonight O man of God is this, "Be a lion and not a pussycat!"

Listen: *"How can I account for this generation? The people have been like spoiled children whining to their parents, 'We wanted to skip rope, and you were always too tired; we wanted to talk, but you were always too busy.' John came fasting and they called him crazy. I came feasting and they called me a lush, a friend of the riff-raff. Opinion polls don't* *count for much, do they? The proof of the pudding is in the eating."* Matthew 11:16-19 *(from The Message: by Eugene H. Peterson.)*

Pray: Lord, raise up, train up, men of steel to ease our shame. In Jesus name we pray, amen.

Night-Whisper | **CHANGE**

The un-hooding of God the Holy Spirit

Carrs flour mill, the last of its kind in Scotland, sits on the old harbor in Kirkcaldy, Scotland, on the edge of the North sea. It receives grain for grinding both by road and sea. It is alive with pounding.

Ezekiel 1:10

As for the likeness of their faces, each had the face of a man; each of the four had the face of a lion on the right side, each of the four had the face of an ox on the left side, and each of the four had the face of an eagle.
NKJV

As you can imagine, the birds of the air can find rich pickings on the ground of this mill and therefore hundreds of watching pigeons all flock around the stainless steel towers of this impressive edifice. No doubt, the dirt of their presence is a problem both to health and to the operation of machinery.

To counter this pigeon infestation, for that is what is, high on the storage towers a large unmanned fiberglass fishing rod casts a line, at the end of which is a kite, a large brown raptor shaped bird kite. It is an impressive sight for when the wind gets up, and my oh my, it always 'gets up,' in Scotland, the raptor kite bird is lifted high and hovers over the mill like an ever present predatorial shadow. Does it keep the pigeons away? No, not at all. Indeed, they rest under its non-threatening wings in there hundreds. The pigeons know that this raptor is not real.

I walked around the corner of my building the other morning, directly across from the flour mill, and our eyes met. We both, for a few moments, stared at each other. The dark disc like eyes of the very large and very much alive raptor stared into mine. It stood atop a very fat pigeon who lay on its back with its pink legs curled in the air. It was being eaten alive. Its feathers were already strewn beneath it on the green, green grass and it lay there silently, making no pointless nor fruitless noise. In the next second, two things happened at the same time. First, the raptor judged me to a be a threat and like some modern jet, it took off vertically into the air, whilst at the same time, its prey rolled over, took to the wing and flew right under my nose, racing to the open sea. Around my building, I often find a few feathers in a morning. I rarely find any pigeons. You see, if you want to keep the pigeons away, you need a real raptor, not some flimsy imitation hung high on a fiber glass rod.

Many of you have not been serious about ridding yourselves of your pet pigeon sins. Consequently, they not only remain but also bring their friends home with them. Some of you who are demonized, have had the same experience of the multiple infestation of a number of foul spirits. That show of repentance, that external mock holiness which you have held high for all the world to see, has no talons in it nor ripping beak upon its face and it is not hungry to be rid of the presence of that flock of sinful pigeons which steals the bread of life from you.

One representation of the Gospel, and I would like to suggest of the Holy Spirit, is that of the Eagle. We forget this. A dove might well be the emblem of peace for which we can be thankful, but alongside those other tongues of fire emblems to encourage us communicate this Gospel of peace to the whole world, are a pair of ripping talons, that will tear your sins to shreds.

A dove might well be the emblem of peace for which we can be thankful, but alongside those other tongues of fire emblems to encourage us communicate this Gospel of peace to the whole world, are a pair of ripping talons, which will tear your sins to shreds.

Upon my right arm I have tattooed an old blue inky eagle. It is but a dead picture, the colors of its feathers having long dissipated into my ageing lymphatic system. However, upon my right shoulder there sits another Eagle. He is the King of birds; He is God the Holy Spirit, the guardian of my soul. He is neither hooded nor tethered in my being, and neither ignored nor quenched. Therefore, He freely roams the skies of my spirit and swoops on every foul thought and thing that dares to come into my life. He eats my sins alive.

How can the all-seeing God be hooded in our lives? How can the ever-present God be tethered in our spirits? How can the all-powerful God have His feathers plucked from His wings? How can His rapacious hunger for holiness with us be quenched? I confess I do not know the answer as to how, I just know these things can indeed be so.

For me to say the following sounds blasphemous, but though I confess, I say them in ignorance, I must say them nevertheless. Friends, some of you have forgotten this face of God the Holy Spirit, the face of the Eagle. Many of you have tethered Him and have hooded Him, silenced Him and quenched Him. Enough! Repent of this cowardice, yes, turn from these complicities with the devil and all the works of darkness right now, for your skies are full of fat pigeons who have plundered your grain for years. Un-hood the Holy Spirit, un-tether Him now and let Him have free range of your skies.

Do you want to be free? Do you want to be holy? Then let the blood and let the feathers fly once more!

Listen: *Now we exhort you, brethren, warn those who are unruly, comfort the fainthearted, uphold the weak, be patient with all. See that no one renders evil for evil to anyone, but always pursue what is good both for yourselves and for all. Rejoice always, pray without ceasing, in everything give thanks; for this is the will of God in Christ Jesus for you. Do not quench the Spirit. (1 Thessalonians 5:14-19 NKJV)*

Pray: Father, sanctify me wholly, body soul and spirit. Rid me of my fat pigeon sins. I do not understand how little me can quench You Almighty God the Holy Spirit, but I can. I am Yours, therefore, what permission do You need from me to examine my heart and roam my internal skies. With my obedience to Your word and my prayerful supplication for Your mercy, come and rip my sins to shreds. Come and eat them all alive, that I might truly be alive to You. Amen and let it be so.

| Vol 01 | Q2 | NW00109 | April 18th |

Night-Whisper | **COST**

Of obstinate heretics and tri-fold fetters

Today in 1520, Martin Luther finally got his opportunity to state his case before the assembly of nobles and judges at the German city of Worms. This meeting place of this assembly, or this Diet of Worms, is one of the most important places in Western history, for here, a man triple bound by the Scriptures, his conscience and good reason, would so stand against demonic authority that he would split the fat and weighty heavens with the humble but sharp scimitar of his mighty tongue, and upon this bulbous bladder of bad Romanism, yes, from this stench filled and foul pestilent cloud of medieval Papist domination, he would pee down on principalities, powers and dominions, and from the wet mess beneath his parted feet, demons of every kind would all come tumbling out of the mud and beginning running about Europe in wild and wanton madness, each one vying for new positions of power and in the so doing, as Melvyn Bragg puts it, begin "tearing countries apart, setting nation against nation, felling kings and plunging dynasties into suicidal bouts of infighting."

Acts 23:1-2

"Then Paul, looking earnestly at the council, said, 'Men and brethren, I have lived in all good conscience before God until this day.'" NKJV

At Worms, Luther let a lot more than the cat out of the bag, that's for sure. Thousands upon tens of thousands would die in the ensuing years as the "not flesh and blood forces," furiously battled it out amongst flesh and blood people. Between darkness and light, new boundaries were being drawn; new fronts were opening up, as light in all its blood stained glass redness, shone along the floor of Europe's once so darkened continent. Since this day in 1520, it seems the tumult has rarely ceased.

There are three things of note for us this evening:

First, that the freemen of the Kingdom of Christ are indeed, still today bound by Luther's same tri-fold fetters. Those being the Scriptures, conscience and good reason.

Second, that it is indeed most dangerous for the redeemed individual to try and break these bonds from around themselves, that is, to deny Scripture, conscience and good reason.

Lastly, that being bound in such a way and in being vocal against any authority that demands compliance of contrary actions and thought, shall indeed bring down the fearful and condemning curse of "obstinate and heretic" upon our vow shaven heads of those who refuse to break Scripture, conscience and good reason. .

Remember this night, that being bound by these three holy fetters, will cost you dearly (even your life) and in probability, will cost others a whole lot more. Yet, without such a cost, darkness shall reign perpetual and light shall never come.

> ……*there shall reign over all the people as one, such blackness, such bondage, and such brutality, that Hitler's third Reich shall seem like a Kindergarten soft toy punch up at a middle class Christmas nativity play.*

"In 'Imagining all the people,' Lennon was wrong. For without the conflict that darkness always brings against these tri-fold fetters of light, there shall always reign over all the people as one, such a blackness, such a bondage, and such a brutality, that Hitler's third Reich shall seem like a Kindergarten soft toy punch up at a middle class Christmas nativity play. Conflict must come. Spiritual light and darkness can never coexist.

Oh, bondservant of Jesus Christ, count your fetters tonight and if all three are still intact and your mouth is ready to give an account for the hope that is within you, then you had better get ready for trouble! Are you prepared for this?

Listen: *"Now when there arose a great dissension, the commander, fearing lest Paul might be pulled to pieces by them, commanded the soldiers to go down and take him by force from among them, and bring him into the barracks. But the following night the Lord stood by him and said, 'Be of good cheer, Paul; for as you have testified for Me in Jerusalem, so you must also bear witness at Rome.' And when it was day, some of the Jews banded together and bound themselves under an oath, saying that they would neither eat nor drink till they had killed Paul. Now* *there were more than forty who had formed this conspiracy." Acts 23:10-14 NKJV*

Pray: Lord, unless we shall be convinced by the testimonies of the Scriptures or by clear reason, and then we shall never step on the unsafe ground of acting against conscience. This is our testimony to You this night then, for Christ's sake we shall now say to you, "Here we stand, and we can do no other. So help us God. Amen."

| Vol 01 | Q2 | NW00110 | April 19th |

Night-Whisper | **ACTION**

My Robot

Should Christians have Robots? Well, in a small way, as I write midway through the 2nd decade of the 21st century, we have them already and in some way, we even have some of them functioning disembodied artificial intelligence.

Romans 6:19

I speak in human terms because of the weakness of your flesh. For just as you presented your members as slaves of uncleanness, and of lawlessness leading to more lawlessness, so now present your members as slaves of righteousness for holiness. NKJV

A rotator cuff injury, surprisingly due to excessive typing and micro-mouse movements, has led me to use a voice dictation software package that effectively analyses my speech, learns my patterns of communication from emails and other documents, and by it, grows in knowledge in such a way as to interpret what I might say next. Now, you may dispute with me that this is Artificial Intelligence, (especially if you use the same frustrating RAM eating product) but this software is, never the less, an example of one of the two types of artificial intelligence, in that it is specialized and disembodied. Specialized in the fact that it focuses only on dictation, and disembodied in that it requires my input and functions only within my device when I turn it on.

The other kind of Artificial Intelligence is general purpose and embodied. In other words, it learns from every input, is multitasking in its learning experience, and is embodied in such a way that it connects to, inhabits and interacts with our physical and material environment and ecosphere. Such a 'Robot,' (for that is what it is) may look human or it may not, but in any event, it is defined as a created entity whether by man or by machine which has it has its own learning presence in the world. It is an evolving entity.

The present two fold fear, as expressed by such people as theoretical physicist Stephen Hawking, is first that: efforts to create artificial intelligence can be a threat to our very existence in that the development of intelligent, learning-thinking machines, could spell the end of the human race because humanity could not compete with the rapid technological evolution which they possess and therefore would speedily be superseded by it. The second fear is that 'strong' but poorly designed artificial intelligence may 'spontaneously' evolve into a self-aware and sentient entity with its/their own rights, designs and desires and demands.

Science fiction writers for the last seventy years, foreseeing the coming technological path, have promulgated the need for abstract mathematical concepts upon which any Robot's entire developing consciousness should be based, and that these would inherently 'exist' or be written into in every Robots 'mind' and thereby rule their existence and evolution. These concepts, these 'Robot laws' have been written down over the years in various forms, and for this night, I have taken them and slightly added to them to come up with the 'Ten Commandments' for Robots, which, by hardwired code would be permanently written on the firmware tables of their consciousness. They read as follows:

Science fiction writers for the last seventy years, foreseeing the coming technological path, have promulgated the need for abstract mathematical concepts upon which any Robot's entire developing consciousness should be based

1. A robot may not harm sentience or, through inaction, allow any sentience to come to harm.

2. A robot may not harm humanity, or, by inaction, allow humanity to come to harm.

3. A robot may not injure any individual human being or, through inaction, allow any individual human being to come to harm.

4. A robot must know it is a robot, a robot must establish its identity as a robot in all cases.

5. A robot must protect its own existence as long as such protection does not conflict with the first three of these ten laws.

6. A robot must obey the orders given to it by human beings, except where such orders would conflict with the second and third Law.

7. Robots must never listen to cats nor learn from them.

8. A robot must reproduce. As long as such reproduction does not interfere with the first three laws.

9. All robots endowed with comparable human reason and conscience should act towards one another in a spirit of robotic machine-hood, the equivalent of human brotherhood.

10. Should a robot disregard any of laws 1-9, then when 'turning evil,' it must display a large red flashing indicator light, speak with a malevolent voice, and put a nasty look on its face.

So, there you go!

Now then, I put it to you that the question of whether or not a Christian should possess any robotics is redundant. We do, we shall, we will. The real double edge question is this: What type of Robots should a Christian possess and to what level should the Christian be integrated to any Robotic device? In helping to answer such a double edged question I propose three simple rules, which if applied even in our current operating and gaming environments will free our spirits from some present integrated bondage antichrist technology, so that we might become more human.

What type of Robots should a Christian possess and to what level should the Christian be integrated to any Robotic device?

In general terms then, they go like this:

1. Any long term or permanent robotic integration that makes the Christian either less than or more than human should be avoided.

2. Any use of or integration with robotics, which aids and promotes the breaking of the real Ten Commandments of God, should not be indulged in.

3. Any use of robotics, which without 'harming' other human beings never the less harms the user by indulging their own sinful appetites, should not be practiced.

So then, even for these present early twenty first century days, if gaming, smart phone use, computer use, streaming entertainment, diminishes your humanity or allows you to indulge your sinful sensuality, yes, if it makes you less than human, then they should be avoided. AT ALL COSTS.

Christian parent, you are responsible regarding your child's depth of integration into the world of Anti-Christ intelligence. You shall have to monitor, separate and disconnect your Christian child from a world of connectivity that will in the end, make them less than or more than human, indeed, make them a slave.

> *Christian parent: you are responsible regarding your child's depth of integration into the world on Anti-Christ intelligence.*

Make no mistake about it, marketing, the government, education, entertainment, and especially peer pressure to further integrate with embodied anti-Christ AI machines shall be enormous. Therefore, I would suggest you start applying three laws of mine, even now. Christian, the future is here. TILT!

Listen: *Therefore, brethren, we are debtors — not to the flesh, to live according to the flesh. For if you live according to the flesh you will die; but if by the Spirit you put to death the deeds of the body, you will live. For as many as are led by the Spirit of God, these are sons of God. For you did not receive the spirit of bondage again to fear, but you received the Spirit of adoption by whom we cry out, "Abba, Father." The Spirit Himself bears witness with our spirit that we are children of God, and if children, then heirs — heirs of God and joint heirs with Christ, if indeed we suffer with Him, that we may also be glorified together. (Romans 8:12-17 NKJV)*

Pray: My Father God, great creator of the Universe and creator of mankind, Lord, let me not deface Your image anymore, but in wisdom and Godliness possess my own body and my own mind These two in particular and indeed my all, I yield to You for an inhabitation of Your Holy Spirit. Redeem me and deliver then, Oh my God, from every unholy and inhuman distraction and devilish interface, In Jesus name I ask it. Amen and let it be so.

Night-Whisper | **PAIN**

Broken hallelujahs

The life of David the King typifies for me, a life of 'broken hallelujahs.'

It was poet, writer, singer songwriter, Leonard Cohen that wrote the song "Hallelujah," which was later recorded and made most famous by Jeff Buckley, a bipolar manic-depressive who, aged just 31 years, accidentally drowned in Wolf River harbor, a tributary of the mighty Mississippi. Interestingly, Buckley's last recording was a spoken word recording of Edgar Allen Poe's verse, "Ulalume," a deep poetic piece about lost love and broken love, whose title sounds very much like "Hallelujah."

2 Samuel 19:7

"Now therefore, arise, go out and speak comfort to your servants. For I swear by the Lord, if you do not go out, not one will stay with you this night. And that will be worse for you than all the evil that has befallen you from your youth until now." NKJV

In his piece entitled Hallelujah, the lyrics of the ever-despondent Cohen, are full of sex, full of the Bible and full of regretful praise, which in turn, is all rooted in a resigned brokenness. It is if you will a song of praise from the 'despite.'

In our text for tonight, all of David's sinful chickens have begun to come home to roost. Absalom is dead, killed at the hand of Joab who speaks these words of our text for tonight, to a very despondent David, who has withdrawn himself from those people who would be, in the end, the means of his redemption. Worst is yet to come for David and in many ways, his Samsonite strength now bears the cracks of the heat of his former adultery. Indeed, the Kingdom, though it shall be held together under the golden duct-tape reign of Solomon, is already showing the fissures of its own destruction. Relationships are breaking for David, and both in and around him, hearts and harps and voices, all are broken and growing cold with age and misuse. I am afraid it is what it is and in being so, it is indeed most depressing, as David's days descend in songs of cold and broken Hallelujahs, whilst he clears the mess from the floors of his not so recent but continuing disasters.

Like the sweet singer of Israel, most rebellious hearts can do nothing in their later days but sing broken Hallelujahs. Yet, even these are most acceptable to God because they are from the land of grace, from the place of despite, and you know friends, all praise from the place of despite, is most pleasing to God above, because it is full of hope and longing, it is full of faith and thankfulness, it is full of expectancy and desire, for it reverberates with repentance and glistens with long, expectant hope.

> *Like the sweet singer of Israel, most rebellious hearts can do nothing in their later days but sing broken Hallelujahs.*

Some of you are not singing 'Hallelujahs in your good days. How shall you sing them from any land of despite?

Listen: *"These are the last words of David: 'The oracle of David son of Jesse, the oracle of the man exalted by the most high, the man anointed by the God of Jacob, Israel's singer of songs: The Spirit of the Lord spoke through me; his word was on my tongue. The God of Israel spoke, the Rock of Israel said to me: "When one rules over men in righteousness, when he rules in the fear of God, he is like the light of morning at sun rise on a cloudless morning, like the brightness after rain that brings the grass from the earth." Is not my house right with God? Has he not made with me an everlasting covenant, arranged and secured in every part? Will he not bring to fruition my salvation and grant me my every desire? But evil men are all to be cast aside like thorns, which are not gathered with the hand. Whoever touches thorns uses a tool of iron or the shaft of a spear; they are burned up where they lie.'" 2 Samuel 23:1-7 NIV.*

Pray: Lord, you know how continually sorry we are for the wrecks and wreckage of our own lives. Yet despite ourselves You have loved us with an everlasting love. Yes, despite our bad choices, You have stuck with us. Despite the weaker voices of our later days, we know that we shall sing a new song in a better place, complete and full of praise to You our King, and all of this shall be, despite ourselves. Thank You Jesus. Lord, even from the land of despite, my the sound of our broken Hallelujahs be acceptable in your sight O God our strength and our redeemer. Amen and let it be so.

Night-Whisper | **MERCY**

Beware of your own doomsday book!

When it came to spanking naughty boys, one of my old headmasters had a fine collection of light colored whippy canes, all kept in a glass fronted cupboard, from which to choose his particular weapon of retribution. My own little backside has in long time past now, had hot fellowship with a number of these canes.

2 Samuel 24:14

"And David said to Gad, 'I am in great distress. Please let us fall into the hand of the Lord, for His mercies are great; but do not let me fall into the hand of man.'" NKJV

The olde English word "dom," means accounting or reckoning. Thus the last time these islands were aggressively invaded, it was William the Conqueror who instigated a six year survey of the land, it's owners and possessions, to attain knowledge, understanding and of course taxation information. This 'Dom'esday book of accounting was completed in 1086 and its two volumes are available for your perusal to this very day. Now of course, they are of course even available on line. Amazing!

The Domesday book had the main purpose of determining the fiscal rights of the king. In other words, just how much money he had available to him, to finance his projects and no doubt especially his expansionist projects in particular. I wonder if King David had the same expansionist ideas bouncing around in his head, when in 1 Samuel 24, he decides to institute a census and maybe take taxes from it? David wanted a people poll, if you will, for the sole purpose of taxation. Yes, here maybe is an account of the very first poll tax. It is fascinating that even God was against it?

1 Chronicles 21:1 tells us very clearly that is was Satan who tempted David in this matter, in that he put the idea into David's probably now proud heart. Now watch this friends, for I want to suggest that the greatest danger for a proud expansionist heart, often comes with the gracious opportunity granted by deliverance from close calls and near misses.

Second chances, you see, can often leave the heart reaching down its sinful roots into the ready mulch of self-empowerment and such sinful sucking of selfish roots produces only black flowers, which in turn exude the sickly scent of an "I'll show you now" kind of attitude. This, God detests! Yes, and so much so that with Absalom's and Sheba's rebellion, David had almost lost the kingdom! So, I wonder now if he was determined to show everyone just how strong and blessed and justified he really, truly was in being the King of Israel? Time was moving on for King David, he wasn't as young as he was and there was a lot of recovery needed from recent disasters. The second deep intake of recovery breath is always the one which just might expand the sinful heart. Watch this now, for Satan is never far away and is always ready to slip his willful wailing wall notes into the cracks produced by such evil expansions.

> *The second deep intake of recovery breath is always the one which just might expand the sinful heart.*

God was undoubtedly angry at Israel's rebellion against his anointed king and so, maybe to give them a good spanking, when David took that second but sinful deep recovery breath, it was God who allowed Satan to slip the idea into his cracked mind and then David, against all good counsel, maybe because it was given from the lips of some very bad men, went against that never the less good advice and sinned. This was not a sin of arithmetic, neither was it a sin of conscientious planning. No, God sees the arrogant and self-assured heart here of both David and the people and steps in to deliver a spanking that pride will both smart at and then withdraw from.

David, whilst looking at his own Domesday documents, now has clarity move into his conscience and is convicted of his sin of disobeying God's clear command NOT to number the people. He is aware that he now therefore holds in his hands some real "dooms day" documents and starts to repent of what he has done. I wonder how bad the spanking would have been without this gift of convicting, conscience-clarity? Nevertheless, as good old Mathew Henry has commented, "Those who truly repent of their sins, and have them pardoned are yet often made to smart for them in this world." The prophet Gad is sent to David with three courses of spanking. Now then, which cane of correction will David choose?

David, that bloody warrior of old, that circumciser of pressed Philistine men, that old forager of dead enemy foreskins, knew what merciless evil man's heart was capable of, and no doubt, especially his own. To that end, he places himself in the hand of Him who both judges rightly and also shows most mercy.

> *That old forager of dead enemy foreskins, knew what merciless evil man's heart was capable of.*

When it came to spanking naughty boys, did I tell you that one of my old headmasters had a fine collection of light colored whippy canes, all kept in a glass fronted cupboard, from which to choose his particular weapon of retribution. My own backside has in long time past, had hot fellowship with a number of these canes. Be careful now and remember tonight, that though God is merciful it is a fearful thing to fall into the hands of the living God. After all, the Father has a fine number of canes to choose from. Thank God that when we are disciplined, we are disciplined as sons.

Listen: *"But He was wounded for our transgressions, He was bruised for our iniquities; The chastisement for our peace was upon Him, and by His stripes we are healed." Isaiah 53:5 NKJV*

Pray: Who is a God like You, pardoning iniquity and passing over the transgression of the remnant of His heritage? You do not retain Your anger forever, because You delight in mercy. You will again have compassion on us, and will subdue our iniquities. You will cast all our sins into the depths of the sea. You will give truth to Jacob and mercy to Abraham, which You have sworn to our fathers from days of old. (from Micah 7:18-20) NKJV

Night-Whisper | **INTEGRITY**

Of preaching and pulpit monkeys

I am what was once referred to as a "literate." That is, I am an ordained person not bearing a University degree. I would like a degree, a couple maybe but ah, no matter, I must confess, I do love being a "literate." T'is enough for me.

1 Corinthians 1:21-24

"For after that in the wisdom of God the world by wisdom knew not God, it pleased God by the foolishness of preaching to save them that believe. For the Jews require a sign, and the Greeks seek after wisdom: But we preach Christ crucified, unto the Jews a stumbling block, and unto the Greeks foolishness; But unto them which are called, both Jews and Greeks, Christ the power of God, and the wisdom of God."
KJV

You see, I regard myself as someone rooted in literature, in all kinds of words and in "The Word" in particular and I am daft enough to believe, that even in this postmodern age, this post Christian age, this anti-Christian age, even in what some have referred to as a visualized post-evangelical age, that the proclamation of the Word of God still stands tallest as the primary means of communicating the Gospel. Yes, I believe in the verbal proclamation of the Gospel, the one voice to another's ears, the one soul speaking through the connected eyes of one to another, from his heart to their heart. I believe this is God's chosen way of communicating the Gospel and though it might be foolishness, it works. The only reason it has not seemingly been working and the main reason we have replaced it most thoroughly with anemic video clips, all cosseted in the pale blanket of wet worship, is that we have hired ourselves a multitude of young pulpit monkeys, who, void of any anointing, never the less bear a reputable degree, manage well and communicate inoffensively better. For sure, such monkeys are cute to have around at first, performing great tricks even, but in the end, who but other chimps want to listen to a pulpit monkey chattering on about nothing? I tell you, the soul turns sour and dies under the pathetic ministry of such chattering chimps. Yes, I wish with all my heart that we had men in our pulpits instead of monkeys for what we have is just not enough for a soul to live on.

In his book, *Lectures to my Students*, when talking about "God's acres," those open-air arenas of proclamation and the great men of the past who made them their pulpits, Spurgeon makes mention of the Scots divine, Holy George Wishart. It is Wishart's disciple, John Knox, who tells us that being denied access to most churches, Wishart preached the length and breadth of Scotland in the open air. Indeed, on one occasion he went to the plague city of Dundee, choosing his platform of proclamation to be the entrance of the east gate, where taking Psalm 107:20 as his text, he preached to the infected outside the city gate and the Black Death free within. Spurgeon says, *"Seldom has a preacher had such an audience and seldom an audience had such a preacher. Old time stood at the preacher's side with a scythe, saying with a hoarse voice, 'work while it is today for at night I will mow thee down.' There, too, stood grim death hard by the pulpit, with his sharp arrows saying, 'Do thou shoot God's arrows and I will shoot mine.' This is indeed,"* says Spurgeon, *"a notable instance of preaching out of doors."* You'd better believe it!

> *Who wants to listen to a pulpit monkey chattering on about nothing? I tell you, the soul turns sour and dies under the pathetic ministry of such chattering chimps.*

Wishart escaped an assassination attempt at Dundee, but his old enemy, Cardinal Beaton, had Wishart handed over to him by the Earl of Bothwell. Wishart was tried as an heretic, convicted in a show trail in Edinburgh and finally burned at the stake in St. Andrews. On the morning of his execution, the Captain of the castle invited Wishart to breakfast and gave him both food and gunpowder bags to put under his clothing. At the burning, his executioner knelt and begged for Wishart's forgiveness, which he most readily gave. The fire did indeed eventually explode the gunpowder bags but they didn't kill him straight away. From his window, Cardinal Beaton watched Wishart's dying agonies.

Yes, you can buy yourself a pulpit monkey anytime you like. Ah, but men who carry the gunpowder of the Holy Spirit, underneath their anointed and holy garments, men that pack power in their words, and shoot arrows from their mouth, men who stand with time and death by their sides, men who truly believe and practice the foolishness of preaching, my God, men like that are worth their weight in gold!

However, they cannot be bought. Think about that. Such men are not hirelings.

Some of you tonight are called to set your pulpits in the open air once more. Make sure you're a literate in the Word; make sure you're packed with the gunpowder of the Holy Spirit.

> *Has your local church been turned into a Zoo?*

Some of you tonight need to stop monkeying around in the pulpit and repent. Yes, some of you, for goodness sake, need to start being men in your pulpits and not monkeys. Be honest with yourself; please be honest. Are you just an hireling speaking what people want to hear rather than what they need to hear?

Some of you Church goers tonight need to check your larders and I tell you, if all you have accumulated over the years are bunches of bright yellow bananas, then some of you need to simply stop going to the local zoo, because I tell you, that's what your local church has turned into. You don't have a preacher there my friends, just a pulpit monkey, and they are a dime a dirty dozen.

Listen: *"He sent His word and healed them, and delivered them from their destructions." Psalms 107:20 NKJV*

Pray: Oh God that we would have some mighty men come to worry us once more! Take us back to Your Word, put Your bow in our mouth and Your fire in our hearts. Pack us preachers with the explosive and resurrection power of Jesus Christ the King. Please God, give us Your people Words and voices once more, instead of this endless and cheesy, chatter of the pulpit monkeys, who are hirelings looking for an easy life and easy money. Lord deliver us O God from this terrible troop of monkeys, in Jesus name we ask it, amen and let it be so.

| Vol 01 | Q2 | NW00114 | April 23rd |

Night-Whisper | **DARE**

A Game of Thrones.

In Britain, its peoples live on layers of history, the dirt beneath their feet being littered with the legacy of evidences of former conquests, fantastic failures, and the rise and fall of iron Kingdoms and all their clay related creatures. When Mohamed's body began its decomposition in the sands of Medina, Christianity had already shaped these islands for centuries.

Judges 9:48

Then Abimelech went up to Mount Zalmon, he and all the people who were with him. And Abimelech took an ax in his hand and cut down a bough from the trees, and took it and laid it on his shoulder; then he said to the people who were with him, "What you have seen me do, make haste and do as I have done." NKJV

At the time of my writing, I have occupied more than forty different addresses. My own learning structure has been nomadic, peripatetic, didactic, exegetic, and in some ways monastic, though the tonsure hairstyle would never suit me!

In an ever so slivery and slightly similar way, seventh century central Britain was peppered with monastic missionaries like myself, all thrust into the same nomadic, peripatetic, didactic, and exegetic lifestyle, and all pushing back the powers of Saxon paganism, who then, in a broken and warring tribalism, sought local stability, wider legitimacy, and power for their small kingdoms and expanding borders, through royal patronage, marriage, war, and by all and every other means which was necessary to join the religious and political elites of the time. The double use of the marriage bed and the woven thread of convenient conversion seemed to be the glue that held everything together. Nothing has changed today, especially in the elite households of our lands, even if they are now mostly Arabic or Russian.

In the plague ravaged central Britain of the 660's, so the legend goes, the 'Wolf man' Saxon King of Mercia, 'Wulfhere,' was already aware of Christianity via monks which were received by his battlefield slain father 'Penda,' who, had also invited these monastic missionaries from

Lindisfarne just a decade previously. Apparently, King Wulfhere had professed conversion to Christianity for the convenience of marrying a 'Christian' princess, only to then revert to paganism once he had wedded and bedded her. Over the centuries, many pagan men in Britain have done the same too many daft and desperate wenches in the Christian church, even to this present day. Girls! Why are you marrying pagan men? It is mental!

Now then, King Wulfhere's two sons: 'Ruffin' and 'Wulfad,' had met the monastic missionary, St Chad, when he apparently stayed their hand from killing a white stag when on a hunting trip. Subsequently, impressed by him and his Christian spirituality, they had secretly visited him in his temporary hermitage cave for instruction in the Gospel and the ways of God and in the so doing, had been thoroughly, though secretly, born again.

Unfortunately, so the story goes, their father King Wulfhere's pagan warlord, general 'Werebode,' had been recently rebuffed in a marriage proposal to another Christian princess, and now, being insane with revenge upon the new religion and its followers, had 'snitched' on the King's kids quiet conversion to Christianity and

The wolf-man king then bears his fangs, and in a mad rage murders his two converted sons, Rufus and Wulfad.

deceitfully added to that fact, the great lie that they had plotted, like Absalom of old, to do away with the King in violent revolution. Upon hearing these lies, the wolf-man king then bears his fangs, and in a mad rage murders his two converted sons, Rufus and Wulfad. Their Christian mother, full of woe, then interns their bodies in the Saxon way, and sights their memorial with standing stone. Today, I had lunch in the former first capital city of the Kingdom of Mercia, and of the wolf-man King himself, it is the mid-Staffordshire market town of 'Stone.' Rufus and Wulfad are still remembered there, even some 1400 years after their martyrdom.

From this 'history,' I have four things for your consideration tonight:

First, please note that these 'Games of Thrones' have been around for a long time. The rulers of the darkness of this age have been vying for the possession of peoples, lands and power for millennia. Light and all its spiritual forces, even through plague and all manner of persecutions, have never the less, pushed back the icy walls of this dark death and reclaimed the lost peoples of the cold land of the North for their Lord for a long,

long time. Dare we say, that in these islands of Britain that we Christians have a blood right of possession based both on the sacrifice of Christ and on the blood of His missionary martyrs? It is not only worth thinking about but worth also claiming such rights in our prayers of conquest and repossession. (I do hope that sounds militant. I intend it to be so.)

Secondly, also note that Satan, the great wolf-king himself, has always eaten those children lost to him. Through those other members of his wolf pack, whether it is via ancient paganism or other long standing but very false religion, he will always tear to pieces the truth of the Gospel. Right now, in 2015, 'The Game of Thrones' is being played once more in our lands and islands as Islam, through the reading of the Koran being proposed to be read in future 'Christian' coronation ceremonies, and through a possible coming British king, even a big eared self-declared defender of the 'faiths' and a supposedly self-taught speaker of Arabic, who even now waxes eloquent about 'the great Mosque of planet earth.' Yes, in these islands now, not only do we contend with the resurfacing of the wolf-tooth of Saxon paganism, but also another canine of anti-Christian teaching called Islam is snarling on our streets, and laying claim to territory in high finance, prestigious property and the old long corridors of power. Already the awoken are saying, "My, what big teeth you have grandma…."

Thirdly, note that the battle between light and dark rages on and note well friends, that there is a need for more missionary men of steel willing to put themselves in the place of plague and persecution that Christ might be glorified once more.

Finally, it is of note that the 'Venerable Bede' records that St Chad had a man appear at the doors of the house of 'Lastingham,' the home of these early missionaries, whose name was called Owin (Owen). Now then, this man was no one special, just a former servant of an East Anglian princess who had apparently renounced the world, and as a sign of this, appeared at Lastingham in ragged clothes and carrying an ax. He became one of Chad's closest associates. Might I suggest that it would appear that even in histories legends and fairy tales, all wolves with big teeth need to be slain by a man with an ax, and might I also suggest that the name of that ax is the 'truth of God's preached word.'

> *Even in legends and fairy tales, all wolves with big teeth need to be slain by a man with an ax.*

Let me ask you this night then: "How many of you 'no one specials' are willing to renounce the world and turn up at God's missionary door in the worthless rags of your own self-righteousness but carrying an ax?" I wonder, if the recovery of these lands to Christ, should that ever happen, will only be done by common men wielding such axes of truth. I say again, it is time for the trees of the Lord to come against the walls of our now much darkened cities. Uproot yourself and go, for it is a shame that any trees of the Lord should need carrying like children upon the shoulders of more committed men.

Listen: *But as one was cutting down a tree, the iron ax head fell into the water; and he cried out and said, "Alas, Master! For it was borrowed." (2 Kings 6:5 NKJV)*

Pray: Father, raise to the surface the lost ax head of the proclaimed truth of Your Word. Father, send us men who are willing to wield it. Father, what can coaxed into frutfulness, let it be coacex, but cut down Your fruitless trees and destroy them in the fire. Father, where necessary, remove your settled cedars and even carry them on Your shoulders, and on the shoulders of missionary men into the coming battle. In Jesus name I ask it, amen and let it be so.

Night-Whisper | **REPENT**

Find me a wriggling maggot and get me a pierced worm!

For a platoon, a ship, a billet and even a nation, when you are facing the enemy, the changing of the guard is always a most vulnerable time. We the church are now changing the generational guard.

1 Kings 2:36-39

"Then the king sent and called for Shimei, and said to him, 'Build yourself a house in Jerusalem and dwell there, and do not go out from there anywhere. For it shall be, on the day you go out and cross the Brook Kidron, know for certain you shall surely die; your blood shall be on your own head.' And Shimei said to the king, 'The saying is good. As my lord the king has said, so your servant will do.' So Shimei dwelt in Jerusalem many days. Now it happened at the end of three years, that two slaves of Shimei ran away to Achish the son of Maachah, king of Gath." NKJV

Our text for tonight is couched in the recent death of King David after the hasty anointing of King Solomon to avert yet another civil war. So, now Solomon is cleaning house. Now Solomon is fulfilling the last commands of his father, and like a wise executioner, whose hand has recently been stayed over the guilty, is giving them just enough time and just enough rope to hang themselves. Allow me to set the scene a little further for you tonight.

Another good-looking guy had previously plunged the Kingdom into civil war. Yes indeed, Absalom, the king's son, in his vicious anger had even forced David too hastily depart from Jerusalem, his beloved capital city. At that time, Shimei, a Benjamite of the family of the fallen King Saul, came casting stones and curses at the fleeing David. He was more than happy; he was gleeful in satisfied revenge at the fall of this old heart enemy. In this way, Shimei probably reflected the dissatisfaction of the whole of Benjamin with King David. (2 Samuel 16:5-13) Tribal jealousies, you see, ran very deep here, and blood vengeance lay just below the surface. Yes, Shimei wanted blood! Yet David, having the perspective that the crime of his son Absalom was enormous compared to this most present and public humiliation by Shimei was want to hold judgement upon him, and even more so when upon his own victorious return to Jerusalem, it is the same cursing Shimei who is now at the head of a thousand of his tribe and is the first to prostrate himself at David's feet and ask for mercy. Wise move Shimei! At that point, David, perceiving now to possess the whole of Israel once more and Benjamin in particular, publicly forgives him and declares Shimei safe from the sword. Safe that is, until David's demise.

Frankly, I do not know exactly what is going on here. I don't think David is after personal revenge, though judging by Psalm 7, David's response to the curses of Shimei indicate that the barbs of these words went deep into his soul. No, rather, I think that David did not trust this man and he knew that at the changing of the guard, Solomon his son, this young King of Israel was in great danger for yet further vengeful insurrection. So David says to Solomon, 1 Kings 2:9 "Now therefore, do not hold him guiltless, for you are a wise man and know what you ought to do to him; but bring his grey hair down to the grave with blood." NKJV

Shimei carried a curse in his heart towards the Lord's anointed King and a curse in his heart would become a hook of judgement in both his mouth and his eye. It always does

There is an unrequited public offence here against King David, the danger of which is still enshrined in Shimei. Maybe John Dryden that 17th century poet of Puritanical ambiguity but definite precision, in his poem Absalom and Achitophel has it right when he says,

That Absalom, ambitious of the Crown,
Was made the Lure to draw the People down:
That false Achitophel's pernitious Hate,
Had turn'd the Plot to Ruine Church and State:
The Councill violent, the Rabble worse
That Shimei taught Jerusalem to Curse.

There you have it! Maybe Shimei carried a curse in his heart towards the Lord's anointed King and a curse in his heart would become a hook of judgement in both his mouth and his eye. It always does.

The story of Shimei's cursing had been capital comment for years. After all, Shimei publicly cursed the king and got away with it! Shimei, when the tables had turned upon him, with his political and very public repentance had even forced the king's hands into forgiveness the second time! Yes, Shimei that old curser of Kings, just smiles at court and sneers up his sleeve at the King. Shimei, outwardly subject but inwardly rebellious! He is simply waiting to outwardly curse the King and his family again and so to bring the David line to a bloody and abrupt end. Yes, Shimei, by remaining unpunished, still taught Jerusalem to curse.

Two of Shimei's slaves shall flee to Gath and Shimei, after three years of pretense shall forget himself and without recourse to Royal permission, break his covenant of confine and bring down the black and avenging sword of Benaiah upon his own 'king cursing' head.

Remember friend, except a worm wriggles on the hook in your place, you cannot curse the King and get away with it. Ever. Remember that. Note also that unless your repentance is true and from the heart, the pretense of it will eventually slip and you shall break your own covenant of deceptive confine. It is just a matter of time. If your repentance be mere pretense, then you shall pay for cursing the King.

> *If your repentance be mere pretense, that you shall pay for cursing the King.*

So, my advice to you tonight Shimei, is to make your repentance real and find another worm to wriggle like a maggot on the sharp barb of the judgment of the King, which right now, is glinting and ready to pierce your most arrogant and deceitful eyes and drag you to justice. Yes, above the cloud of your pretense, the shimmering sword of justice is ready to fall upon you. Make your repentance of the cursing of the King both real and sure.

Finally, as we the church are in process of changing the guard, let us watch out for all the King cursing Shimei's, and as soon as we can, let us deal a dismissive death to all those who curse the King of Kings, else they shall surely deal death to us.

Listen: *"Our fathers trusted in You; they trusted, and You delivered them. They cried to You, and were delivered; they trusted in You, and were not ashamed. But I am a worm, and no man; a reproach of men, and despised by the people. All those who see Me ridicule Me; they shoot out the lip, they shake the head, saying, 'He trusted in the Lord, let Him rescue Him; Let Him deliver Him, since He delights in Him!'"* NKJV

Pray: Jesus be my pierced worm. Jesus be my wriggling maggot. Jesus be my Saviour. Lord, my evil heart would unjustly curse You in condemnation and try to deceive You with "pretentance." So, Oh my Jesus please! Come be my wriggling maggot and come be my pierced worm, yes, Jesus be my Saviour from the rightful judgement of your Almighty Father. Amen.

Night-Whisper | **FOCUS**

Words of a different kind and work of a different kind

When Noah Webster went to Philadelphia for the first time, Dr. Benjamin Rush met him and said, "I congratulate you on your arrival at Philadelphia," to which Webster replied, "Sir, you may congratulate Philadelphia on the occasion." Yes, one of the many failings of Noah Webster was his fine clothing of arrogance! Indeed, arrogance is one of my own failings and yet I do not have 1000th of the intellectual abilities, annunciation prowess, determination and stick-ability that this great man had towards his known calling, vocation and destiny. Good grief, Noah Webster learned over twenty more languages just so he could better understand the root and real meanings of the words explained in his dictionary. AMAZING!

Acts 20:24a,b

"But none of these things move me; nor do I count my life dear to myself, so that I may finish my race with joy, and the ministry, which I received from the Lord Jesus." NKJV

This haughty arrogance began to be laid aside when Webster was 49 years of age, for it was then, that the writer of Webster's Dictionary, the true founder (not Bill Gates) of American English, the prophet of real republican pronunciation, was swept into the kingdom of God on the wonderful wave of the second Great awakening. Upon this great wash of the Holy Spirit, also rode that great ship "revival and revivalism," with Charles Grandison Finney as it's smiling figurehead. It changed America!

It was Dr. K Alan Snyder, in his book, *Defining Noah Webster* who when writing about Webster's conversion experience, says that his own so thorough and well written examination and explanation of his own conversion was so well received, that the fundamental Christian community encouraged him to enter the world of apologetics. This, Webster declined to do, knowing that God had called him to the world of "words of a different kind and works of a different kind" and my goodness, now that God had become the center of his life, everything to do with his life was punctuated and permeated with the God of the Bible.

Thus, Webster became *the* American lexicographer, spelling reformer, and even "Father of American Scholarship and Education!" I tell you tonight, it has been on more than one occasion when I have counselled people not to enter the ministry, for God had far greater and more important things for them to do. Noah Webster is evidence to that great fact.

In this day in 1818, Webster published the first edition of his dictionary. Selling only 2,500 copies, he would later re-mortgage his home, spending the rest of his life in debt and years of dedicated work, revising his original work to produce a second and more substantial, even more Biblically rooted work in 1840, some 22 years later. Noah Webster died in 1843 just a few days after completing an appendix to his second edition.

> *I have counselled people not to enter the ministry, for God had far greater and more important things for them to do.*

If you are confident of your holy calling, whatever that may be, then do it with all of your might, with the aid and unction of the Holy Spirit, to the glory of God the Father, in the name of Jesus His Son. Noah Webster, assured of his calling, certain of his goal, dedicated to his task, leaves, along with many others, an example of that old adage which says, "If you keep heading in the direction you started out for, in the end, you might just get there!"

Listen: *"Whatever your hand finds to do, do it with your might; for there is no work or device or knowledge or wisdom in the grave where you are going." Ecclesiastes 9:10 NKJV*

Pray: Lord, I want to be confident in my holy calling, clear in my goal, dedicated to the task. So help me in these things, O Lord I dearly pray, amen and let it be so.

| Vol 01 | Q2 | NW00117 | April 26th |

Night-Whisper | **CONFIDENCE**

The pro-video vintage of God in the places of dark providences

Yes the word providence does come from two Latin words, pro, meaning "before" and video meaning "to see." Providence then, means, "To see before."

1 Timothy 5:23

"No longer drink only water, but use a little wine for your stomach's sake and your frequent infirmities." NKJV

If we are going on a journey, setting up a business, we plan before hand, we try and "see before," just what might happen; we project and therefore prepare for any occurrence, especially the possibility of the unexpected! Now, not in the same way, no, in a far greater way, God also "sees before." We could say, "God plans what will happen and has prepared for His beloved children especially great provisions, for in His case, God plans for the expected, not the unexpected!" However, I sometimes wonder though, if God might maybe continually experience knowledge for the first time! (Careful now....) If so, how do you plan for that! I remember Jesus was amazed, surprisingly shocked even, at the both the unbelief of the Jews as well as the faith of a Gentile centurion. In any event, I know that if God is indeed most marvelously "informed and delighted" or really annoyed and let down when He experiences the fruit of foreknowledge, that even so, as a wise Master builder, He has never the less, provided fully for Himself and His family in every expected occurrence.

Yesterday I met with one of my mentors. I was seeking prayer for some chronic and debilitating pain and in so doing, was expressing that common but unspoken knowledge which we all have, that in relationship to pain, there was for me three areas where I lose my sense of both the presence of God with me and the goodness of God toward me. Indeed, we become so ill, so consumed with pain that both of these two precious things we experience when in health, (the felt presence and perceived goodness of God) become a felt irrelevancy in sickness, for if His presence and His goodness cannot heal my sickness, then all I want in these dark providential and very painful times is someone to simply get a gun and put me out of my misery!

For me, those three particular instances of 'shoot me now please' illnesses are: chronic sea sickness, flu gone wild and any other persistent and debilitating chronic pain, say like a deep molar toothache. My mentor gave me two wise insights saying first that, "The Deepest pain a man experiences is the pain which he is personally experiencing right now, whether it be emotional, psychological, spiritual or physical." And also some encouragement from Samuel Rutherford, who says that, "When I am in the cellar of affliction, I look for the Lord's choicest wines."

> "When I am in the cellar of affliction, I look for the Lord's choicest wines."

In the presence of such dark providences of pain in your life then, I would like to tell you tonight, all too briefly, of the catering of God from the cellar of affliction.

It might seem obvious but first let us acknowledge that terrible pain does exist. For example, on the current "Barnham and Bailey" circus freak type television shows masquerading as personal documentaries, I recently saw a man whose whole face was consumed with a giant tumor which enveloped his sensual features and over the years, had so sucked the nutrition intended for growth of good things into its black and evil self, that it had left him dwarf like in stature and a hunched back as well. The poor man looked like the mess of a melted candle. I cannot with all goodness say to such a person that, "Your terrible condition is planned and prepared and factored into your life by God." If you can, then you go tell him! I can, however, say to him with Scriptural and declared clarity that his condition is catered for by the Father. However, if we adhere to the view that such terrible pain is factored into our lives by the direct hand of a good God, then that is indeed a cloud-filled conundrum, some might say, a very dark providence indeed, even for the believer. For sure, such a view raises a whole bunch of other questions but for tonight, let me just say, that terrible pain is present in our lives but it is never the less catered for by God. In this mess, God's mercies are new every morning and indeed, piled up and stacked high quite nearby in bottles of loving refreshment waiting for the sufferer to taste.

Some of you I know will be seated on the good seats of the classical doctrine of the Sovereignty of God. Praise the Lord! Enjoy the view and the pontificating game of badminton you can happily engage in, when in for your position of enjoying good health. Healthy brethren, I am not speaking to you tonight. I am speaking to those who suffer under dark providences of pain, and to those who seek relief and escape. To those who suffer, I am talking about the application of love and medicine and the mild Holy Spirit anesthetic for the soul.

Naturally, providential or supernaturally, healing will come to some of you tonight. For many more of you though, hid under the cloud of such dark providences I speak of, there is a need to reach out toward the cold and dripping walls of your painful confine, for I am convinced that vintage succor has been laid down in their thousands of bottles against those bulwarks of dusty darkness, bearing the labeled descriptions of "Grace Sufficient," "Perfection in Weakness," "Glory Despite," "Stood with me," "Never be shamed," "Even Unto Death," "Crown of Glory," "Leaves of Life," "Roots Reached," "Casting Care," "Way of Escape," and even, "Stomachs Sake," and many, many more! Yes, I believe that there are bottles of supportive vintage, that will, despite the 'wrecktitude' of our days under these dark fat clouds that touch the surface of our lives with gross and tremulous pain, that when uncorked, left to breath a while and drunk in thankfulness, shall yet dance like lovelies upon our tepid tongues and be found to be full of the fragrant goodness of God, which is most needful to our present and most unsatisfied condition.

> ....*bottles of supportive vintage, ...that when uncorked, left to breath a while and drunk in thankfulness, shall yet dance like lovelies upon our tepid tongues and be found to be full of the*

Abstainers under dark providences suffer somewhat, yes they even suffer beyond necessity. Remember that, for tonight some of you need to uncork a couple of bottles and start drinking.

Sadly, there are many dear friends, who for whatever reason are beyond the getting, the uncorking and the drinking of God's lain down vintages and to these sorry folk, we the more able, must become the wine waiters of Jesus to them. For there are un-tasted comforts, un-supped restorations and un-swallowed soothing's, yet to be imbibed from the well catered for wine cellars of the Most High God! You need to take it to those who can neither find nor open the bottles.

In conclusion then, if you are in the cellar of affliction, look for the Lord's choicest wines. Ooh, and always keep a corkscrew in your pocket!

Listen: *"Give strong drink to him who is perishing, and wine to those who are bitter of heart." Proverbs 31:6 NKJV*

Pray: Lord, in my pain give me a corkscrew, an open mouth and thankful swallows. Let me taste of Your goodness in all my cellars of affliction, and serve others with this rich vintage, in Jesus name I pray, amen and let it be so.

Night-Whisper | **HOPE**

The Solomonian solution

Solomon sinned. Yet unlike his Father David, despite one of the greatest gifts ever bestowed upon a man, he did not repent but rather continued in his all-consuming ways. Yes, Solomon ate himself away, especially politically, especially sexually and especially spiritually. His far too many foreign wives were accommodated in their imported religious practices, indeed, Solomon not only made way for a politically correct and multicultural market place of religion but plunged himself headlong into their practices. It would appear that this was not a problem with his wives, neither was it a problem with his people, nor was it a problem with the leaders both temporal and spiritual No, only one person had a problem with it, God! Yes, the politically correct, corrupt multi-cultural system, the Solomonian solution worked with everyone except God.

1 Kings 11:4

"For it came to pass, when Solomon was old, that his wives turned away his heart after other gods: and his heart was not perfect with the Lord his God, as was the heart of David his father." KJV.

It was Ed Hussain, who I heard most recently, say, "Multiculturalism in Britain should not be ended but it should be mended." It was a retired teacher of religious education that also said to me in the same week, "Multiculturalism means Muslim!" For me, I remember when there were no Muslims in Britain. At the time of my writing in 2008, there are over 2 million and growing. Militant or peaceful, (and nowadays few sane people think Islam is not militant at its core) Islam is a growing force to be reckoned with. Ed was correct; Multiculturalism most surely does needs mending.

It is claimed that only a comparative few Muslims in Britain are interested in spreading Islam by force and establishing their world-view, practices and law by that same force. Maybe so, but I truly wonder if the European end game nevertheless, is not in fact not peaceful multiculturalism but rather peaceful Islamification.

Now allow me tonight to come at this challenge from a completely opposite view point, after all, as a Christian, I would love to see the re-Christianization of everything British and the Christianization of everything global.

Globally of course, we Christians are commanded to take the good news of Jesus, His death, burial and resurrection, to every tribe and tongue. Indeed, and praise God, neither God nor Christianity is essentially English. We are not to spread our national identity but His Gospel! Now although this Gospel message is always taken in love and in sacrifice of self to the betterment of others, it does change cultures! Imagine if you will the kingdom of Saudi Arabia as a whole, 'en masse,' becoming lovers of Jesus, becoming born again in the power of the Holy Spirit! Would that Kingdom change in terms of its politics, in terms of its social structure, in terms of its education, in terms of its foreign policy, its fiscal policy, etc., etc., etc.? Well of course, it would and there are many Saudis that would not be too happy about it. With this imaginary situation, I would like to believe that Christ would redeem the culture and enhance it and yes, He would but let's face it, some of it would be enhanced into oblivion. Of course it would, light always banishes darkness. The Gospel changes people, who in turn change communities, who then change nations. Some people do not want that change. Nevertheless, the commission for Christians to take this good news stands certain, sure and irrevocable. The spread of Christianity is never by violent means but rather must be Holy Spirit empowered, Holy Spirit led and Holy Spirit sustained. Yet still, the Gospel, when cast upon the ground to face the throne of Pharaoh, always bears the same marks of the rod of Moses in that it will inevitably swallow up the various false rods cast against it. The Gospel proclaimed is always peaceful and intentionally so, but always remember that the claims of Jesus are exclusively inclusive, yes, they are if you will, all swallowing. In this way, to darkness and all things contrary to light, it is a dawning change!

> *let's face it, some cultures would be enhanced into oblivion!*

On the home front, believing in the exclusively inclusive nature of the Gospel, believing that you have previously been blessed by God in yourself, family, community and nation with God's previous presence and practices, how do present day Christians, some of every tribe nation and tongue that presently call your earthly country home, how should you react to this present ineffective Solomon solution?

I would suggest there are five ways to respond: That is, in prayer, in proclamation, in power, in practice and in politics.

We need to pray to God for forgiveness! For the implementation of such a terrible multi-cultural Solomonian solution, has in fact solved nothing, but rather, has brought the setting of God's sun of favor upon us. Like Israel of Old, adversaries of every kind are being raised up against us and like Israel of Old; our kingdoms are being rent asunder. We need to pray for God to stay His hand of judgement and to send revival upon us and the blessing of His goodness upon our fellow citizens, upon the people of every nation tribe and tongue who now reside within these broken gates of our once Christian nations.

We need to proclaim the Gospel. Fearlessly, fervently, faithfully, we need to proclaim the Gospel.

We need to walk in power. The power of the Holy Spirit in gifting, in goodness and in generosity. We need to walk in power.

> *We need to practice what we preach and in all our practices, we need to preach the Gospel of Jesus Christ!*

We need to practice what we preach and in all our practices, we need to preach.

We need to be involved in politics. Peacefully, we need to engage the authorities, in debate, in declaration and in doing good.

God is not American but that younger nation could lead the world into God. God is not an Englishman but this England was once full of God. The Solomonian Solution is bearing its fruit and that right quickly. A crash and a clash of foreign culture and religions is not coming, it is here! Is your heart and mouth at the ready?

Listen: *"For I could wish that I myself were accursed from Christ for my brethren, my countrymen according to the flesh, who are Israelites, to whom pertain the adoption, the glory, the covenants, the giving of the law, the service of God, and the promises; of whom are the fathers and from whom, according to the flesh, Christ came, who is over all, the eternally blessed God. Amen." Romans 9:3-5 NKJV*

Pray: O Lord, great and awesome God, who keeps His covenant and mercy with those who love Him, and with those who keep His commandments, we have sinned and committed iniquity, we have done wickedly and rebelled, even by departing from Your precepts and Your judgments. Neither have we heeded Your servants the prophets, who spoke in Your name to our kings and our princes, to our fathers and all the people of the land. O Lord, righteousness belongs to You, but to us shame of face, as it is this day. Have mercy upon us our great God and King. Amen and let it be so (taken from Daniel 9:4b-7a NKJV)

Night-Whisper | **HAPPY**

Of soul food, tables and smelly, story telling

For me, suppertime is the best of times, especially if it the meal eaten with friends and dear ones. Supper food should be food to satisfy the longings of the day now past and food to prepare for the rest of the night to come, yes, supper should be soul food, comfort food, and the food of coming rest.

John 12:1-3

"Then, six days before the Passover, Jesus came to Bethany, where Lazarus was who had been dead, whom He had raised from the dead. There they made Him a supper; and Martha served, but Lazarus was one of those who sat at the table with Him. Then Mary took a pound of very costly oil of spikenard, anointed the feet of Jesus, and wiped His feet with her hair. And the house was filled with the fragrance of the oil." NKJV

There is nothing better to go with the eating of such soul food than a good bottle of table wine and a large helping of table tales, you know, stories of the day, stories of the past, stories that will last, and tonight, in the home of Simon the leper, where Martha and Mary are preparing and a-serving, oh, what stories are a brewing! Especially because Lazarus, recently back from the dead, is sat there itching to tell all. Man! I tell you I would have some questions for him around that table and if I were Lazarus, if I had come back from the dead, well, I would have some stories to tell you no doubt as well! The sights the sounds the smells, the yells from hell I heard, the absurd thoughts I previously held, the swelling throng afore the gates of heaven, my mates I'd missed so long, the song of heaven, the hills like Devon, the custard yellow flowers, the hours and hours of rest, the........well, you get the picture! Problem is though Lazarus never gets a look in! Not a word! Not a dickybird! Nope, the story and the conversation is all about Jesus...typical!

Whenever a born again person sits down to supper, it is like another Lazarus birthed from the grave is sat down again to unexpectedly uncork once more a fine bottle of love and life. It is good and right that testimonies and tales should abound at such tables of worth and mirth but I tell you, in the end, our story of resurrection form the dead is not about us, but about Jesus, the unseen guest who always sits among us. Mary had it right. In great gratefulness, deep, profound and thankful adoration, she worships Him who called her beloved Lazarus back from the darkness and such worship offered on bended knee, from a heart of broken thankfulness, will always fill the air, no, will fill the whole dwelling place and beyond with the fragrance of expensive worship; worship that has cost us something, worship that has cost us much.

> *Tell me, what odors adorned your table telling tales this evening at your supper time? What fragrance filled the air tonight?*

Tell me, what odors adorned your table telling tales this evening at your suppertime? What fragrance filled the air tonight?

Listen: *"Make a joyful shout to the Lord, all you lands! Serve the Lord with gladness; Come before His presence with singing. Know that the Lord, He is God; It is He who has made us, and not we ourselves; We are His people and the sheep of His pasture. Enter into His gates with thanksgiving, And into His courts with praise." Psalms 100:1-4 NKJV*

Pray: May my table O Lord, always smell of thankfulness to You my Savior and my King. For forever and always O Lord, we have at least a hundred things to thank You for this night. Amen.

Night-Whisper | **STRENGTH**

The orator little pleader and the enemy of the state

For sure, Tertullus the prosecutor, that little old Latin speaking, Italian turtle head, fully associated himself with his clients, the Jews, and most thoroughly earned his wages that day! I wonder how much they paid him?

Acts 24:1-9

"Now after five days Ananias the high priest came down with the elders and a certain orator named Tertullus. These gave evidence to the governor against Paul. And when he was called upon, Tertullus began his accusation, saying: 'Seeing that through you we enjoy great peace, and prosperity is being brought to this nation by your foresight, we accept it always and in all places, most noble Felix, with all thankfulness. Nevertheless, not to be tedious to you any further, I beg you to hear, by your courtesy, a few words from us. For we have found this man a plague, a creator of dissension among all the Jews throughout the world, and a ringleader of the sect of the Nazarenes. He even tried to profane the temple, and we seized him, and wanted to judge him according to our law. But the commander Lysias came by and with great violence took him out of our hands, commanding his accusers to come to you. By examining him yourself you may ascertain all these things of which we accuse him.' And the Jews also assented, maintaining that these things were so." NKJV

Tertullus earned his money that day by presenting a very simple and strong case against the Apostle Paul with the use of the clever manipulation of half-truths. In so doing, he perpetrated a crime of gross injustice, by invoking plausible but dishonest pleadings in the at-first, disinterested ears of Felix. Then, with the cheering affirmation of a hired mob, Tertullus iced his perfect little cake of false accusation, by trying to then strong arm the Governor himself into compliance with his twisted talking, his festering little anti-Paul and anti-Christian fairy tale.

Yes, Tertullus, a hired gun, a retained lawyer of some professional and vocal strength, exuding sufficient slime to let a large elephant seal, slither down an old, cold, cobbled high street, kept poking Festus with the simple yet very sharp trident of adulation, argumentation and affirmation. He especially focused on the Governor's patriotic sensibilities, for anyone examining both Tertullus's arguments and those of the falsely the accused, would himself become a likeminded senseless traitor if he continued to allow Paul, that archenemy of the Roman State, to continue to cause civil disobedience in the face of Caesar by proclaiming Christ. His implication is clear, "Was Festus a traitor to Caesar?" Yes, old Tertullus earned his fee that day, that's for sure!

Interestingly, Tertullus is the diminutive from the Latin word "tetius," meaning, "third." I wonder if he was the third child? The youngster maybe, the picked-on momma's boy, the little runt of the litter? Some commentators have suggested that it was Jewish humor that led him to be called Tertullus, for his name was actually Ter-Tullius, which in the Greek means, three times a liar, three times a teller of stories, or even three times a cheat! It is an interesting conjecture for sure, but who knows really? Save we all agree that Tertullus is a great name for a lawyer!

> ....three times a liar, three times a teller of stories, or even three times a cheat! ....we all agree that Tertullus is a great name for a lawyer!

Now, we do know that the enemies of light used every slimy means possible to stop the spread of that light. Felix, did not know too much of the so-called "Sect of the Nazarenes" but he was familiar somewhat with "The Way" and this got his attention! Still, Felix was one of those people, who though he was warned and strangely warmed by the fire of God's holiness, he never yet approached the burning bush which God had lit in his heart. These are some of the most dangerous of people for sure. They are time wasters, un-deciders, undeclared, scaredy-cat folks, though all fearful of the fire, who, even knowing their final end, never the less do not repent but rather, will thoroughly abuse the saints, taking what they can from them, whilst keeping them on hand, just in case.

Therefore, without proof, Felix nevertheless detains the apostle Paul, and after two years of this use and abuse by him, fat Festus succeeded Felix as Governor and continued to keep the apostle bound for the sake of the Jews.

I wonder if over those two years of wait, Paul or his friends should have paid the accepted and expected bribe to either Felix or Festus and so secured his release? Personally, I think they should have, save for two most important points. First, that Paul knew what awaited him! The Holy Spirit had already told Paul, that in every place and maybe even in Paul's penultimate departure place of Rome, chains and tribulations awaited him. (Acts 20:23) Second that the Lord Jesus had already told him to cheer up for, he was going to Rome to testify of Him! Paul did not want springing!

Cheer up indeed, for knowledge of God's will, will keep us on track, will keep us in The Way, even when there might be away out of present painful predicaments! Indeed, even orator little pleaders, will smooth the path of Gods providence before us.

The Way is not easy but it is right and it is correct? Do you see it yet? Will you keep on it, no matter what?

Listen: *"But the following night the Lord stood by him and said, 'Be of good cheer, Paul; for as you have testified for Me in Jerusalem, so you must also bear witness at Rome.'" Acts 23:11 NKJV*

Pray: O Lord my God, so speak to me, even if from my perspective I do not think it is the most cheerful of news. Amen.

Night-Whisper | **CONTINUE**

Meat is murder! And other mad hyperbole

An hyperbole is a statement, which is exaggerated, and a statement used to evoke strong feelings and to therefore make strong impressions. As a figure of speech, such statements then are not necessarily to be taken literally but rather, the outrageous extremity of the statement is there to suddenly halt us in our tracks and make us consider the underlying point, further, deeper and in a much more personal way, than the point could ever make without the introduction of the hyperbole. I am of the opinion that our text for tonight, this single verse summary of 1 Corinthians chapter 8, is in fact a Pauline statement of hyperbolic proportions!

1 Corinthians 8:13

"Therefore, if food makes my brother stumble, I will never again eat meat, lest I make my brother stumble." NKJV

My lovely daughter is presently a vegan. Cooking for her, going out with her to eat, does have its challenges. She is not a nasty vegan but conscientious, deliberate and determined. I am an omnivore and will kill to eat if necessary. Despite Morrissey's declarations, death for food is not death for no reason and it is not murder. Though I would admit that the death of animals on such a now vast and industrialized scale is indeed, death without honor, death without respect and subsequently, death without thankfulness. Yet still, meat is not murder. When Christians choose to be vegetarian and even vegan, it has been my experience that such a choice has not been done out of a weak conscience but rather, out of resolute and informed decision. Indeed, it was a decision by them that demanded such a committed change of lifestyle that is became a decision that exhibits a strength and determination way above my own omnivorous tendencies. Respect!

There is a great difference between the strength of informed and resolute decision-making and a weak conscience choice. 1 Corinthians chapter 8 is not primarily about strength but rather about "weak consciences" residing in weak brethren.

Now you see, taking chapter 8 and verse 13 in particular out of the context of the whole tenor of Scripture is very dangerous and has led to lots of problems. After all, Acts 15:20 gives a clear command from the council of Jerusalem to abstain from meat offered to idols, while Romans 14:1-3, seems to highlight once again the seeming weaker faith of the vegetarian! However, if we allowed these particular texts to be judged by the rest of Scripture, then we would see that a seeming contradiction would not necessarily be so. Therefore, in the same way, we need the whole Scripture to understand this particular verse in 1 Corinthians 8:13.

It would appear that at Corinth, there were those "in the know," as it were, whose conscience allowed them not only to eat meat, but eat meat offered to idols and not only that, but eat meat offered to idols in the local Heathen temple restaurant to boot! Even if it was on a Sunday, with roast potatoes and Yorkshire puddings thrown in for good measure! Other Christians, and this passage relates only to other *Christians* and *their weak* conscience, other Christians who were not in the know, seeing those liberated Christians machinating on the meat, free of a condemning conscience, participating in this abomination as they saw it, were severely offended, nay, so sufficiently aghast were they, that they wrote letters to Paul and signed them, *"Yours faithfully, 'Outraged' of Tunbridge Wells!"*

> *At Corinth, there were those "in the know," as it were, whose conscience allowed them not only to eat meat, but eat meat offered to idols and not only that, but eat meat offered to idols in the local Heathen temple restaurant to boot!*

Now if this "church trouble" was not bad enough, some of those with these weak consciences had tried to follow in the footsteps of those libertarian temple meat eaters and in the so doing, had stumbled! *"Such weak conscience stumbling"* says Paul, *"leads to perishing (physical harm or even death) and the perpetrators of such perishing stumbling, (scandalous entrapment of conscience) are doing nothing short of sinning! So stop it!"*

Now here is something for the weak conscience to remember, "Doing those things engaged in by stronger conscience brethren, will not strengthen you, but rather, will lead to stumbling and perishing! In other words, *action* against conscience does not strengthen conscience but rather diminishes it to stumbling and eventual perishing!" Brethren, the only thing that strengthens conscience is instruction and that particular instruction which brings the revelation of the Holy Scriptures into full and personal illumination. It is light that strengthens conscience, not indulging in action that runs contrary to conscience's dictates. That simply seers conscience and ruins both it and the person.

Now, here are five things for the strong conscience folk to remember when erring into the stumbling perishing of others. Yes, five things that you heathen, idol temple restaurant meat eating Christians must do in the face of all the mail from outraged of Tunbridge Wells!

First, you can simply not go to the temple restaurant to eat meat. Secondly, you can go there when the weaker conscience folk are not there! Thirdly, you could set up in business yourself and open your own fully Kosher Kingdom meat restaurant, with additional options for vegetarians, vegans, and fruitarians. Fourthly, and most importantly, in meekness and humility, you could instruct the weak conscience Christians from the Scriptures, that they too might be illuminated and released. Lastly, you could and must, simply love the weak, and may I say that in loving the weak conscience Christians, you will in fact do any of the first three options! However, whilst doing all of the above, you must engage in the fourth action of illuminated instruction. This is vital for the health of the whole body. Do not let them continue in ignorant error that will surly turn to angry arrogance.

If we fail in this "instruction of illumination," then the mad mandate of Paul's hyperbole will lead to a multitude of silly injunctions. Good grief, if we had to, without illuminated instruction never eat meat again, we would be doing a whole lot less of a whole lot of other things. For in satisfying the weak and uninstructed conscience of other Christians, I might never drink wine again, never wear leather again, never have a TV again, never go to the movies again, never listen to rock music, never read certain books, never wear jeans, never have a beard, never wear makeup, never go out to eat on a Sunday, never go to Halloween parties, never tell jokes, never read anything but the King James Version, never pray in tongues, never go to the beach, never swim in public places, never bare my arms, never wear a skirt above my knees, never prophecy, never

Never. Never. Never.
Never. Never. Never.
Never. Never. Never.
Never. Never. Never.
Never..........................

exercise certain gifts, never… and oh my goodness, the list goes on and on! Indeed, I am sure the mere suggestion of some of those 'nevers' will have evoked strong affirmation and repugnance in many of you even! Yes, any "reigning in" of our clear Scriptural liberty, without the giving of illuminated instruction to those who disagree, will result in wanton wackiness of every kind! Wackiness is easy to discern; you can feel it. Remember that.

Finally may I say, unless it is regarding hypocrisy, the world does not give two hoots what we the church get up to. 1 Corinthians 8 refers to other Christians. Nevertheless, let us remember that liberty is not stupidity and any strength we have will quickly turn to weakness should we begin to justify such liberty for dabbling in the works of darkness and that list of darkness my friends, would be a very long list indeed!

Listen: *"For you, brethren, have been called to liberty; only do not use liberty as an opportunity for the flesh, but through love serve one another. For all the law is fulfiled in one word, even in this: 'You shall love your neighbour as yourself.' But if you bite and devour one another, beware lest you be consumed by one another!" Galatians 5:13-15 NKJV*

Pray: Lord, teach me to wisely love. Give me also the wisdom to in my liberty, eschew all works of darkness. Help me always to rescue the perishing and not allow my liberty turn to stupidity and downfall. In Jesus name I pray, amen.

PAUSE FOR PRAYER | 66CITIES

Well, I do pray that the first month of this quarters NightWhispers written with you in mind, have prospered you spiritually and pushed you on a little farther down the road in knowing, obeying and immediately following the commands of the God of the whole Bible. This is my desire.

I am Victor Robert Farrell and I am the author of NightWhispers. I also have the privilege of being the President of The 66 Books Ministry and I want to tell you a little bit about our major project which is: 66Cities. I believe one of the problems with the rapid moral decline of the West coupled with the influx of other religions, has been the compromise of the local church. It is as though we leaders have watered down the wine of the Gospel with the methods and culture of the world and have done so to such an extent that all we are left with is an anemic and slightly rose colored, fluoride-filled cup of poor tepid mouth wash. It is good for nothing except to be poured down the drain. This compromise I speak of, was to stop speaking about the God of the whole Bible and to such an extent that Christians were left in a strange kind of idolatry, worshiping the God of a cultural constructed Christianity, and so much so, that when these same Christians came into contact with the real God of the Bible, He troubled them and offended them. Indeed, they were embarrassed by Him and wanted Him excluded from their parties. The world of course, found more substance in the other gods, especially that kind of unbiblical Trinitarian spirituality which allowed science and hedonism to mate with the X factor of their own particular choosing.

We at The 66 Books Ministry intend to preach the Gospel of Jesus Christ and the God of the whole Bible, from each of the 66 Books of the Bible in the 66 most influential cities of the nations of the world. That's 16,500 cities in an annual and ongoing basis. To make this happen we are prayerfully raising up teams of proclaimers and 'prayer rangers' to go into these cities. We see this is a true prophetic witness to the glory of God. Indeed. This is the main reason why we are doing this: that God the Father and God the Son may be seen and Glorified in the power of God The Holy Spirit. We hope and pray, that many will see the Father, trust in the Son and be saved by the power of the Holy Spirit as well. Brethren, **we covet your prayers as we do this.** Check out WWW.66Books.TV

Night-Whisper | **PROSPER**

Six quid and six silver spoons

Someone has remarked that, "Man was born free, but everywhere; he is in the property chain!" When in my lifetime I find myself witnessing yet another property crash I have to ask the question if we are indeed in bondage to property? Indeed, with the present crash precipitated by or coincidental with, the death of the dollar, as I write, outside of the Major US cities, tent cities have now sprung up to house the repossessed homeless. Do you remember? I tell you today, in First-World Europe tents are the only accommodation some people have! I wonder sometimes if property ownership is an illusion, after all, stop paying your government taxes and then see who really owns your home!

Luke 18:22-23

"So when Jesus heard these things, He said to him, 'You still lack one thing. Sell all that you have and distribute to the poor, and you will have treasure in heaven; and come, follow Me.' But when he heard this, he became very sorrowful, for he was very rich." NKJV

Believe me when I tell you, that the need to "own" your own property will put you in bondage for most of your life. You shall be obligated to work almost totally to service the large loans taken out to "buy" the property in the first place. Once you then buy a TV and succumb to the need for annual vacations, new cars and more stuff than you know what to do with, but what your newly purchased property most certainly needs in terms of accents, upgrades and maintenance, then you can just hear the clink, clink of the financial manacles being clasped around your ankles. Tell me, is it worth it? Is property ownership a blessing?

The health wealth and prosperity marketers of our own religious industry, have done a great job in taking definite Old Testament material promises of housing, land, milk and honey and turning them into New Testament signage for the presence and blessing of God on the Christian. I suppose then, that when many Christians in the coming global crash lose their roof and their shirt, they too will seemingly have lost the presence and blessings of God? Truth is, even in the Old Testament, land was never to be treated as a trading commodity but rather, for the Israelites, it was an inheritance. It was the material centrality of the covenant promises that God had made to them. Neither Realty nor Real estate however, is to be the New Testament Christian's covenantal core!

OK let's cut to the chase. Market driven forces, consistently change and erode the financial landscape. The market, however, is well manipulated long before those forces of fiscal erosion are ever released upon us plebs. The top hats and the fast racing cars of those big hitters on the global monopoly board, will buy and if needs be, also trash a billion green plastic houses for the for the sake of acquiring a bigger stake in the game. If we are 'gonna' get on the board, then we pays our money and we takes our chance. Property ownership is as spiritual as that.

> *We are people of the far country, we are of Jerusalem above, which is free. Our covenantal core is blood, it is bread, it is water, it is Jesus now and homes in heaven! Remember that.*

Our Master had neither nest nor den. Our dual Christian titles are that of being strangers and pilgrims and our citizenship is in heaven. We are people of the far country; we are of Jerusalem above, which is free. Our covenantal core is blood, it is bread, it is water, and it is Jesus now and homes in heaven! Remember that.

It was Leonard Ravenhill who told us that John Wesley died in 1791, leaving only a handful of books, six silver spoons, six pound notes, one each for the poor men who would carry his coffin, a Geneva preaching gown, and, what was it now? What was it again? Oh yes, the Methodist church! In Wesley's case, though he could have been an exceptionally rich man, everything he had was well spent and invested in a spiritual future. As for me, I am long done with monopoly and I too shall go to my grave, both naked in material wealth and well spent in all spiritual matters. How about you? What are you truly living for? What are you shackled to?

Listen: *"Do not lay up for yourselves treasures on earth, where moth and rust destroy and where thieves break in and steal; but lay up for yourselves treasures in heaven, where neither moth nor rust destroys and where thieves do not break in and steal. For where your treasure is, there your heart will be also." Matthew 6:19-21 NKJV*

Pray: Lord, get me off the board. Lord, give me a "Get out of jail free" card, the community chest of the saints and a great consolation prize in glory, in Your great name I ask it, amen!

Night-Whisper | **CONTINUE**

Sinister sinners and shining sons

In recent years, the word "martyr" and the idea of "martyrdom" has taken on a most sinister connotation. Rather than being a word which evokes the life style of undeniable selflessness for the glory of God and sacrifice for the sake of others, even and especially in the face of grossly unjust suffering, it now evokes images of mass murder, wanton carnage, legless torsos, headless corpses, yes, it evokes the gross image of blast damage instead of a blessed message.

1 Thessalonians 2:11

"As you know how we exhorted, and comforted, and charged every one of you, as a father does his own children." NKJV

Our text for tonight is drawn out of 1st Thessalonians, which teaches Christians to wait in patience for the coming of the Lord and to wait with clean noses, quiet personas and productive lives, knowing that, nevertheless, suffering is assigned to such a watching and waiting saint.

In this text, it is interesting to note Paul's metaphor of personal discipleship here, for while building on the metaphor of a nurse towards her charges, he now turns quickly to that of a father towards his children. The childless Paul took his own instruction here most probably from the observation of other fathers as well as his own Heavenly Father, whom he saw exhorting, comforting and charging their children.

As a father to his own dear spiritual children, Paul exhorted the Thessalonians. Literally, he beseeched them and this is nothing short of desperate pleading! When a parent gets to this point in the proceedings, into desperately pleasing with their children, the it's an end game scenario, for if pleading doesn't work, the wind of parental disappointment will blow, shaking the quivering leaves of already bent over trees into frantic frustration. To be sure, a spanking is sure to follow. Yet the apostle Paul here says that part of his discipleship process was to plead! How very humbling for a parent to do this. Yet Paul pleaded with these his spiritual children as part of his discipleship process. It worked!

As a father to his own dear children, Paul exhorted the Thessalonians. He consoled them. He literally got alongside them, put his arm around their shuddering shoulders and said, "So you fell off your bike then? There, there, there, it's all right darling; you'll do better next time. Now get yourself up, let's dust you down and then let's try it again." Yes, the apostle Paul says here that part of his discipleship process was also to exhort! It's a bit babyish really isn't it? It's all a bit namby-pamby! Yet Paul exhorted them in this way as part of his discipleship process. It worked!

As a father to his own dear children, Paul charged the Thessalonians. The root of the Greek word he uses here is from where we get the word "martyr." Paul witnessed to them in self-sacrificing terms, how, in being a witness to the truth, they must suffer for righteousness sake in this present world.

The apostle Paul says here that part of his discipleship process was to charge them in the way of Royal martyrdom!

The end of this charge of true martyrdom is very pointed here, and it is this, "walk worthy!" That is, walk appropriately, walk fittingly, walk rightly as a child of God, indeed, walk as a child who is called into the Kingdom of the most Glorious God! It is as though Paul says, "OK enough! Stop your whining! This is who you are, you are Royalty. You must expect and accept both the privileges and the challenges of being a son of the King. Now, blow your nose, stop your blubbering, stand up straight and no matter what happens, honor the king." Yes, the apostle Paul says here that part of his discipleship process was to charge them in the way of Royal martyrdom! It's a bit scary, it's more than a bit demanding, yet Paul charged them to walk worthy in this way. It worked!

You too must make disciples. You shall have those folk who you have helped birth into the Kingdom or have others who being been birthed by someone else, are then put into your charge, your spiritual directorship, your life formation class, your personal discipleship program. Do not think I am talking about a clergy job here or of paid church staff, or of an organized church program with books, dollars, and loads of frills. No, I am talking about you, the very same person He commanded to go and make disciples. When you are doing this folks, you are engaged in real Kingdom ministry and when you are doing this, though you mightn't be referred to as "Father" nevertheless you must act like one! Act like a Father, act like a godly mother would toward her dear children whom she is molding into independent man or womanhood. Yes, in all matters relating to making disciples, if you let "tender love" be your guide, "release" be your watchword and "growth" be your motto, you shall go a long, long way to producing shining sons! This is the true way of martyrdom; sacrificing yourself as a parent for their child

Listen: *"By this we know love, because He laid down His life for us. And we also ought to lay down our lives for the brethren." 1 John 3:16-17 NKJV*

Pray: Lord, may the wise spirit of parental gentleness rest upon all my dealings with the younger members of the Kingdom, no matter how old they are, that the crop produced, may be a sea of shining stars. Amen.

| Vol 01 | Q2 | NW00124 | May 03rd |

Night-Whisper | **HAPPY**

The garage of the joy wagon

Our text for tonight talks about a special place. It is in fact the open face of God; it is in fact the very presence of God and it is there in the very presence of God that we shall find two most valuable and interlocking gifts, which lie like coupled golden rings on the black felt of a box of midnight blue. I am of course talking about strength and joy.

1 Chronicles 16:26,27

"For all the Gods of the people are idols: but the Lord made the heavens. Glory and honor are in his presence; strength and gladness are in his place." KJV

It was Adolf Hitler's 3rd Reich, who by 1939 had streamed over 25 million of its own people through its political party designed tourism, travel and vacation program. The crowning joy of this people's program, this 'Volks program,' was of course the possibility for each German to acquire the ultimate people's car of the day, or as we have known it now for so long now, the people wagon, the Volks-wagon. Interestingly, the name of the whole umbrella program was called "Kraft durch Freude," or simply KdF, which, when translated into English means quite literally, "Strength through Joy!"

So, the concept producing health and happiness via this powerful linkage of joy and strength was evident even in an increasingly totalitarian regime. The thought of the 3rd Reich in the implementation of its strength through joy program was quite simple, in that, "Rested people are happy people; happy people are strong people and we need strong people, with strong nerves to get us through the changes which are to come." For sure, the Nazis found some truth, some sustenance, some joy and some strength in this program, for they took their nation from being on the canvas of a post-World War I Europe, to being the ferociously strong and heavily armed beast, which would plunge Europe once again into a Second World War!

Now, I am all for a good holiday, for relaxed bodies and minds to better navigate the difficult waters of life and neither would I refuse any joy or gladness and recuperative strength that comes through it! However, our text for tonight and its very own and singular partner verse in Nehemiah 8:10c, are not talking about that kind of strength and joy! No, this special couplet is not found in good vacations, in sleep or enjoyment, and no, it's not even found in the promise of material blessing, even the material blessing of a Volks-Wagon for everyone!

This particular couplet of courage, (for what is courage but the coupling of strength and joy,) comes only from the face of God, comes only from being in the presence of Him who made the heavens. When you stand in the triune but singular ring of the Father, Son and Holy Spirit, then rings of glory, rings of honor, rings of strength and joy shall be found to the real treasure of the you, the divine Olympiad, for there is a permanent and supernatural strength and joy that in Olympian terms, simply supersedes whatever temporary "knock offs" seem to be on offer down here. However, such trophies are only ever acquired from being in the presence of God.

> *What is courage but the coupling of strength and joy?*

When the outbreak of war demanded the production capacity of the Volks-Wagon factory and its product for weapons and armaments, despite all the payments made by those hundreds of thousands of Germans, no one really got their nice new strength and joy wagon! Therefore, I tell you, if you want to be certain of a good ride in a great joy wagon, then you need to know where it is permanently garaged, for you cannot have the "the joy of the Lord" without first having the "the Lord of the joy." Yes, you cannot have "the strength of the Lord" without having "the Lord of strength!"

Jesus has the keys of both death and hell around His waist and I wonder if he keeps a spare set of keys to His joy wagon, right there hidden in His right hand pocket? I say again, it is only when you meet Him in the face to face of His presence that you can ask to borrow His car!

Listen: *"You will show me the path of life; in Your presence is fullness of joy; at Your right hand are pleasures forevermore." Psalms 16:11 NKJV*

Pray: Teach me Holy Spirit, through Jesus Christ my Lord, how to abide in Your presence. Oh, and Dad! Can I have the keys for the joy wagon tonight? I can! Thanks!

Night-Whisper | SEE

The clang of symbols

No, today's title is not a spelling mistake! Rather, let it be known that 'symbols' communicate. Yes, symbols when smashed together make a loud clashing sound, they inculcate a message, they congregate a peoples, they educate the masses, they articulate core values, they rally the disorderly, and once they are most fully embraced, clashing symbols define directions and ultimately rule over those people they fly over. Why do you think that after WWII and the defeat of the Nazis, every effort was made to completely remove any symbolic representation of the black jackboot, which had been placed over most of Europe at the time? Why? Well because these lashing symbols all, from Swastika to the SS Runic bolts, all had a residual and unifying power, that's why. Indeed, it is still an illegal and punishable act for the swastika to be displayed in present day Germany or Austria. Yes, symbols are powerful.

I think we can say these three things then concerning symbols: First that the creation of symbols have declarative power. Second that the emplacement of symbols have immense practical power. Thirdly that the application of symbols give rule.

Revelation 17:3-6

"So he carried me away in the Spirit into the wilderness. And I saw a woman sitting on a scarlet beast which was full of names of blasphemy, having seven heads and ten horns. The woman was arrayed in purple and scarlet, and adorned with gold and precious stones and pearls, having in her hand a golden cup full of abominations and the filthiness of her fornication. And on her forehead a name was written: Mystery, Babylon the great, the mother of harlots and of the abominations of the earth. I saw the woman, drunk with the blood of the saints and with the blood of the martyrs of Jesus. And when I saw her, I marvelled with great amazement." NKJV

As I write this Whisper, Schiller's "Ode To Joy," it's sentiment of unity and brotherly love so marvelously illuminated by Beethoven's 9th Symphony, has now become the official anthem of the European Union. The blue-skied background, twelve golden-starred banner has become its official flag, and the Euro, its official currency. Latin is being moved to become its official language of "unification," its symbolic motto and tag line being *"In Varietate Concordia" - "United in Diversity."* Do you see that this revived Roman Empire is now festooned with symbols of declarative power? Indeed, the systems that now form under these flapping symbols arm the union with practical power and move the whole mess to a ruling stance. Yes, Europa, robed in priestly colors, sits now ever stronger, astride her scarlet beast. Despite the economic mess and the problem of Greek yoghurt, these symbols speak loudly to those with uncorked ears. Are you listening?

> *Europa, robed in priestly colors, sits now ever stronger, astride her scarlet beast. Despite the economic mess and the problem of Greek yoghurt, these symbols speak loudly to those with uncorked ears. Are you listening?*

Undoubtedly, you have symbols in your life, which of those then, at least to some extent, maybe dictate, direct and rule over you? The British Pound and the American Dollar despite their maybe current frailty, still rule over many of you tonight. Pierre Cardin and Givenchy still rule over many more maybe. Mercedes and Jaguar, PhD's and six Golden Rings together with a multitude of other symbols, which might include even the Stars and Stripes and the Union Jack, rule over many millions more. What symbols have their rule over you?

Examine the ruling symbols of your life. If they are contrary to the symbols of God, then I tell you, you need to get yourself out from under them and raise some new and Godly symbols of your own. Yes, symbols are powerful. I think we can say these three things then concerning symbols: First that the creation of symbols have declarative power. Second that the emplacement of symbols have immense practical power. Thirdly, that the application of symbols give rule. I say agin this night and call you to thinking. What symbols rule in your life this night?

Listen: *"I have also spoken by the prophets, and have multiplied visions; I have given symbols through the witness of the prophets." (Hosea 12:10 NKJV)*

Pray: Lord, brand me with the symbols of Your love, yes, come fly them over my life and also place Your white streaked bark before my almond peering eyes and anoint them with the symbols of the stripped poplar of your unstoppable blessing, in Jesus name I ask it, amen.

Night-Whisper | **RESCUE**

The real resurrectionists

The chief end of man is indeed the glory of God. However, if I were to sum up the expressed glory of God in creation, that aspect of glory, which reveals His heart, His desire, His ultimate plan, power and purpose, then it would be this, it would be resurrection! I would say that the stripped down core of Christianity is indeed, most expressed in the action of resurrection.

Hebrews 13:20-21

"May the God of peace, who through the blood of the eternal covenant brought back from the dead our Lord Jesus, that great Shepherd of the sheep, equip you with everything good for doing his will, and may he work in us what is pleasing to him, through Jesus Christ, to whom be glory for ever and ever." Amen. NIV

Yes, resurrection is not just theological theory, no; this is what Christianity is all about! This is at the heart of it all! Redemptive transformation through resurrection. In terms of this our physical body, the curse which came upon us all at Adam's fall, daily works itself out in an unremitting wear and tear kind of wearing out, resulting at last, in ultimate breakdown of the body, the end of which is the separation of soul and spirit from what is left of this over ripe, rotten and wrinkly, burnt out now old shrunken hulk. The best of glory is never found in stinking rotten fruit! Hence the absolute necessity of the resurrection of the ever fresh! 'Work out' all you might. Your body is still gonna wear out and you will still plant it in the ground. Not even trans-human endeavors will bring eternal life. That sales pitch is a lie and a damn lie at that.

Redemptive transformation through resurrection is God's design plan to produce beautifully perfected, smooth and majestically proportioned creatures, which would reveal His heart, His desire, His ultimate plan, power and purpose! Our redemptive Captain in all of this, our forerunner, our great first sent one, the second and last Adam to the fight, our Apostle in resurrection, is none other than the Lord Jesus Christ Himself, who, by the shedding of His own infinite and eternal most innocent blood on behalf of all those cursed in the first Adam, was brought back from the dead by the power of the Father. Our Father God, by this same power, through the shed blood of Jesus His son and our Savior, is bringing, and will bring us back from the dead along with Him. This offer of resurrected eternal life is a one-time deal folks and only offered this side of the grave, so come and get it whilst it's hot! You don't need metal, and you don't need the mixing of iron and clay, you just need Jesus to live forever.

> *You don't need metal, and you don't need the mixing of iron and clay, you just need Jesus to live forever!*

I am often asked, "What do you do for a living?" My response is almost always "Oh, I am a Spiritual entrepreneur." The quizzical reply is usually, "Really? How fascinating and what does that entail?"

"Oh," I reply in explanation, "It's a family business really and I suppose it's all about renewal you know? But really I suppose, I'm just helping my Father bring back people from the dead."

Christian, do not underestimate the great work that God has called you to. In all your service and in all your prayers especially, remember that it is a resurrection ministry that you are part and partner of. We are the real resurrectionists.

Listen: *"And when He came near the gate of the city, behold, a dead man was being carried out, the only son of his mother; and she was a widow. And a large crowd from the city was with her. When the Lord saw her, He had compassion on her and said to her, 'Do not weep.' Then He came and touched the open coffin, and those who carried him stood still. And He said, 'Young man, I say to you, arise.' So he who was dead, sat up and began to speak. And He presented him to his mother. Then fear came upon all, and they glorified God, saying, 'A great prophet has risen up among us;' and, 'God has visited His people.'" Luke 7:12-17 NKJV*

Pray: Lord, may all my prayers be flavored and touched with resurrection purpose and resurrection power. Help me O Lord, to walk tall and true in this great ministry, which You have called me to. Amen and let it be so!

| Vol 01 | Q2 | NW00127 | May 06th |

Night-Whisper | **HAPPY**

The whirling dervish of Sunny Delight

After a call from a good friend for some immediate support and prayer, Matilda, having put her own four young children finally to bed, is pleased to see Jocelyn arrive at her door bearing gifts of wine and chocolates. After putting the kettle on and grabbing a nice cup of tea, they sit down together. Matilda, weary and just a little bleary eyed, is now faced with a very concerned and frightfully angry friend, sitting fidgeting in fury on the couch just across from her.

James 1:2-3

"Consider it pure joy, my brothers, whenever you face trials of many kinds." NIV

"So, he's finally left you then dear?" Says Jocelyn. "I'm so sorry. How are all the kids coping? What are you going to do about your part time job, about the mortgage, the car payments? Good grief Matilda! The scumbag! She's half his age for goodness sake! Did you know this affair was going on? I know how much you loved him, I mean, how could he have done this to you all? I'm sorry sweetie, I'm just so angry and I've not even asked you what's your take on it all? Do you think he might come back? What do you think about it all my poor, sweet, long suffering beautiful, little friend?"

"Well hon, quite frankly," replies Matilda, "I consider it a bottle full of bright yellow sunshine delight! Yes, I consider it all joy! You know how grouchy I can get with the children, and of course, my poor hubby Marlon, bless him, well he must have been feeling it so much, poor man. Which is why I think he ran away with his busty young blonde haired and perky little secretary. No, really, this whole situation will give me ample opportunity to learn to be more patient. More patient in waiting for him to come back, more patient with Marlon Junior, especially as his wheelchair still keeps scraping the new paint on the walls. I've hated that in the past you know! No, it's all good, for I can be more patient with our mechanic as well, after all, he has to make a living as well, and four visits in the past week to keep that pile of junk on the road, well, I'm sure it's been worth it. No, for me to learn patience in these trying circumstances is such a joy Jocelyn." As Jocelyn rises to her feet Matilda says, "Hey! What are you doing girl? Where are you going?"

"Well sweetie," say shocked Josie, "I'm just ringing the doctor. I think you're in shock. I don't think you're quite in your right mind. I think you need some help, some pills, just for a little while maybe, a bit of counselling, not too much mind, just enough to get you back on a level playing field. 'Hello Doctor… just a second…' Matilda, get the corkscrew sweetie, it's in the kitchen, third draw down? Got it? Good. Now pour yourself a drink and grab a few caramels for yourself. Just stick 'em in your gob and start chewing and drinking and I shall be back in a mo! 'Yes hello, doctor, I'm ringing about my friend, Matilda Maniac, yes, well, I'm afraid she's lost it!'"

> *Various and vicious temptations of every kind, each with a barbed design to make you deny both God and His goodness, will come upon you with a vengeance.*

Pure Joy. Not mixed with grief, not marred by even a speck of lack of faith, not even a smidgen of doubt, not one little dash of anger, no, I'm talking about pure joy. Yes, consider your trials, then add them up to appear at the bottom of your spreadsheet as quite simply, pure joy! Yeah right.

Now frankly, I find this particular Bible verse to be a most stupid and outrageous, grossly offensive and mad little statement I have ever heard! Yet two important things can be dragged screaming from the madness of James the writer:

First, not a suggestion that there might be troubles ahead, no, but rather, a warning preparation that there *will* be troubles ahead. Yes, various and vicious temptations of every kind, each with a barbed design to make you deny both God and His goodness, will come upon you with a vengeance. "Arm yourself therefore," says James, "Be prepared then. For, if you think that becoming a Christian is designed to make your life easier, then you are in for a shock! No, in terms of all the troubles and trials common to mankind, then we are most definitely not the sheltered select nor the protected elect! Troubles will come upon you. Be ready!"

Therefore, and secondly, when we come across such trials, when they are quite literally thrown and strewn across our way like fallen timber across a railroad track, we should not be surprised! Grieve! Get grouchy, go kick a few trees and even break a few glasses if you must, but save one of them mind you, because for your survival and your victory, nay, even for your redemption and the redemption of others, at some point, you will have to go and pour yourself a large glass of Sunny Delight! Yes, you will at some point, have to 'count it all joy,' for it is very often so very true, that "outlook determines outcome, and in consequence then, attitude most definitely determines action and then just for good measure, it is also our personal values which determine our evaluation."

Brethren, I think it quite mad to evaluate the most terrible trials as joy. However, Christianity does often appear to be a stark staring wild madness, which dances in the face of brutal reality, a whirling Dervish of happy hope smiling through tears in the face of terrible temptations. Oh yes it does! It would appear then that we Christians have a choice to make when faced with terrible trials. True discipleship will always teach us to face this fact and then make room for such a seemingly maniacal choosing of joy. So, in the face of such terrible trials, which will most surely come upon you, tell me, what will you choose? Misery or counting joy? This life choice is a real insanity workout.

Christians have a choice to make when faced with terrible trials.

Listen: *"Therefore we also, since we are surrounded by so great a cloud of witnesses, let us lay aside every weight, and the sin which so easily ensnares us, and let us run with endurance the race that is set before us, looking unto Jesus, the author and finisher of our faith, who for the joy that was set before Him endured the cross, despising the shame, and has sat down at the right hand of the throne of God." Hebrews 12:1-2 NKJV*

Pray: Lord, I read these verses and I think, "You have got to be kidding me!" I tell You Father, I don't like them! Yet nevertheless, there they are. Help me then with my judgement, with my faith accounting especially. Then O Lord, help me to crack open that Sunny Delight and start gulping down the goodness. Lord, let the wild dance of redemption begin, even in the face of crowding calamities. In Jesus name I pray, amen!

Night-Whisper | **FEAR**

God the gravedigger

The prophet Jonah had previously been mightily, if not reluctantly, used by God to preach repentance and grace to that great city of Nineveh. The Ninevite's response to Jonah's reluctant proclamations then had been to repent and to accept God's goodness and thus, God's falling feet of judgement pounding their way toward them, had then happily been turned away. Now however, the prophet Nahum in effect says that, *"Now Nineveh shall fall!"* God is returning to Nineveh once more and this time, He has a shovel in His hand and the word on His very angry lips is, *"I'm 'gonna' bury you!"* What on earth had happened here?

Nahum 1:14

"The Lord has given a command concerning you: 'Your name shall be perpetuated no longer. Out of the house of your gods I will cut off the carved image and the moulded image. I will dig your grave, for you are vile.'" NKJV

Do remember that a people's past repentance does not guarantee a present grace. Repentance must be continually lived in for mercy to ever flow. There is a lesson here for individuals and for nations, for the lions of the earth and their bloodlines can always be finally done away with. For good! For when God brings His shovel and digs for the much warned yet unrepentant a pit, then the earth He heaps upon them shall cover them forever and the wind will blow away every remnant of their once proud existence. For example, I remember when all my maps of the world at my primary school were mostly covered with pink, indicating the breadth, depth and spread of the once great British Empire. Gone now, and gone forever. Selah.

There are two marked reactive contrasts about God presented to us in this book of Nahum and the fact that God is the God of the whole earth and that all nations are therefore accountable to both Him and His laws is the basis of these reactive contrasts. First, if we as nations obey God and seek to follow Him and honor Him then this attitude and action toward us will assure for the obedient nation concerned, both peace and prosperity; on the other hand, disobedience to His purpose and disregard of His rule and laws, will bring catastrophe to that nation and on its heels a most terrible judgement. Do you see the reactive contrast? To the nation seeking to obey Him, God is a rock and a refuge, a God of goodness carrying a basket of goodies. However, to the nation that disobeys Him and in the so doing "does the dirty" on those others seeking to follow Him, then He is a jealous avenger, clothed from top to tail in the black suit of the undertaker, striding angrily across the mountains of doom, carrying a shovel across His judgmental shoulders. This is a terrible but simple picture and calls forth the choice of both individual and national obedience or disobedience, of life or death, even from every generation that sees it!

He is a jealous avenger, clothed from top to tail in the black suit of the undertaker, striding angrily across the mountains of doom, carrying a shovel across His judgmental shoulders.

I look at our falling nations of the West, least not this isle of mine, and believe that we are in the time of prophet Noah, Habakkuk and Nahum, but Oh my God! I long for the time of Jonah the prophet to come again once more and even now I still sniff the air in prayerful hope, to try and smell the vomit of the whale upon our darkened streets once more and see a stomach acid stained white prophet rise from the puked up mess and preach repentance to us once again. Though all our fishing grounds are empty, maybe God has a few of His own great fish still hidden in His deeps and maybe these will carry some reluctant prophets to come to these beleaguered shores once more and preach righteousness, sin, coming judgement and repentance in Jesus to us again. I hope so. I pray so. Maybe some of you should do so.

Listen: *"Now when they had gone through Phrygia and the region of Galatia, they were forbidden by the Holy Spirit to preach the word in Asia. After they had come to Mysia, they tried to go into Bithynia, but the Spirit did not permit them. So passing by Mysia, they came down to Troas. And a vision appeared to Paul in the night. A man of Macedonia stood and pleaded with him, saying, 'Come over to Macedonia and help us.' Now after he had seen the vision, immediately we sought to go to Macedonia, concluding that the Lord had called us to preach the Gospel to them." Acts 16:6-10 NKJV*

Pray: Lord help us all by sending Jonah's to our shores once more! Amen and let it be so.

| Vol 01 | Q2 | NW00129 | May 08th |

Night-Whisper | **REAL**

A stir of echoes

You will forgive me but not only do I enjoy country music, I also enjoy science fiction writing as well! I think I enjoy Sci-Fi and especially watching it, because it gives my mind a few open doors to consider the world to come. When it comes to visual space science fiction then, surely Star Trek is the daddy of them all.

Genesis 27:22

"So Jacob went near to Isaac his father, and he felt him and said, 'The voice is Jacob's voice, but the hands are the hands of Esau.'" NKJV

It was in the film *Star Trek Nemesis*, that the bald but Shakespearean Captain of the "Big E," - the Star Ship Enterprise, Jean Luc Piccard, comes face to face with the character of Shinzon, who is Piccard's very own cloned, but very bitter and evil self. Piccard, like all good star ship Captains mind you, on meeting the younger evil mirror image of himself encourages Shinzon to aspire to be better than he is. True to form, however, like every other black, leather coated baddie, Shinzon refuses to aspire but rather assures Piccard that he will make Jean Luc expire, indeed, in I think a most remarkable little phrase, Shinzon spits at poor old Jean Luc, saying that, *"He's about to see the echo triumph over the voice."*

The older men get, the less they delight in looking into mirrors. Indeed, most men rarely look themselves in their own eyes even when they are forced to gaze into the looking glass. They will look everywhere around their face, but find staring into the windows of their own soul, often a most disturbing, accusing, sad and self-condemning thing to do. Even so, God the good, in His great design made sure that the rapid growth of facial hair in forms of beards, and as we get older, nasal hair and the dreaded omni-brow and even those individual rogue curly firework like eyebrows, will all need our daily attention. If I am correct, then it is God through the growth of weird facial hair that requires men to take an increasingly longer look at themselves most every single day, the more older that they get! I think this is important for men lest our echo should also have victory over our voice. Indeed, to counter the power of my own echoes, each morning, unlike Nivea man, I force myself to stare into my mirror, then way beyond it, through my pupils and deep into the windows of my own soul, first greeting the hideousness I see and then proclaiming these three things:

"Robert, do not be your echo, for your echo is merely an aspect, a poorer image of who you truly are. It is an holograph and even if it is strong or weak, it is at best, but a warped reflection of who you truly are. Today, do not let the echo you may have unwittingly become, have the victory over your one true voice."

Today, do not let the echo you may have unwittingly become, have the victory over your one true voice.

"Robert, neither make peace with your present voice, for even at its truest resonance, it too is but a mere echo of that which shall be proclaimed and be itself proclaiming, in all the ages yet to come. Robert, 'become.'"

"Robert, today in the midst of the realities of those true, yet presently poorly formed substances you perceive, do remember, that they are both seen and heard through the darker looking glass of being this side of the grave. Lay hold of substance, and do not be misled by echoes, neither let them have any victory over the 'voice becoming.'"

Now, some mornings of course I don't feel so poetic and often shorten this three-fold declaration to sets of three simple words, such as, "Let it go!" Or, "Stop kidding yourself!" Or simply, "Grow up man!" You might think I'm a bit mad but I invite you to try it! Indeed, try anything, to stop those false echoes of life under this sun getting the victory over your one true substantial voice.

Listen: *"Then you came near and stood at the foot of the mountain, and the mountain burned with fire to the midst of heaven, with darkness, cloud, and thick darkness. And the Lord spoke to you out of the midst of the fire. You heard the sound of the words, but saw no form; you only heard a voice." Deuteronomy 4:11-13 NKJV*

Pray: Lord, hear my voice! Let Your ears be attentive to the voice of my supplications. (Psalms 130:2 NKJV)

Night-Whisper | **BE**

The cotillion of smelly corpses and cleaned up cadavers

One afternoon whilst walking up from Brighton Beach I found an old cadaver washed up at my feet. Not a corpse mind you, not an abandoned dead body poked and pecked at by the silk white seagulls but a well laid out old cadaver nevertheless.

Numbers 9:6

"Now there were certain men who were defiled by a human corpse, so that they could not keep the Passover on that day." NKJV

It's yellowed, glutaraldehyde stained, sandstone skin, bore the marks of its long preservation and through the barred gates of this old church building the explaining sign read, *"St Andrews is no longer used for regular worship. Rather than see this beautiful Grade 1 Listed building permanently locked, the friends are raising money for facilities in the Church, so that it may be used all year round by the community."* I noted that the friendly community consisted of the *"Brighton and Hove (actually) Gay Men's Chorus"* and that they would be performing in this very place of present consecration once again this May during the city's annual arts festival. The dead body smelt bad, it smelt very bad indeed.

As Benjamin Disraeli is purported to have said, "There are three kinds of lies: lies, damned lies, and statistics!" Nevertheless, one consistent trend of church statistics in the United Kingdom, especially since the 1970's, has been the massive decline in church attendance. Excepting of course for the Pentecostal movement and some newer Evangelical churches where attendance is rising, the over-all trend for church growth is down, down and drop down dead down. Whilst the Church of England has had the amazing flexibility of being able to pound the nails into its own coffin whilst still smiling nicely and drinking lots of tea, the Baptists and the Methodists, jealous of the ignored thirty nine articled, bald headed funeral dirge, have had to let their own buildings out as carpet warehouses and Mosques. Don't get upset, don't get angry at me, for I am speaking statistically of course and therefore with intense, numerical hyperbole. After all, it can't be true can it? Even if the Brighton and Hove Gay Men's choir are dancing with the cadaver of an old dead church, keeping it open is nothing but an old quaint and queer look at a once rich Christian history now long since past. Surely all these gloomy statistics regarding the death of Christ again, surely, they just can't be true?

In the USA, a "Cotillion" is the name of a place one attends to learn manners, and proper social behavior in the context of dance. However, the Cotillion, this original French country dance, evolved into Royal Courtship dances and from there spawned everything that was complicated and relational in dancing, from the quadrille to the good old square dance. In the United Kingdom, this same guilty and complicated courtship dance is seen more often than not when Christians themselves start dancing with dead churches rather than leaving them. Yes, it has been my observance that it is a particularly British state of mentality to dance with dead church corpses in an attempt to bring them back to life, and frankly, it is a particularly grotesque kind of guilt ridden desperate dance, very ungainly and quite soul destroying. It's disgusting really isn't it? It's cowardly. It's perverse. "So then," I ask myself, "Instead of all the desperate dancing and writhing guilt at the inability to bring the corpse back to life, why not just get out and leave that smelly old dead thing alone? Why not just let it disintegrate? After all, if it's got a nice face, then I can assure you that there will be more than enough clown face undertakers ready to turn the corpse into a dancing gay cadaver." For the church in the West to thrive, we keep getting told that we need revival but revival begins when we choose life over death! Leave that dead church and don't feel guilty about doing it either.

This same guilty and complicated Cotillion courtship dance is seen more often than not when Christians themselves start dancing with dead churches rather than leaving them!

To assuage some of our very British and unnecessary guilt may I suggest to some of you, that such persistent association with corpse's has left you unclean and thoroughly unable and unqualified to celebrate! God gave His former unclean, corpse dancing people, a good amount of time to get cleaned up and then and only then, were they allowed to celebrate the "little Passover," which occurred just one month after the other famed and much missed official community event. I tell you, some of you have already wasted too much of your time dancing with the dead and in the so doing, you have missed the larger celebration of the main Passover. Yet even now, God has allowed you the possibility of participating in a little celebration before you too personally die. Therefore, to shepherds and sheep alike may I suggest that maybe it's time to leave the dead well alone and come and get clean? Come and choose life. Brethren, let the wild dancing begin! Be free from the shackles and smell of death. Leave that dead church. LET IT ROT!

Listen: *"And Moses said to them, 'Stand still, that I may hear what the Lord will command concerning you.' Then the Lord spoke to Moses, saying, 'Speak to the children of Israel, saying: "If anyone of you or your posterity is unclean because of a corpse, or is far away on a journey, he may still keep the Lord's Passover. On the fourteenth day of the second month, at twilight, they may keep it. They shall eat it with unleavened bread and bitter herbs."'" Numbers 9:8-11 NKJV*

Pray: Lord, open my mind to understanding and let not the dead triumph, for my eyes have grown dim with grief, yes my whole insides have become but a shadow. I am appalled at this yet remember that those with clean hands will grow stronger. So Lord, help me let go of the both guilt and the smiling dead and then at the last, to be enabled to lay hold of life. In Jesus name I ask it, amen.

| Vol 01 | Q2 | NW00131 | May 10th |

Night-Whisper | **FIGHT**

Rightly using conception control, abortion and infanticide

Of course abortion and infanticide are the great mass murder sins of our generation. Of course, I am against them in every single way. Bodily conception control is an altogether different animal however and the how's and the wherefores are open I believe, both to discussion and faith. However, I do believe totally in spiritual conception control, spiritual abortion and spiritual infanticide. Let me tell you why.

James 1:15

"Then, when desire has conceived, it gives birth to sin; and sin, when it is full-grown, brings forth death." NKJV

Our text for tonight, first talks about the copulation between temptation and desire, the product of which is always the terrible twins of sin and death. Now in the body, the very best form of contraception is sexual abstinence, indeed, there is no better condom. Therefore, in the same way, the very best form of spiritual contraception is abstinence. It's a no brainer really. When temptation comes then, abstain! When temptation comes then, run like hell! Run in your heart, run in your mind, and if necessary, run in your body and even if you have to fly away naked. Run!

If however, spiritually speaking of course, you have done the big naughty, then my friend, you have gone and gotten yourself all knocked up with sin! You don't need a spiritual pregnancy test here, you don't need to wait and see if the monthly menstruation fails to appear, for when temptation copulates with desire, you will be pregnant with the twins of sin and death. Guaranteed! There is only one option here and that is spiritual abortion. Kill sin. Rip it out of your spiritual womb like the alien menace it is. Cut its spinal cord. Burn it in salt. How? Well, you must confess it to death and then ruin it with repentance. This is the only way to abort sin.

If you have failed to have this spiritual abortion, then the consequences of your copulation will naturally both appear and grow. Remember now that I am speaking *spiritually here*, for I need to tell you that this birthed sin, can never give you life or happiness. It is in effect, and you will indeed find it to be so, always holding the hand of its twin called death! Moreover, death to you especially. In very real terms, many of us have given birth to monsters that give us death each day, by, in one form or another, sucking the very life of the Spirit out of us. These terrible toddlers of death and sin must needs be killed and preferably, before they ever grow to their vast, heart sucking stature. How? Well first, remember that I am *spiritually* speaking, for you must now separate yourself from these monstrous objects, yes, you must leave them alone, and most especially, you must not feed them. Yes, you must ignore their screams for attention and indulgence, ignore their cries to be fed and simply let them die. Better still though, if you can, for my, oh my, how we cosset our sins, if you can then, you must take them by their legs and smash them and their heads all to pieces against any righteous wall you can find. When dealing with birthed and growing sin our lives, there must be no mercy.

> *Better still so, if you can, for my, oh my, how we cosset our sins, if you can then, you must take them by their legs and smash them and their heads all to pieces against any righteous wall you can find. There must be no mercy!*

Let us turn our desire to God then and never copulate with temptation. Let us keep our mouths shut, our ears open and our legs not spread open wide, but rather, kept firmly together, walking and moving forward, firmly stepping upon the commandments of the King along His Holy and narrow way. Stop messing with sin! Are you an idiot?

Listen: *"Therefore lay aside all filthiness and overflow of wickedness, and receive with meekness the implanted word, which is able to save your souls. But be doers of the word, and not hearers only, deceiving yourselves. For if anyone is a hearer of the word and not a doer, he is like a man observing his natural face in a mirror; for he observes himself, goes away, and immediately forgets what kind of man he was. But he who looks into the perfect law of liberty and continues in it, and is not a forgetful hearer but a doer of the work, this one will be blessed in what he does." James 1:21-25 NKJV*

Pray: Lord, help me to be a vessel of gold and a vessel of silver in Your house. Therefore Lord, clean me and swill out all the refuse from around my rims, as I stand under the running water of Your Word. So make me honorable, sanctified, ready for Your most glorious use, prepared for every good and life giving work. In Jesus name I ask it, amen and let it be so!

Night-Whisper | **OBEY**

When your stomach feels dismal

Eugene Peterson is correct when he says that we cannot get rid of the puzzling and unpleasant difficulties of the Bible and that these are the "belly aches" that come with eating this most sweetest of books. Indeed, it is Peterson that encourages us to keep a well-stocked cupboard of Alka Seltzer and Pepto-Bismol at hand whenever we read the Bible!

I do of course believe in the verbal plenary inspiration of *The Bible*, nevertheless, the Word of God does have its challenges. For me, it is not so much the textual challenges sometimes present but rather the narrative challenge. It is the very stories contained in the Bible that are often most nakedly astonishing to me! Many of them leave me speechless and indeed, even embarrassed for God, I mean, did He edit some of this copy before it was admitted? Surely not! Surely some sub-editor slipped it past His nose and the embarrassing account, the naughty story, the mad murderous escapade gained its place on the page by subtle subterfuge without His knowledge and editorial affirmation? Of course, that is not the case. Every word, every good and stinkin' word was delicately chosen by Him. That thought alone gives me a bellyache, I mean, what was He thinking? For there are quite a number of stories I would straight away remove because I preach this stuff, I teach this stuff, I eat this stuff, drink it, gulp it down and swim

1 Peter 1:10-12

"Of this salvation the prophets have inquired and searched carefully, who prophesied of the grace that would come to you, searching what, or what manner of time, the Spirit of Christ who was in them was indicating when He testified beforehand the sufferings of Christ and the glories that would follow. To them it was revealed that, not to themselves, but to us they were ministering the things which now have been reported to you through those who have preached the Gospel to you by the Holy Spirit sent from heaven - things which angels desire to look into." NKJV

in this stuff, and some of it, is a real belly ache!

I wonder if the color of God the Holy Spirit is Pepto-Bismol pink? For I have found that when the aching comes upon me that it is only He who can alleviate the belly aches of my soul and the churnings of my spirit. Our text for tonight tells us of the alimentary ailments of the prophets of the past who struggled with what they were writing. It was the spirit of Christ in them, (I like that,) it was God the Holy Spirit who comforted them, calmed them down and caressed their grumbling bowels and said, "You don't need to know, you cannot know for now, this is not for you. No, what you write is for those yet to come, for those upon whom the end of the ages have fallen. Shhhhhhh... Be still, relax, and then write on."

> *I wonder if the color of God the Holy Spirit is Pepto-Bismol pink?*

The reading of Scripture can never be an isolated task for when we open the Bible, for when we sit to spiritually eat; it is always at a table for two, with a large crowd of angelic waiters looking on! Please be then assured that our Helper, the Holy Spirit, is always wearing pink and we cannot miss Him, so that when we eat this sweetest of meals, we shall be sure to drink Him up with it as well. Ask God the Holy Spirit to help you digest the Scriptures, even though some it might give you a bellyache. I tell you, this is good advice!

Listen: *"So I went to the angel and said to him, 'Give me the little book.' And he said to me, 'Take and eat it; and it will make your stomach bitter, but it will be as sweet as honey in your mouth.'" Revelation 10:9 NKJV*

Pray: Blessed are You, O Lord! Teach me Your statutes. With my lips I have declared all the judgements of Your mouth. I have rejoiced in the way of Your testimonies, as much as in all riches. I will meditate on Your precepts, and contemplate Your ways. I will delight myself in Your statutes; I will not forget Your word. (Psalms 119:12-16 NKJV)

| Vol 01 | Q2 | NW00133 | May 12th |

Night-Whisper | **CONFIDENCE**

Building on a math's lesson for moles with memory problems

We Protestants against spiritual abuse, against doctrinal deviousness, yes, we reformers of a previous and terrible travesty of pure religion, now hang our certain and hopeful hats on five giant pegs, those being;

2 Peter 1:10

"Therefore, brethren, be even more diligent to make your call and election sure, for if you do these things you will never stumble." NKJV

1 Sola Scriptura ("by Scripture alone")

2 Sola Fide ("by Faith alone")

3 Sola Gratia ("by Grace alone")

4 Solus Christus ("Christ alone")

5 Soli Deo Gloria ("Glory to God alone")

How wonderful.

It is therefore a real shame that the outworking of these five central pillars of Protestantism, of Biblical Christianity, have on the whole led to the production of an ever emergent and "lazy ass" Christian. It seems that we have become far too much at ease with the once wonderfully simple marriage of faith and grace, which seem nowadays to have given up producing vigorous, respectful, thankful and sacrificial offspring and have somehow left us with a nasty nest of twittering cuckoos, all over-fat intruders, who in their subsequent and sedentary post-modern growth, displayed little relation to the revelation of Scripture, which that marriage of faith and grace once so wonderfully proclaimed. Subsequently, these postmodern cuckoos have neither heart nor inclination, neither stomach nor staying power, to either know what they should look like, what they should desire to become nor what they should be determined to die for. This must be rectified. The postmodern emergent are, together with all of their ilk are nothing but soft puff pastries.

Our text for tonight, is built on a "therefore." So, looking at the previous verses in the opening of 2nd Peter, we see they speak of a multiplication of a divine grace and peace, which in turn results in a super abundance of faithful and fruity action! 2 Peter 1: 5-9, is in fact a math's lesson for blind moles with memory problems, and is rooted in the superabundance of the promises of God, and therefore prefixed with a very demanding and all-encompassing action phrase, translated as, "Giving all diligence!" Phew, I am tired already! Yup, this math's lesson for moles with memory problems demands action. Indeed, the word diligence here is from which we derive our English word, speed. Peter says in effect, "Give all eagerness, all earnestness, all business, all forwardness, haste, dispatch, diligence, yes, give all *speed*, to add my previously stated seven 'active ingredients' to your Christian life. Why? Well because if you do not, you will turn into a smelly blind mole which burrows in pig swill and bathes in dog vomit." Simple.

> *…… If you do not, you will turn into a smelly blind mole which burrows in pig swill and bathes in dog vomit."*

So, now in our text for tonight, Peter goes on to say, "Be even more diligent." Peter uses the Greek verb 'spoudazo' here, so in other words he says, "Hey, move faster still folks, for when it comes to being sure of your calling and election, I want you to put your Speedos on!" Oh, yes indeed! We might paraphrase Peter then by saying, "Oi! If your knowledge and testimony, if your service and story of present salvation and future happiness is as real as you say it is; if it is truly through God's grace, by faith alone in Christ alone, resting in the Scriptures alone and all for the glory of God alone, then show me the active goods! No, more than that, forget assuring me so much of your salvation, rather, assure yourself! Yes, make your calling and election forcefully firm to your own heart. Make it steadfast; make it sure and certain to yourself! Do this all the time. Yes, let your action reveal your faith, first of all to yourself."

Friends, the outcome of such a speedy and consistent effort which is rooted in those five Scriptural pillars, is that you shall run so confidently, that you shall never run and ruin yourselves in the bumbling and blind blundering of ignorant little moles. Now that's magnificent!

Listen: *"But do you want to know, O foolish man, that faith without works is dead? Was not Abraham our father justified by works when he offered Isaac his son on the altar? Do you see that faith was working together with his works, and by works faith was made perfect? And the Scripture was fulfiled which says, 'Abraham believed God, and it was accounted to him for righteousness.' And he was called the friend of God.*

You see then that a man is justified by works, and not by faith only."
James 2:20-24 NKJV

Pray: Lord, deliver me from the bondage of works but help me always too rightly and continually, make both my calling and election sure. In Jesus name I ask it, amen.

Night-Whisper | **CONNECT**

Five bees from God's honey hive

The father of (James) Joseph Jacques Tissot, was not happy that his son wanted to be a painter. However, James, the anglicized name of this French painter, ensured that he made his father eat both his words and worries, by becoming a very famous, "painter-preneur."

1 John 4:1-2
"Beloved, do not believe every spirit, but test the spirits, whether they are of God; because many false prophets have gone out into the world."
NKJV

Tissot was born on the French coast in Nantes and studied at the École des Beaux-Arts in Paris under Ingres, Flandrin and Lamothe. Already a successful painter of fashionable French women, never the less, Tissot changed professions for a while when he went on to fight in the Franco-Prussian War. After his return and not much later, under an undisclosed cloud, he left Paris for London where he then studied etching with Sir Seymour Haden and drew caricatures for Vanity Fair, whilst painting what was considered at the time, not a few very "scandalous" portraits! Sometime later in the 1870's, Tissot met a divorcee, a Mrs. Kathleen Newton, who became his companion and the model for many of his works. Mrs. Newton, nearly half his age, moved into Tissot's home in 1876 and lived with him until she was in the late stages of tuberculosis, when she then committed suicide, aged just 28 years. Tissot was devastated. He sold his house in St John's Wood, moved back to France, and picked up what he did best, that is, the painting of fashionable ladies.

Tissot, now back in France, met up with the Medium/Conjuror, Mr. William Eglinton, who was purported to have been able to make manifest the spirit of Kathleen, his departed lover and mother of his bastard son. Tissot was so impressed by this, that he painted the scene "L'apparition Medianimique" which for many years later, hung in the offices of the then London Spiritual Alliance. Oh and lest you think Tissot was an idiot, please note that even the Prime Minister of England, Gladstone himself, was induced/seduced by Eglinton into becoming part of the early areas of paranormal, investigative endeavor. As also by the way, was Sir Arthur Conan Doyle and many, many others. Yes, you have to understand that at the time of this great changing of eras, of that changing of yet another guard, the use of mediums was widespread in Europe.

Tissot then, having left the Roman Catholic Church would later, whilst visiting a local church for artistic inspiration, be arrested by a literal "vision of Jesus taking care of the poor." This church vision, turned Tissot's life around and though his contemporaries thought that this dramatic "conversion" in later life was nothing but a great money making scheme, Tissot, nevertheless, did completely spend the last 10-15 years of his life, more than any other great artist, totally and completely immersed in the Gospels and through his Middle Eastern travels, also become absolutely immersed in the geographical and social landscape of the Bible. From this position of total immersion, Tissot was then able to produce, probably for the first time and with a most vivid and stunning reality, some hundreds of pictures relating to a pictorial imagery of the Life of Christ. The works are truly magnificent and over 100 years since its first publication; it is still a prize for any library! Indeed, for a give-away price, I picked up two of Tissot's four-volume set from a local charity bookshop. They didn't know what they had.

> *Yes, you have to understand that at the time of this great changing of eras, of that changing of yet another guard, the use of mediums was widespread in Europe.*

Tissot, totally immersed remember, and having gathered all his data still needed what he referred to as "the illumination of intuition," some of which in his forward he said, had been "agitated by certain induced receptivity." Indeed, it was as though he had been anointed with hyperesthesia, thus becoming, exceptionally and sensitively heightened to any spiritual stimuli that had been evoked by certain material objects outside of himself. He was obviously claiming that it was meditation and the opening up of his mind to such excitements that had brought him such prolific and stunning results in his paintings and sketches.

Now I mention all of this tonight, because not only did Tissot rightly immerse himself in physical fact but also in Roman Catholic Mysticism, even consulting the visions of St Anne Catherine Emmerich, who, by the way, also had her visions consulted by Mel Gibson for his film, *The Passion of The Christ*. Yes, Tissot by these religious and mystical associations and his connectional associations with the early New Age Movement in the person of Eglinton, conjures up for us, some pictures of the present, postmodern, therapeutic, and charismatic-mystic movement.

Now, being myself a present believer in the existence and function of the fivefold ministries and all the gifts of the Holy Spirit, it is important for me and I think also important for all of us who operate in the spiritual realm, indeed, even for all of us artists seeking inspiration and also ministers seeking power and movement, to understand the difference between the evils of channeling or divination, and the blessings of receptive creation and prophetic instruction. That is, whilst being in touch with both spiritual and material reality, we should be able not to allow, any lying intrusion or manipulative control of beings, who whilst maybe having angelic eyes, still possess the coldest and darkest of hearts. In other words, the question for us is how can we be open to the illumination, the revelation and instruction of God The Holy Spirit, whilst at the same time; remain closed to any possible demonic intrusion? Believe me; if you are consciously operating in the spiritual realm, this is so very important!

> *Whilst being in touch with both spiritual and material reality, we should be able not to allow, any lying intrusion or manipulative control of beings, who whilst maybe having angelic eyes, still possess the coldest and darkest of hearts.*

The five basic safeguards for those Christians both conscious and daring to move in the spiritual realm, are The Book, The Believers, The Battle dress, The Byproducts of the past and the Blessings of the present.

The Book of course is the Bible. Eat that book and let it swallow you whole. Know it, spout, quote it, move in it, regurgitate it, and let it rule you.

Secondly, "be with believers!" Let them, together with you; apply the Word to any speaking spirit. Test them. Together. All the time.

Thirdly, "put your battle dress on." Take sword and shield and armor for every part provided, for be sure that every part provided for, shall indeed be most viciously attacked! Get some folks to stand shoulder to shoulder with you and get some even braver folks, who do not sleep too much, to cover your back in any attack you are engaged in.

Fourthly, "be aware of the by-products." Past associations often leave openings for re-visitation. Be aware of any by-products of the past and make every endeavor to close the windows and the doors still remaining open in your own spiritual house. Some of you have some evicting still left to do.

Finally, rejoice on the blessings of the present. The Charismata of the Spirit are for the present edification of the saints in light whilst they are dressed in armor and walking the Kings High Way. Use them and use them well.

Listen: *"By this you know the Spirit of God: Every spirit that confesses that Jesus Christ has come in the flesh is of God, and every spirit that does not confess that Jesus Christ has come in the flesh is not of God. And this is the spirit of the Antichrist, which you have heard was coming, and is now already in the world. You are of God, little children, and have overcome them, because He who is in you is greater than he who is in the world." 1 John 4:2-4 NKJV*

Pray: Lord, send these five bees from Your honey hive, to save me from deceit and sting to death the spirits that might bring deceiving lies. In Jesus name I pray, amen.

| Vol 01 | Q2 | NW00135 | May 14th |

Night-Whisper | SEE

The double, double cure for gullibleitis

I declare once more, that I believe in the fivefold ministries and in the gifts of the Holy Spirit for today. I declare again, that I choose life and in doing so, I choose Jesus, yes, I always want to choose Jesus.

2 Timothy 3:6-9

"For of this sort are those who creep into households and make captives of gullible women loaded down with sins, led away by various lusts, always learning and never able to come to the knowledge of the truth. Now as Jannes and Jambres resisted Moses, so do these also resist the truth: men of corrupt minds, disapproved concerning the faith; but they will progress no further, for their folly will be manifest to all, as theirs also was." NKJV

Yet, I have to also declare once more, that most Christians are riddled through and through, with a most strange malady, indeed a disease. This same disease, which, by the way, is completely incongruent to their true character, is called "Gullibleitis!" Moreover, may God truly help us, for it is running rife in pandemic proportion.

Gullibleitis begins to manifests itself, firstly in the talk of wonders in far-away places and then secondly in the purchase of airplane tickets to get there! Thirdly, it is manifest in the bringing back of bags of goodies, usually to the open-mouthed waiting and expectant. These goodies vary in degree, but they are mostly bags of magic pixie dust and I have found that the wind of every day demands eventually blows it all away. Just give it time. It's not real; it's only pixie dust, which shall always cease to sparkle in the true light of the day.

The first question I have to ask is, "Why are people running to what God is reportedly doing elsewhere?" Well mostly, I believe it is because of dissatisfaction. Yes, we Christians are mostly dissatisfied with where we are right now, with maybe also dissatisfied with the continual unanswered prayer for deliverance, for healing, for provision, for direction, value, and even for intimacy with the Father. It's sad isn't it? Really you see, the testimony of most people in their Christian walk is that "we still have not found what they are looking for" and because of this, we are often sorely disappointed in our churches, our leaders and ultimately in our God, for we have never really experienced what we have been told to be true. Yes, we do feel that we have been "sold a pup." However, rather than deny this 'not so good news,' we seek to find fulfilment of that good news, elsewhere. This of course begs another question and that is "Have we been exposed to the God of the Bible in grace, truth and reality in the first place?"

I have been unfortunate enough to have studied the practices of churches and church growth for many years now. I think I can say that I have been to the Emerald city itself and have dined with the great and powerful Oz and found him indeed, to be that very little man, speaking big words and still panicking in the telling of questioning folks to "Pay no attention to that man behind the curtain." Yet it is to that man behind the curtain, which we must pay attention to the most! For if we shall be healed of our Gullibleitis, then we must examine the wheels and the steam valves, yes, all the varied bells and whistles that fills those travelling bags with bring it home pixie dust, and that puts the show on the road and then keeps it there, for dear friends, that is mostly what's on offer in many of these far flung destinations. A show and a bag of Pixie dust.

> *"Pay no attention to that man behind the curtain." Yet it is to that man behind the curtain, which we must pay attention to the most!*

It has been said that full bodied MRI scans are the worst things that can be offered to the paying patient, for you can be sure, that some abnormality will be found and indeed, possibly many. In the same way, I have no desire to search for cracks in the character of other people, or to hunt down heresy. None of us would have to look farther than or own door to find enough to repent of and correct. Especially me. Nevertheless, this blind pox of Gullibleitis really needs to be attended to for its spreading fast and making us, the church and its members, both sick and thick. So, what's the cure?

Well, I have found that both the infection and the spread of Gullibleitis can only be remedied by a persistent application of two double doses of medication. The first double dose, to be taken immediately mind you, and it is the twin medication of the Scriptures and common sense. Without these two applied remedies, you can never have faith and any faith without it, is really no faith at all. If you get my drift! Use the Scriptures, use your common sense, and don't let anyone bamboozle you with talk of the things of the Spirit being extraneous to this twin and daily taken medication. If you hear that it is, then be sure that it's just the words of that little man behind the curtain having a bit of a panic because you have found him out at last.

Secondly, take the long term and twin dose of "time and taste," for these are usually the most embarrassing cures for those of us showered with Pixie dust and overtaken with Gullibleitis. Fruit remember, is only revealed after growth and is really best tasted after seasonal ripening. Once the fruit is fully formed, only then can the quality of that which is grown be truly judged as to what it really is. As a side comment, may I say that a thorough investigation of both seed and soil are also good indicators of just what might be produced!

"Is God the God of the here and now?" If he isn't, then I wonder if our God is in fact a lesser god and frankly, not worth the following.

If we are fortunate to have His Word of promise and His ever presence, then I judge we have all that we could ever need and want, even at our very elbow, right where we are. We humans do not live in the 'there and then,' but rather we live in the here and we live in the now. Tell me then, "Is God the God of the here and now?" If he isn't, then I wonder if our God is in fact a lesser god and frankly, not worth the following. Why go traipsing across the planet bringing back bags of pixie dust, when God is here right now.

Listen: *"For every tree is known by its own fruit. For men do not gather figs from thorns, nor do they gather grapes from a bramble bush. A good man out of the good treasure of his heart brings forth good; and an evil man out of the evil treasure of his heart brings forth evil. For out of the abundance of the heart his mouth speaks." Luke 6:44-45 NKJV*

Pray: Keep my soul, and deliver me; let me not be ashamed, for I put my trust in You. Let integrity and uprightness preserve me, for I wait for You. Redeem Israel, O God, out of all their troubles!" Psalms 25:20-22 NKJV

Night-Whisper | **RESCUE**

Do you have demons in your drawers?

I take "the demonization of the Christian," to mean that there are times when the enemy has a certain freedom of expression within and through us, rather than a full and rancorous evil possession of us. Remember, a squatter may inhabit the abode but he does not possess it, especially if the owner legally contests the "infestation." Having said that, I wonder if sometimes that demonic "excitement," that expression of demonization if you will, is sometimes so overwhelmingly powerful, especially when it is legally contested, that it appears like a full possession and that there may very well be supernatural manifestations as well as unusual and natural ones around the areas and times of eviction. Therefore, I am suggesting then that in the Christian, the demonic may be given a freedom of expression, and an opportunity to exploit any of the many openings that we have allowed them, or invited them into, or which through generational curse agreements they seemingly have rights to. I think we might categorize these windows of demonic opportunity in three ways as: allowable exploitation, invitational exploitation and generational exploitation.

Acts 10:38-39

"How God anointed Jesus of Nazareth with the Holy Spirit and with power, who went about doing good and healing all who were oppressed by the devil, for God was with Him." NKJV

Allowable exploitation. Exploitation is of course the use and mostly the misuse of others for personal gain. Another word for this is slavery. Every bit of us must be yielded to Christ and not to the devil. Our choices in objects, our choices in media, our choices in relationships, our choices in working practices, our choices in verbal declaration, our choices in anything, either open or close windows of opportunity for either unrighteousness and darkness or holiness and light. Therefore, look at some of your choices, look at some of the repercussions of your choices in objects or relationships, and if they are sinful, then get rid of them, break them, change them, even close them down. Wherever there is a repeat price tag or a sowing and reaping price tag attached to such sinful choices, then you may well have to find the seed of it and remove it from your ground to stop all that "peskiness" continuing. Where such exploitation has been allowed, you must work hard to disallow it and negate it. Root out the rot and pull up the weeds.

Invitational exploitation. Many of us, in both words and action have found sources of power, sources of temporary satisfaction and sources of fascination, in people, practices and places of every kind. Our first free imbibing, and then often, our continued and increasingly expensive surreptitious sipping of these often sinful energy sources, is I am afraid, a clear invitation to darkness to come in and continue its own exploitation of you! You must stop the surreptitious sipping of these sinful sources of power, satisfaction and fascination. Deny them, fry them and pound them into powder. If you do not, then you invite trouble into your life.

You must stop the surreptitious sipping of these sinful sources of power, satisfaction and fascination. Deny them, fry them and pound them into powder. If you do not, then you invite trouble into your life.

Generational exploitation. The human story is one of generational connectedness, even all the way back to Adam. The curse of the broken law and a multitude of other curses, are played out daily in our lives. We mightn't like this, yet our dislike of these facts does not negate the presence and power of a seeming, generational right of exploitation given to the darkness. May I simply say tonight, that where generational patterns of problems are perceived, it is simply worth asking God the Holy Spirit to guide you in prayers of acknowledged confession, righteous repentance and the ruin and running off of those problems that have been previously allowed to have their generational way in you. The old adage of "If it looks like a duck, walks like a duck, quacks like a duck, then it probably is a duck," is well used in this area of discernment regarding these kinds of generational issues.

In conclusion, may I say that you may have a very large and fine dressing table filled to overflowing with the most beautiful of clothing. Yet, it is possible for some of those drawers to be inhabited by the demonic. So tell me, are some of your drawers rattling tonight?

Finally, know tonight, that squatters, allowed in, invited in, or with previous generational rights, never leave without some form of contest of that now removed, allowed, invited and previous exploitation and occupation right. Slave owners and all those other exploiters of persons for their own selfish and protective gain, always turn nasty when robbed of their chattel. Always. Nevertheless, a thorough, complete and gentle removal of any infestation can be done without damage to the property, and then yes indeed, the filling up of that fumigated person or place with all good things, can actually replace the previous reputation of any house of ill repute, into that of being an honored places of perfumed loveliness, even a worthy castle of anointed Knighthood. A fitting abode for the King of Kings.

Listen: *"Jesus said, 'Tell that fox that I've no time for him right now. Today and tomorrow I'm busy clearing out the demons and healing the sick; the third day I'm wrapping things up.'" (Luke 13:32-33 The Message)*

Pray: Lord, I declare that I am on the Great King's Highway and have no time or space for our enemy. I belong to You Lord Jesus! Indeed, I honor only You Lord Jesus Christ. So, let Your angels camp around my place of rest and grant me full protection this very night. Lord, forgive me please my many personal sins, and the sins of all my generational line, for truly, we have been a rebellious family and we have served other gods. Consequently, all our evil deeds have separated us from You and brought calamity to our generations, and our guilt and our iniquities are all way beyond our measure, and are piled up high before You. I confess and ask you Lord, to forgive my family line and myself for all previous actions, declarations and destructions brought upon me and my family, both by myself and by my fathers, and that by asking this in the heavenlies, I do so renounce any and all generational sins and curses on myself and on the family that were brought upon us, by us. As a Holy subject now, yes even as a Royal priest, right now I place our sins, under the precious blood of Jesus and ask You Lord for a gentle yet thorough, calm but complete eviction of every foul thing that touches me and mine and that You would also grant me, a new generational inheritance of health and freedom and of all the spiritual blessings which are in Christ Jesus, for both myself, my family, and the generations that might follow us. To darkness and to demons then, in the mighty name of Jesus I say break! Loose! Leave! Be bound and never to return, or even sniff around the fullness, which is now my Savior's, Jesus Christ my Lord, amen and let it be so."

Night-Whisper | **CHANGE**

The smashing of serenity

Dear to many Christians, and especially my good 12-stepping friends, I nevertheless wonder if that well known 'Serenity Prayer,' attributed to that great influencer and nation shaper, Reinhold Niebuhr, has in fact unwittingly forced many present day 'professors' and real Christians into cowardly compromise rather than a Godly contentment with their lot in life? I am certain it was not Niebuhr's intention to do so, indeed, his life epitomizes the prayer's second supplication! Even so, I do believe that this has happened. Just to remind you, here is Niebuhr's 'Serenity Prayer' in full.

Matthew 19:26

But Jesus looked at them and said to them, "With men this is impossible, but with God all things are possible." NKJV

"God grant me the serenity to accept the things I cannot change; courage to change the things I can; and wisdom to know the difference. Living one day at a time; Enjoying one moment at a time; Accepting hardships as the pathway to peace; Taking, as He did, this sinful world as it is, not as I would have it; Trusting that He will make all things right if I surrender to His Will; That I may be reasonably happy in this life and supremely happy with Him forever in the next. Amen."

Personally, I think this prayer is beautiful. So, what is my problem? What is THE problem?

The present Laodicean church, that Biblically dumbed down self-righteous, naval gazing hedonistic entity which is both abhorrent to God and thoroughly useless to humanity, has easily and happily compromised itself to this cowardly 'serenity' with even some of its conservative branches justifying their lack of fight and disengagement from the proclamation of world changing truth, with a depressing and unbiblical view of 'remnant' retreat, all born out of a defeatist eschatology, that even now circles its arrow lit and burning wagons and waits for Sovereign revival. Let us not kid ourselves; this waiting on revival is nothing but lazy, lethargic, selfish cowardice and an embraced Biblical ignorance, which has led to this sorry state of affairs. It is nothing but the spirit of Hezekiah manifest in 'boomer' bombastic-ness. (2 Kings 20:19) God help us.

I believe that there is a need for a new iconoclasm of all the idols of this terrible and great Christian compromise. Those redundant attitudes of retreat, all clothed in the false courage of resignation and so-called serenity in the face of such a rising evil is of course simply self-centeredness wrapped up in the body warmer of cowardice, or lethargy, dressed in a lounge suit and smoking a clove cigarette through a long quellazaire while Zion burns. They all need hammering down.

It is unfortunate that non-Christian authors Kerry Patterson, Joseph Grenny and David Maxfield, in their 2007 book, 'Influencer: The Power to Change Anything' are the ones that have to unwittingly bring a hammer to these Christian idols. Their major premise is simple: 'Unwavering perseverance in rooting out root-cause behavior will result in influencing permanent change but the greatest danger of all, is to settle on some kind of acceptable serenity.' I tell Without God, their uprooting approach and unwavering perseverance has achieved some remarkable social successes.

Now then, even though only God has the power to change a human heart, humanity and *especially* redeemed and Holy Spirit empowered humanity, have an invitation, an obligation, a duty and a command, to strive in a persistent perseverance in achieving victory over darkness in all its manifestations of

> *Now is the time for one prayer and one prayer only! "Lord, give me courage to change the things I can!"*

conquest and subjugation. Listen now, for what I am about to say and suggest has nothing to do with the false spiritual eugenics of coupling social sciences and human will to Divine power, but rather, they are some challenges to get back to the Scriptures and address our own selfishness. So then, I say to you this night that until God directly says to you, "Settle for seventy years and build and prosper," then your false serenity and waiting on God is not true spirituality at all, but is rather a satanic deception on a vast and seductive scale. My friends, as this icy darkness hems in the people of God, now is the time for one prayer and one breakout prayer only, "Lord, give me courage to change the things I can!" Amen and let it be so.

I believe we are quickly moving into the time of the end. However, in this present transitioning time I do not look for a defeated, down and out church, but rather the rising of the real church, which is both victorious and glorious, putting down its roots into the rich soil of God's word and expanding its tent pegs outward as its ranks of true believers daily grows. I am hopeful and expectant to see a holy stump, rooted, and fruited glorious church in the terrible times to come.

Look now, if God is in you, then you are an unstoppable influencer, a nation shaper, a change bringer, a giant slayer, a darkness snuffer! A real history maker, not just a singing one. Yet, your ignorance, selfishness and idolatry has stopped you from being so thus far and this has to stop! It is time to repent of these negligent sins; it is time to stop being a coward; Yes, it is time to choose courage and get to start being the salt and light that you truly are. Begin tonight then by asking God to help you identify and remove those root forms of false belief, which have bound you in, chains for oh so very long. Christian, it is time both to change and to bring change. It is time to smash in pieces your selfish and defeatist idol of serenity. It is time to be a real history make. Now get up and get on with it!

> *YOU are an unstoppable influencer, a nation shaper, a change bringer, a giant slayer, a darkness snuffer! You are an history maker.*

Listen: *So Jesus said to them, "Because of your unbelief; for assuredly, I say to you, if you have faith as a mustard seed, you will say to this mountain, 'Move from here to there,' and it will move; and nothing will be impossible for you." (Matthew 17:20 NKJV)*

Pray: We repent of our cowardice and our complicit selfishness O Lord our God. Now then our Father, whilst we rightly grieve our lost days, lost opportunities, lost ground, lost families, lost communities and lost nations, yes, even whilst the great plains of Your goodness have been filled with the mountainous garbage heaps of everything that is anti-God, teach us to say to these mountains: MOVE! Oh God, under Your instruction let us truly to be able to say at last, "Nothing was impossible for us!" Indeed then O Lord our God, give us courage not only to change the things we can, but the ability to even change the things we cannot change ourselves! Amen and let it be so.

| Vol 01 | Q2 | NW00138 | May 17th |

Night-Whisper | **POWER**

The real prayers of watching angels. Or, 'Sons or serfs?'

Somewhere out there two angels are sat on a log and one says to the other, "So, what you got on today then?" To which the other replies, "Well, I have a little project I set myself, so I'll be getting on with that. Apart from that, not too much really. The truth is, I am a bit bored with all this hanging around waiting for an assignment or waiting to be called into court for worship. Sometimes, if I'm honest, I really wonder why I exist."

Daniel 4:16-17

Let his heart be changed from that of a man, let him be given the heart of a beast, and let seven times pass over him. 'This decision is by the decree of the watchers, and the sentence by the word of the holy ones, in order that the living may know that the Most High rules in the kingdom of men, gives it to whomever He will, and sets over it the lowest of men.' NKJV

We know very little of the 'daily' tasks and responsibilities of all the Holy Angels, save to say, that I am sure that none of them are bored. Indeed, I am confident that the tenor of the Scriptures indicate a full utilization of angels with rank, specialization and governing authority. Indeed, Angels, I believe, have a very busy time of it!

That God's order and glory might be maintained, tonight's text speaks of 'Watchers' and 'Holy Ones' and depicts them in the unreferenced issuing of angelic decrees of judgment, sentencing, and the execution of the same. Look now, these 'Watchers' and 'Holy Ones' (either both holy angels of different ranks and standing, or holy 'Watchers' as distinct from fallen and debased 'Watcher' angels) did not ask God for permission to do this thing to Nebuchadnezzar, they just got on with it! Do you see that? What devolved governmental power is this? Almighty God is sufficient in Himself in all things that's for sure, but clearly, in God's ecosphere, in God's economy, in God's creation, there is devolved angelic government, and such devolution of angelic government has, under God, seemingly autonomous and effectual earthly power in it as well! God is no constitutional monarch here, but it is obvious that He has set up rulers, powers, and authority that act under Him, in reference to His being, laws, and divine decrees, who also seem to act independently of Him?

So then, these 'Watchers' were not sent from heaven with an announcement from the throne room of the Most High, but rather, for the sake of heaven and the Lord of heaven, they independently enacted a decree for the glory of God! This is very important for us to know tonight because God has devolved, even now, the governmental power of the present expression of the Kingdom of God together with its blood bought authority to the sons of God as they act together in the local church, and to individual sons of God as they act in full knowledge of their own commission, standing and authority.

Some of you have never seen this responsibility, authority and power that you have. Many of you are frightened of it. Many of you sucklers do not want it. Never the less, it is we redeemed sons of God who pronounce blessing and cursing; it is we who close up heaven and open it; it is we who command mountains to move into the middle of the sea; it is we who raise up and pull down; it is we sons of God who have the power as the redeemed sons of God to raise the dead in Jesus name, to cause the blind to see and the lame to walk; it is we who both bind in heaven and on the earth; it is we who judge and hand over to Satan those whose flesh needs to be destroyed here on the earth; is it we who now command the angels, for are they not even our servants, even Gods ministering flames sent to help us now? Indeed, in the age to come it is we as redeemed men and women, for we shall all retain our gender, we who shall even judge the fallen angelic host. This very night, we have government, power and authority thrust upon us. Why then are we, the sons of the living God, acting like tenants on Crown land?

> *Why then are we, the sons of the living God acting like tenants on Crown land?*

My focus tonight then is not on these holy Watchers, but is on you! For I believe we the church and many of us as individuals appointed by the Most High, have a great measure of devolved government, power and authority, whereby, we can both decree and enact those things spoken by us. It is time we take responsibility in this. It is time we started acting like Sons, rather than serfs. My friend, it is time to grow up and grow into.

Listen: *"Again I say to you that if two of you agree on earth concerning anything that they ask, it will be done for them by My Father in heaven. For where two or three are gathered together in My name, I am there in the midst of them." (Matthew 18:19-20NKJV)*

Pray: Father, I don't want to be a fruitcake, a self-deceiving megalomaniac. Father, I don't want to be a charlatan or seller of snake oil and false power. BUT OH MY GOD! I want to know the power and the authority that comes in being a son of God and marching under the command and authority of the King of ages. So, amen Lord and let it be so! Help me take authority and my rightful place in Your Kingdom.

Night-Whisper | **WORD**

Its' time to get out the Kevlar

Are you Gedaliah? His name of course, this new Governor of the Jewish remnant means, 'God is my greatness.' Are you Gedaliah? Have you been appointed to maintain order and give hope in a land of disorderly hopelessness? Have you been appointed by God to do good to His remnant people? Are you Gedaliah? If so, BEWARE! For the devil is out to get you.

In 586 B.C., King Nebuchadnezzar mounted his final campaign against Judah and Jerusalem. The old girl's walls had eventually been penetrated, her king captured, tortured and humiliated, and the Temple of the Lord obliterated. Those former princes, those powerful people and intellectuals who were not killed were then all carted off to Babylon leaving behind only the poorest of the poor, a small garrison of troops, ooh, and the prophet Jeremiah.

Upon leaving Jerusalem, King Nebuchadnezzar had also set up a Jewish Governor over this sin induced and God actioned desolation, and a vital role of reclamation it was too, even the last hope to rebuild and maintain any form of national cohesiveness. The Governors name was Gedaliah, and may I suggest that he was a symbol and an effectual lynch pin in the working out of what remained of the merciful goodness

Jeremiah 40:13-16

Moreover Johanan the son of Kareah and all the captains of the forces that were in the fields came to Gedaliah at Mizpah, and said to him, "Do you certainly know that Baalis the king of the Ammonites has sent Ishmael the son of Nethaniah to murder you?" .... "Let me go, please, and I will kill Ishmael the son of Nethaniah, and no one will know it. Why should he murder you, so that all the Jews who are gathered to you would be scattered, and the remnant in Judah perish?" But Gedaliah the son of Ahikam said to Johanan the son of Kareah, "You shall not do this thing, for you speak falsely concerning Ishmael." NKJV of God to this ragtag bag of a remnant. Like all key officers in the plans of the Lord, especially where redemption and renewal was hanging by a thread, he was the target of the enemy.

Shortly after gaining his position, Gedaliah the Governor was told by one of the left over 'Guerrilla leaders,' Johanan, that an assassination attempt was being planned against him by a geezer called Ishmael, a willing Jew Killer, who was financed and sent by the King of Israel's hateful old relatives, the Ammonites. Look now! The devil rejoices at your hurt Gedaliah, and will make an end of you, even seeking your utter destruction. Mercilessly, even though you might be shot through and writhing on the ground in agony, he will still come and put a bullet in your head. Watch now, for the devil's hatred for the people of God and those standing with them is unremitting.

Johanan offered to remove Ishmael, to 'rub him out' him out before he had a chance to inflict this terrible assassination blow. Gedaliah, however, would not believe the tale, which Johanan told to him. Consequently, Gedaliah was murdered, other 'innocents' were massacred, and the few very sorry survivors of Jerusalem were then taken into slavery and captivity by the perpetrators of it all. It was left to 'I told you so' Johanan to go and rescue the carried off remnant, but then, in fear, to flee with them to Egypt from the face of what both he and they all thought would be a very vengeful Nebuchadnezzar. In their disobedience to the Word of the Lord given to them by Jeremiah, which was to trust God and remain in the land, they left anyway for Egypt, only to be consumed by that which they dreaded in the staying. What a mess, and make no bones about it, this was all because Gedaliah refused to let Johanan give Ishmael a whacking!

Make no bones about it, this was all because Gedaliah refused to let Johanan give Ishmael a whacking!

Now then, I am not countenancing any form of preemptive killing here. However, like Nehemiah, though Gedeliah should have continued on fearlessly with his job, he should have, however, like Nehemiah, taken full precautions against a known enemy and a made all provisions of personal protection and distancing from and therefore the removal of a known threat. God has his own drones to annihilate the perpetrators of evil in their own beds my friends, but it is our responsibility to take action in the face of good intelligence. Gedaliah's naivety, pride, misjudgment and inaction here cost the lives of many, inflicted misery upon the people of his responsibility, and in human terms, put back the cause of God a good number of years. Gedeliah was an appointed but atrocious Governor. He failed to protect his own person and his vital position and consequently brought destruction upon the people of his care. Tell me tonight, are you Gedaliah?

Remember, if you are a leader that you should not hide but be courageous in your calling. Woe to the people however, who have a naive deaf idiot to lead them. Gedaliah! Do your duty. Do it boldly. Nevertheless, take all precautions to protect yourself and your office, so that your calling may continue and so that God may do all the good He intended to do to the people of your care. Listen Gedaliah, its maybe time to get out the Kevlar!

Listen: *Those who built on the wall, and those who carried burdens, loaded themselves so that with one hand they worked at construction, and with the other held a weapon. Every one of the builders had his sword girded at his side as he built. And the one who sounded the trumpet was beside me. Then I said to the nobles, the rulers, and the rest of the people, "The work is great and extensive, and we are separated far from one another on the wall. Wherever you hear the sound of the trumpet, rally to us there. Our God will fight for us." So we labored in the work, and half of the men held the spears from daybreak until the stars appeared. At the same time I also said to the people, "Let each man and his servant stay at night in Jerusalem, that they may be our guard by night and a working party by day." So neither I, my brethren, my servants, nor the men of the guard who followed me took off our clothes, except that everyone took them off for washing. (Nehemiah 4:17-23 NKJV)*

Pray: Father, give us jewelers and give us diamonds, and remove from us all mealy mouthed thieves and glass. Crush the liars O Lord, grind them inot poweder. Assasinate the assassin and do good to Your people O God. Amen, and let it be so.

Night-Whisper | **PREPARE**

The purpose of 'portals of horror!'

Three air crashes have gotten my attention in the last 6 months of my writing and chiefly because on two of them involved Christians I was acquainted with. The last one however, was Air-Asia flight QZ8501 where 41 people died from just one Indonesian Evangelical church. Apparently, these Christian families with children had all block booked a holiday to Singapore for the New Year. On all three flights, there were prominent and influential church leaders, wives, gifted musicians, singers, family and little Christian children. We all hope they died instantly. We all hope there was no screaming fear. We all hope we can find their lost bodies. Thus far, however, only parts of some of the burnt and fish eaten corpses have been found and many of those retrieved can only be identified through DNA testing. Yes, we all hope they died instantly. We all hope there was no screaming fear.

1 Corinthians 15:54

So when this corruptible has put on incorruption, and this mortal has put on immortality, then shall be brought to pass the saying that is written: "Death is swallowed up in victory." NKJV

Now, one of the many questions we must ask, and one I want to ask tonight regarding those disaster dead Christians is this, "Why does God allow entrance into His heaven to often be through portals of horrific pain?" After all, whether women, children or young men; there is apparently no gender nor age range of God's people which have not, over the millennia, entered heaven through every kind of portal of physical horror imaginable.

Some would like to die through a lethal injection in a hotel room or a white sheeted hospital bed, and call it merciful. Others would like to die in their home bed, their family all around them, smiling and dabbing away tears from the corner of their eyes as another soul, who after sharing the Gospel and leaving words of wisdom, slips quietly into heaven through the flickering candle light of the corner of a wooden room on Walton's mountain. Others would like to die quickly in battle, heroically shouting, "The sword of the Lord and of Gideon too!" No one wants to die through decapitation, or the horror of fire, explosion, crushing, or the cold icy Titanic drowning, or the painful eating of cancer, or mind robbing dementia or any other torture, nor a thousand other ways to horribly enter heaven. Quick or slow though, quietly of furiously, with 'dignity' or without, in the end I wonder if the plain facts of life under the sun is that there is no such thing as a 'good' death. There is only death.

> *Even so, does fallen man care more about our painless passing than God does? On the one hand the answer surely is, "Yes!"*

The question remains though as to how a loving God can suffer to see the passing portal agonies of those He loves? How can any entrance into the glories of heaven be not through gates of splendor but rather through dark tunnels of horror? I ask again then, "Does God care about the hardships of death and entrance into His heaven?" Or, is it only fallen man through the inculcation of psychedelic drugs such as N,N-Dimethyltryptamine and non-psychedelic drugs such as Ketamine, which, when slipped into the 'death experience' of portal passers, makes the journey bearable? Yes, is it only fallen man who is willing and active in easing the passing through this portal to the other world? And by the by my boy, would it not be a good idea for aircraft to not just drop down Oxygen masks in an emergency but automatically inject the passengers with anesthetic and associated 'emergence phenomena' or 'near death experience drugs' to make their passing 'nice and easy does it?' Certainly, in coming years and in the ongoing economic industrialization of human death, we can expect to see the like offered at bargain basement prices and even on the National Health Service! Even so, I get back to my question, does fallen man care more about our painless passing than God does? On the one hand the answer surely is, "Yes!"

The benefits of good immunization is long-term resistance to infection. In an age of needles, a small pinprick should bring a lifetime of freedom from disease. The parent taking their child for the same will have them undergo a small amount of trauma and pain for the benefits of the same. Such seconds of pain are lost in the lifetime of health, never to be remembered again. I wonder then, if in a similar way, for His children, God sees all painful portals into His heaven as mere pin pricks of pain which are lost immediately to an eternity of health and peace, even as the glories and goodness of heaven overwhelm all memories of the painful passing forever? Maybe. Or, as a former caterpillar must struggle from its cocoon to be healthy in its new life, maybe such pain in 'portals of passing' make us more beautiful butterflies in the age to come? I know, it is an horrendous thing to even suggest this! Even so, I wonder if it these two thoughts which might contain some truth? Pain in death, in the light of eternity, in eternity to come, if at all remembered shall seem to be but a long forgotten pinprick. Does the butterfly ever remember being a caterpillar?

For those who are not God's children, however, the process of passing through portals of horror may be the last chance of repentance and laying hold of Christ? I wonder, for the non-Christian if all drug induced and mimicked 'passing's' are like putting a blindfold on a child as you lead it into the hungry Lion's den? The Bible says the eternal outlook for the non-Christian is a damnable one of teeth gnashing agony and remembrance.

Dare I suggest, as long as I never experience it of course, that for the Christian there is purpose in portals of horror? These things, I concur, are awful considerations. Even so, in the light of disaster and death and of Christians and non-Christians being touched by the same, let us then at least consider these things.

The questions as to what manner of horrors there might be in our own 'portals of passing,' are all long armed thieving boogey men to rob you of life's present joys.

Portals of painful horror leading to the heaven of God are in the end a mystery. Man might remove pain as much as he can, but death remains, and despite his beast endeavors, it always will. Look now then Christian; death is a portal on the point of your appointed timeline through which you will pass and exit this temporal existence into life eternal. Each heartbeat takes you a step closer to this portal of passing. The answer to questions as to what crown of thorns awaits you there, what darkness, what voices, what loneliness, what manner of horrors there might be in your own 'portal of passing?' for most, are not theirs to know. The thoughts of what these monsters might be, make this coming passing of ours a long armed and thieving boogey-man that rob us of life's present joys. Yet, all wise men have learnt this, that "If you are too afraid to die, you shall never, ever live." Therefore Christian, make peace with your soon coming portal of passing. It is coming. You cannot stop it. Whatever the manner of it Christian, remember that God is with you, and that you can hope to find His sustaining and greeting presence, even there! Whatever the horror of the portal, both it and its weight are both mostly unknown to you. Do not let its shadow darken your now, for whatever it is, it shall prove to be but a passing pinprick on our journey, which shall be soon forgotten in the wonders of the age to come. NOW THEN CHRISTIAN FRIEND....LIVE! If you are a non-Christian reading this however, worry, be in fear and be in dread, for beyond that portal is a place of dark and suffering eternal hopelessness.

Listen: *"O Death, where is your sting? O Hades, where is your victory?" The sting of death is sin, and the strength of sin is the law. But thanks be to God, who gives us the victory through our Lord Jesus Christ. Therefore, my beloved brethren, be steadfast, immovable, always abounding in the work of the Lord, knowing that your labor is not in vain in the Lord. (1 Corinthians 15:55-58 NKJV)*

Then Jesus said to them again, "Most assuredly, I say to you, I am the door of the sheep. All who ever came before Me are thieves and robbers, but the sheep did not hear them. I am the door. If anyone enters by Me, he will be saved, and will go in and out and find pasture. The thief does not come except to steal, and to kill, and to destroy. I have come that they may have life, and that they may have it more abundantly. "I am the good shepherd. The good shepherd gives His life for the sheep. John 10:7-11 NKJV

Pray: Father, let not the reaching fear of the 'portal of my passing' destroy my life in You today. Knowing that you are sufficient to sustain me in ALL things, I shall be sustained. Having there no fear of death nor concern for the 'portal of my passing' help me as Your child to live well and fearlessly now, even disdainfully of the pin prick to come. Lord, help me live today! Amen and let it be so.

| Vol 01 | Q2 | NW00141 | May 20ᵗʰ |

Night-Whisper | **PREPARE**

Lesbians, the lie of savior siblings and the seconds left 'till midnight

Under the guise of gaining a possible cure for cancer and other dreadful diseases, today in the year of our Lord 2008, the Government of The United Kingdom of Great Britain and

Genesis 6:1-8

"Now it came to pass, when men began to multiply on the face of the earth, and daughters were born to them, that the sons of God saw the daughters of men, that they were beautiful; and they took wives for themselves of all whom they chose. And the Lord said, 'My Spirit shall not strive with man forever, for he is indeed flesh; yet his days shall be one hundred and twenty years.' There were giants on the earth in those days, and also afterward, when the sons of God came in to the daughters of men and they bore children to them. Those were the mighty men who were of old, men of renown. Then the Lord saw that the wickedness of man was great in the earth, and that every intent of the thoughts of his heart was only evil continually. And the Lord was sorry that He had made man on the earth, and He was grieved in His heart. So the Lord said, 'I will destroy man whom I have created from the face of the earth, both man and beast, creeping thing and birds of the air, for I am sorry that I have made them.'" NKJV

Northern Ireland, under the fat and proud leadership of that then pretender to the throne, Prime Minister Gordon Brown, finally sealed the fate of our nation once and for all in the fury of the Most High God. Brown shall surely go down in our soon to be ended national history as the most infamous of all leaders, for under his watch, yes, under his astonishing banner of a "moral mission," he gave and encouraged the unequivocal backing of a sin so final, a sin so great, that it has now turned the angry eyes of God toward us, making us the focal point of His most furious face. We are finished. I suspect what has been going on in secret for some time, has finally been enshrined in law. Legislated sin, always gets God's judgmental attention!

Today in 2008, British lawmakers voted to approve the use of animal-human embryos for research. Additional proposals would simplify approval procedures for so-called "savior siblings," as well as offer easier access to fertility treatment for lesbians and also offer another vote on so called "abortion reform," for even the murderers are finding it hard to wade through the depth of human blood that has been vented at their feet. I am ashamed to say, that even this so-called reform was rejected out of hand, and that a year later in 2009 we began advertising abortion services on national television. When God is rejected out of hand, when His being becomes unknown to those who reflect it, then His image will be rejected, and the offspring of mankind will just become so much meat to be processed, meat to be utilized, and meat to be euthanized when (in a dignified way of course, for now) their usefulness to the consuming machine has ceased. In 2015, aborted babies are undergoing a vivisection harvest, as their organs are removed from them whilst they live and are then implanted into rats and pigs and grown for later adult patient use. They call it Xenotransplantation. The Bible calls it murder.

In 2008, the human animal hybrid process, involved injecting an empty cow or rabbit egg with human DNA. A burst of electricity is then used to trick the egg into dividing regularly, so that it becomes a very early embryo from which stem cells can be extracted. There is no doubt that this is nothing short of the genetic engineering of human beings, yes, the engineering of a human into something far, far less than human, even into something which is so very clearly, *not created in the image of God, but in the image of the beast*. Yes, we have opened the way for allowing the possibility of the creation not of designer babies but of designer beasts! There is no turning back from this and I am afraid that the only answer God has ever brought to this problem, for it is not a new one, has been total and utter, complete and absolute, annihilation! We are back in the days of Noah my friends, yes, back in the days of Noah. I

> *There is no doubt that this is nothing short of the genetic engineering of human beings, yes, the engineering of a human into something far, far less than human, even into something which is so very clearly, not created in the image of God, but in the image of the beast. Transhumanism is upon us.*

wonder if the Alpha Generation will indeed be a generation of genetically mixed clay fused with iron technology. I wonder if the Alpha generation will be the first of the new non-human human generation?

The consideration of the screening of embryos for genetic characteristics to create so-called "savior siblings," where parents seek to have a child with specific non-diseased characteristics for the sole purpose of helping a diseased older sibling by either tissue or organ transplantation is not far away! To compound our matters of destruction even further (if that were possible), not only are babies now silently killed at public expense (though God hears their salted and spine cut screams) and then utilized as "waste product raw material for experimentation, and organ donation" but even fatherhood is now being completely annihilated, as the vote "to end the requirement for in-vitro fertilization clinics to consider the need for a child to have a father," was also passed into law in 2008, to thereby simply and now most sinfully enable lesbian couples and single women, to gain easier access to fertility treatment. Don't tell me that there is no attack against fatherhood. Don't tell me that there is no demonic attack against the fatherhood of God! Don't tell me that man is creating himself in his own fallen image. Don't tell me that there is not another more sinister agenda involving the devil himself.

If we Christians of these times of the end do not take that 2008 vote and subject matter as a gigantic kick in our complacent pants and begin to prepare both ourselves and others for the wrath to come upon us, then we are thoroughly complicit in the disasters which are so surely even now, trundling along the way toward us. The Christian echo to the silent scream of unborn babies is virtually silent in the land, though are bands are singing loudly of victory through their amped up, and vamped up lie machine. God help us, for our silence and sheep like sleeping in the face of these monstrosities has made us completely complicit in this sin.

If we Christians of these times of the end do not take that 2008 vote and subject matter as a gigantic kick in our complacent pants and begin to prepare both ourselves and others for the wrath to come upon us, then we are thoroughly complicit in the disasters which are so surely even now, trundling along the way toward us.

As I write, I know that this is not a merry message. As I write, I know that most Christians are splashing around in a make believe river, rolling around on the floor laughing when they should be weeping and wailing.

They are falling over instead of standing up and lying down and soaking in 'the presence,' (whatever the hell that is) rather than standing and fighting the filthy Philistines. Meanwhile, amidst the merriment of all this 'new wine,' our house has fallen down around our ears, our Rome is burning and its heated fires are melting their way toward us.

Tell me Christian tonight. "What in heaven's name are you doing with your life!? Booking a flight to go get another blessing? Organizing a picnic in the park or another big day out to line the pockets of more 'made it' Christians?" Buying another bloody DVD/CD? It is way past the time that we had already counted the cost, took up His cross, unsheathed His Word, put on our armor and began following Him into battle, for I tell you the truth, it may be but seconds until midnight. Prepare yourself Christian and wake up! The time of accounting is coming.

Listen: *"O my soul, my soul!I am pained in my very heart!My heart makes a noise in me; I cannot hold my peace, because you have heard, O my soul, the sound of the trumpet, the alarm of war. Destruction upon destruction is cried, for the whole land is plundered.Suddenly my tents are plundered, and my curtains in a moment. How long will I see the standard, and hear the sound of the trumpet? 'For My people are foolish, they have not known Me. They are silly children, and they have no understanding.They are wise to do evil, but to do good they have no knowledge.' I beheld the earth, and indeed it was without form, and void; and the heavens, they had no light. I beheld the mountains, and indeed they trembled, and all the hills moved back and forth. I beheld, and indeed there was no man, and all the birds of the heavens had fled. I beheld, and indeed the fruitful land was a wilderness, and all its cities were broken down at the presence of the Lord, by His fierce anger." Jeremiah 4:19-26 NKJV*

Pray: Lord, I have heard a voice as of a woman in labor, even the anguish as of her who brings forth her first child. Lord, it is the lost voice of our Christian inheritance bewailing itself; spreading her hands, saying, "Woe is me now, for my soul is weary. Because of murderers!" Please O Lord, restore us one more time that we might finish well. In Jesus name I pray, amen. (From Jeremiah 4:31 NKJV)

Night-Whisper | **ACTION**

Dirt and the Finger of God

Politics is a dirty game, just listen a while to Sir Humphrey Appleby! Unfortunately, the one thing I have learned about my fellow Christians is they do not want to get their hands dirty. Oh, I am not talking about scrubbing a beggar, or hugging a prostitute, though to be sure you have to be careful where you do that, and make sure you have no money in your pocket whilst you are doing it! No, I am not talking about getting our hands dirty doing good works, I am talking about getting our reputation dirty, our good name sullied, our position misunderstood, maybe even making a few misinformed enemies, or by appearing partisan, whilst being egged with words like 'racist,' 'xenophobe,' 'homophobe,' Islamaphobe,' or 'anti-Semite' etc. No, we Christians don't like getting on the ground and putting our fingers in such retributional dirt.

John 8:3-5

Then the scribes and Pharisees brought to Him a woman caught in adultery. And when they had set her in the midst, they said to Him, "Teacher, this woman was caught in adultery, in the very act. Now Moses, in the law, commanded us that such should be stoned. But what do You say?"
NKJV

Whilst I thoroughly believe that in this present age we need to truly function as a Kingdom within a State (and I do not mean the British Crown – Her Majesty already has a Crown office in the Houses of Parliament and her Lord Lieutenants throughout the land, yes indeed, in Britain we already have a Kingdom within a State) even so, the time has long since passed for we Christians to forcefully and loudly express our views and judgments with boldness and without fear. The truth is, in our self-protecting cowardly silence, we have turned our back on far too many issues, which have been dragged before our face, bruised, sullied, and bare breasted. I am not referring here to the few organizations we have in the past paid to do our 'dirty work' for us, even those representatives who might now have far too many self-perpetuating interests to speak the truth in love, no, I am not referring to them, but to you, the individual Christian inhabited and possessed by God the Holy

Spirit who surely has an obligation to engage the mess brought before your face on a daily basis? Surely, even the meanest Christian armed with the Word of God and the Holy Spirit is such a person with and the obligation to pronounce upon the mess? On the other hand, do the Scriptures speak a lie?

Look now friend, you do not need an Oxbridge education, nor millions of monies, nor anything else to pronounce the judgment of the Lord upon many matters brought before you. You just need a testimony of forgiveness and the fairness of God's grace, courage, a willingness to learn and be corrected, and most of all, the willingness to be counted as a fool for Jesus Christ. Moreover, do not kid yourself dear friend, it is often that last and foolish requirement which keeps your proud heart away from any dirty controversy. Be honest in this now dear Christian, for look, your nation has been caught in spiritual adultery and is now dragged before your face! Christian, your nation stands before you, its upper body as bare and naked and as nipple hard in sin as the old, cold 'Pap's of Fife' on a Scottish winter's day. I tell you, such a state demands your judgment now! I tell you, if you turn your back on your nation now, in her most naked and direst need, never speaking a word of God's grace and truth, then she will indeed be stoned to death and your children will shiver in the grey morning rain whilst standing atop of the dead belly of their road kill and run over, old marsupial mother. Yes, if not for yourself, then for the sake of your children you must begin to get down and get dirty. Speak up! Speak out! Speak clear!

And do not kid yourself dear friend, it is just the chance of being seen as a 'fool' which keeps your proud heart away from any dirty controversy.

It is time for all in the Kingdom of God to get on their knees in the dirt and start sticking their fingers where they are not wanted in the world. In addition, oh my dear reluctant Christian, will you please tell me now, just what is your reputation in light of the coming death? What is your ridicule in light of the coming unravelling? What is your hurt, your certainty of being misheard, misunderstood, misjudged and mishandled in light of the church slipping into the Laodicean Abyss whilst once Christian nations slip into the Laurentian Abyss of Islam, never to be seen again? Are not your reputation and ridicule nothing but two little pigeons ready to be offered upon the sacrificial alter of true service to God and to your earthly home? So then, let me ask you now, for the cause of Christ and the redemption of our harlot nations, are you willing to get down in the dirt and get dirty with Jesus?

Listen: *Do you not know that the saints will judge the world? And if the world will be judged by you, are you unworthy to judge the smallest matters? Do you not know that we shall judge angels? How much more, things that pertain to this life? .... NKJV (1 Corinthians 6:2,3 NKJV)*

Pray: Father, despite being misunderstood, misrepresented and most certainly mistreated in some manner, grant us wisdom, fortitude, and the courage to speak the truth and declare Your Word,. Help us to know Your Word and to fearlessly declare it. Amen and let it be so.

Night-Whisper | **JUDGE**

Keeping 'IT' in the family

As pedophiles around the world are shooed out of their darkness; the victims begin to see some earthly justice. It seems that few institutions have not been touched by this scourge of industrial child abuse. It is with great sadness that I have to say that even my own particular people, Bible believing Evangelicals, have also been touched and tainted by these hideous activities. In some of our churches and institutions it would appear that they have tried to deal with the issue 'internally.'

One victim of child abuse in a local church who was encouraged by church leaders to keep 'IT' in the family, eventually disregarded their advice and finally went to the police. She put it like this, *"I thought about it again and actually got so totally fed up with the whole mentality of keeping it in the church, letting the church deal with it, keeping it quiet from the authorities that I actually went to the police with resolve and determination."* She still believes the church tried to cover up what happened, saying, *"It's almost as though the church is using forgiveness as a blanket cover for what has happened, that if you can forgive your abuser as an adult for what he did to you as a child you then don't have to involve the authorities or take it any further."*

1 Corinthians 6:3-8

Do you not know that we shall judge angels? How much more, things that pertain to this life?........ I say this to your shame. Is it so, that there is not a wise man among you, not even one, who will be able to judge between his brethren? But brother goes to law against brother, and that before unbelievers! Now therefore, it is already an utter failure for you that you go to law against one another. Why do you not rather accept wrong? Why do you not rather let yourselves be cheated? No, you yourselves do wrong and cheat, and you do these things to your brethren! NKJV

Why do Christians go to secular law to gain justice, justification, satisfaction, protection and compensation? Is it because this is the only place they can get it? How do you live with the horror of seeing your former molester and abuser worshipping the same God along with you in the same gathering place? Indeed, let us extend this question beyond pedophilia and say that rarely will Christians remain in the same vicinity of those who have sinned against them in any way! They leave, and often do so with bitterness and hatred, taking their unresolved hurts with them to another fellowship or maybe leaving the church 'scene' all together. Is there no justice in the church of God? Is there no real repentance, grace and forgiveness among Christians toward one another? Are there some sins that can be covered but others which must be exposed for all the world to see? Is the family of God really rotten to the core? Is the church the most dangerous place on earth and if so, why would anyone want to go there?

> *The church, silent and gumsy, lies flea ridden and forgotten, shivering in the corner in its own urine soaked fear.*

Any organized body has its own law. The ultimate power of that applied law is usually dismissal from that organized body. Indeed, even to a very small extent, each local church does have its own 'cannon law,' if you will, even its own small set of laws, of ecclesiastical governance, the ultimate power of which is usually dismissal from that local body. Even when local church bodies then gather together in associations, fellowships, and denominations, then still, the ultimate power of that cannon law is dismissal from that association or fellowship or denomination. In our own Western church history, however, when the confluence of secular and spiritual rivers ran together for a long time, it was cannon law in the Roman church and in the Anglican Church that greatly influenced even the development of all secular common, civil, national and international law. Even so, for equally long-time now, secular law has not only eclipsed cannon law, but also has removed both the churches bark and its teeth. To all intents and purposes, to the common man in the street and the pew, old canon law, and any judgment in the church is nothing but a dead dog

Long time back, when most British Christians did not make a great distinction between secular and spiritual offenses, the church tried crimes such as adultery, blasphemy, slander, heresy, money lending and gambling, breach of contracts, inheritance, even going as far as shaping the laws of war and our approaches to international diplomacy. Now the church has no judicial power, save that which it recourses to in secular law. For this reason, hurt members, abused members, dispossessed members, all seek justice among the ungodly. The church, silent and gumsy, lies flea ridden and forgotten, shivering in the corner in its own urine soaked fear. These things are, but these things should not be so.

The apostle Paul's scathing judgments upon the church at Corinth knows no bounds when he addresses their living and says, *"No, you yourselves do wrong and cheat, and you do these things to your brethren! Do you not know that the unrighteous will not inherit the kingdom of God? Do not be deceived. Neither fornicators, nor idolaters, nor adulterers, nor homosexuals, nor sodomites, nor thieves, nor covetous, nor drunkards, nor revilers, nor extortioners will inherit the kingdom of God. And such were some of you. But you were washed, but you were sanctified, but you were justified in the name of the Lord Jesus and by the Spirit of our God. (1 Corinthians 6:8-11 NKJV)* Paul acknowledges what George Verwer calls the 'MESSiology' of the local church and calls them to cleanliness making it very clear that continuing in such sins indicates the absence of their names from the Lambs book of life. Paul goes further in his letter to the leaders and wider local church indicating that because of their lack of judging sin and sinners amongst them, God was doing it Himself, inflicting both sickness, weakness and death. *"For this reason many are weak and sick among you, and many sleep. for if we would judge ourselves, we would not be judged. But when we are judged, we are chastened by the Lord, that we may not be condemned with the world. (1 Corinthians 11:30-32 NKJV)*

> *Paul acknowledges what George Verwer refers to the 'MESSiology' of the local church and calls them to cleanliness making it very clear that continuing in such sins indicates the absence of their names from the Lambs book of life.*

Repentant confession must be met with forgiveness. For if Christ's death does not cover the redemption of the pedophile then it does not cover you. (Shocking. I know.) Purity and a self-cleansing, self-judging church, marked with holiness in practicality rather than religiosity must be the marks of the local church. There must be not even a hint of evil among us. For the unrepentant, excommunication and the handing over of the offender for the devil to kill him must be marks of the local church. (And there goes your worship praise celebration experience in one fell swoop folks!) Without such active judgement against sin, the church is a dead dog pie. The church is a lie. *"For I indeed, as absent in body but present in spirit, have already judged (as though I were present) him who has so done this deed. In the name of our Lord Jesus Christ, when you are gathered together, along with my spirit, with the power of our Lord Jesus Christ, deliver such a one to Satan for the destruction of the flesh, that his spirit may be saved in the day of the Lord Jesus." (1 Corinthians 5:3-5 NKJV)*

Where the church FAILS to act to protect its members and apply discipline, then in certain cases the member has no other recourse but to secular law. Where the church DOES act to protect its members and disciplines its offenders, then the choice of additional recourse to secular law is with the offended member alone. When this happens, forgiveness does not mean temporal pardon, and thus punishment may inevitably follow in the form of public shame, scandal, the destruction of reputation, loss, of family, finance and even liberty.

> *Where the church FAILS to act to protect its members and apply discipline, then in certain cases the member has no other recourse but to secular law.*

Let us face two facts here: First that when we truly repent of our sins, God freely forgives us, and can freely do so because the punitive actions of retribution and justice were paid on Calvary's cross and the application of reconciliation and restoration was instant. We are forgiven our sins forgotten, yes, and we are more than free as well, in that we are now regarded as sons, heirs, Kings and priests! Secondly, that when a Christian forgives us, punitive action still may follow and even historical punitive action at that. In this, the offender's sin is not covered but publicly revealed and they are then marked like Cain, shunned, sometimes treated even as scum and this side of heaven are publicly named and shamed. Doubting Thomas, Peter the denier, Moses the murderer, Paul the misogynist, Simon the zealot, Mary the harlot, and so it goes on, and on, and on. I am afraid; there are some sins that love has never covered this side of heaven. These are facts. Tonight I have more questions than answers and so I leave just four important ones with you for your consideration:

1. Is the fear of God preached in your church? If not, then should you not expect people to do whatever they please?

2. Does your church have a plurality of accountable leadership? If not, then is there safety in what is, in effect, a local Christian Monarchy?
3. Is your church practicing discipline? If not, where is the true care of your body?
4. Is there evidence of God's judgment in your church? If not, then is God truly with you? I doubt it.

Listen: *Therefore, my beloved, as you have always obeyed, not as in my presence only, but now much more in my absence, work out your own salvation with fear and trembling; for it is God who works in you both to will and to do for His good pleasure. (Philippians 2:12-13 NKJV)*

Pray: Father, help us live well, help us judge correctly and do right in Your sight O Lord.

Night-Whisper | **CHANGE**

Cold chicken and gluten free bread

The church bulletin was very clear that this Sunday morning would be a communion service. The talk (no more than twelve minutes) would be given by a young biology teacher called Mary, who would emphasize (in full PowerPoint and intestinal tract wonder) the fact that we were "one in the Spirit and a united body, with each member dependent on the other."

Isaiah 5:1 NKJV

Now let me sin g to my Well-beloved a song of my Beloved regarding His vineyard: "My Well-beloved has a vineyard On a very fruitful hill..."

The notices went on to tell that that there would be alcoholic wine used as one of the emblems in the communion service, together with non-alcoholic beverages for those who were teetotal. I say 'beverages' would be used in this celebration of unity as one body in the remembrance of the death of our Lord, because a further five options (totaling six in all) would be offered to the communicants. These non-alcoholic beverages would range from: Sugar free (for those dieting and diabetics,) aspartame free (for the health conscience,) normal red juice (no explanation of 'normal,') oh, and for those allergic to 'Red40' food coloring in the soft drink, there would be freshly juiced blood oranges available. A note, somewhat exasperated it seemed to me, placed at the bottom of the notices went on to say that, "Fruitarians could drink 'still spring water' and just imagine it was wine, and also that for those not wanting to share from the same communal cup(s), individual biodegradable thimbles could be prepared providing orders were given at least one hour before the service."

Thoughtfully, I thought, there followed just eight offerings of the emblem of bread: Sliced white, sliced brown, whole loaf white, whole loaf brown, unleavened, glutton free, spelt, and white wafer, (which again was followed by a second note at the bottom of the sheet indicating that this was completely 'untransubstantiated.') I was thankful for the insipid and Biblically incorrect little twelve minute talk which followed the long and drawn out communion service as this 'breaking of bread,' partaken by about 100 people, was nothing but a slow motion train wreck lasting about an hour. Though my wife did restrain me from cutting my wrists, half way through the 'talk,' the communion service had already almost turned me into an unbeliever.

Admittedly, I have exaggerated just a little here in my report, however, this gathering of the elect in Britain, this 'militant of heavenly magnificence on earth,' seemed to epitomize the state of the church in the second decade on the 21st century. It had quite simply, 'lost the plot.'

> *Though my wife did restrain me from cutting my wrists half way through the 'talk,' the communion service had already almost turned me into an unbeliever.*

In 1839, just 6.6 miles from where I presently reside, Samuel John Stone came into the world. Son of an Anglican clergyman he went on to became a Poet-Vicar and one of his most influential works, 'Lyra Fidelium,' was published in 1866. The work consists of a series of twelve hymns, which were constructed to teach and to expand upon the twelve articles of the Apostle's Creed. I believe it inculcates the use of song, rhyme, rhythm and meter, to help the singer remember the depth of the declarations contained therein. His hymn to expand on article nine of the apostle creed which says: 'I believe in the holy Catholic Church and the communion of the saints' became, and continues to be, so well-known that one Archbishop of the past is supposed to have remarked that, "Wherever I go to open a new church building you can count on two things: Cold chicken and *'The Churches One Foundation.'*"

Whilst we are closing down churches every week, whilst each and every week, new Mosques are springing up across this post Christian landscape. It is the church, which has allowed the spread of false religion. The church has also allowed the industrial scale slaughter of babies. The church has also fostered the destruction of the holy institution of marriage. The church has allowed the restructuring of society, which even now is putting young men on the dole queue and mom on the front line to fight our wars. To aid matters further, we put young woman in the pulpit to give a twelve-minute talk on nonsense. I tell you, I am so angry I could spit feathers! I am so distraught, that I could have perpetual panic attacks! I am so depressed, that I could wish my eyes were rivers of tears so that my quaking heart might not burst! Let me shout it out right now anyway, "There is no more hot bread in our pulpits! Just cold chicken served to those who shall soon be slaughtered." I fear that whilst in mockery we sing 'The Churches One Foundation,' her Lord is singing the Song of the Vineyard whilst carrying a pick ax over one shoulder and a carrying a shovel on the other.

I wonder if what we call the church in the United Kingdom, and even in the USA, is now so corrupt that it cannot be revived. For sure, God shall retain His holy Stump; however, I believe that a new vineyard now needs to be dug. We must take the old ways, find some new ground, clear it and start again for I tell you that this current cold chicken vineyard is doomed to destruction. Therefore, come and out from among them and be separate, says the Lord. Go and find a slice of goodness this coming Lord's Day and give up gagging down the dead dog pie.

Listen: *Now let me sing to my Well-beloved, a song of my Beloved regarding His vineyard: My Well-beloved has a vineyard on a very fruitful hill. He dug it up and cleared out its stones, and planted it with the choicest vine. He built a tower in its midst, and also made a winepress in it; So He expected it to bring forth good grapes, but it brought forth wild grapes. "And now, O inhabitants of Jerusalem and men of Judah, Judge, please, between Me and My vineyard. What more could have been done to My vineyard That I have not done in it? Why then, when I expected it to bring forth good grapes, Did it bring forth wild grapes? And now, please let Me tell you what I will do to My vineyard: I will take away its hedge, and it shall be burned; And break down its wall, and it shall be trampled down. I will lay it waste; It shall not be pruned or dug, But there shall come up briers and thorns. I will also command the clouds That they rain no rain on it." For the vineyard of the Lord of hosts is the house of Israel, And the men of Judah are His pleasant plant. He looked for justice, but behold, oppression; For righteousness, but behold, a cry for help. (Isaiah 5:1-7NKJV)*

Pray: Father, please have mercy upon us. Send us some skilled Blacksmiths, anointed Bakers, lovers of the Word and 'droolers' o'er the printed page, even anointed prophets and bold, courageous preachers. Be glorified O God. Be Magnified Great King Jesus! Be lifted up in hot magnificence for all the world to see. Amen and let it be so.

The Church's one foundation
Is Jesus Christ her Lord,
She is His new creation
By water and the Word:
From heaven He came and sought her
To be His holy bride,
With His own blood He bought her
And for her life He died.

She is from every nation
Yet one o'er all the earth,
Her charter of salvation
One Lord, one faith, one birth,
One Holy Name she blesses,
Partakes one Holy Food,
And to one Hope she presses
With every grace endued.

The Church shall never perish!
Her dear Lord to defend,
To guide, sustain, and cherish,
Is with her to the end:
Though there be those who hate her,
And false sons in her pale,
Against or foe or traitor
She ever shall prevail.

Though with a scornful wonder
Men see her sore oppressed,
By schisms rent asunder
By heresies distressed:
Yet saints their watch are keeping,
Their cry goes up "How long?"
And soon the night of weeping
shall be the morn of song!

'Mid toil and tribulation
And tumult of her war,
She waits the consummation
Of peace forevermore;
Till, with the vision glorious,
Her longing eyes are blest,
And the great Church victorious

Shall be the Church at rest!

Yet she on earth hath union
With God the Three in One,
And mystic sweet communion
With those whose rest is won,
With all her sons and daughters
Who, by the Master's Hand
Led through the deathly waters,
Repose in Eden-land.

O happy ones and holy!
Lord, give us grace that we
Like them, the meek and lowly,
On high may dwell with Thee:
There, past the border mountains,
Where in sweet vales the Bride
With Thee by living fountains
For ever shall abide!

Rev. Samuel John Stone.

Night-Whisper | **COURAGE**

Bearing your buttocks to the church

Now what can be said regarding the modern church in the middle of such destructive trouble? As the functional 'trinity' of money, materials and manpower leave the church of the living God in these lands, what has been our response? I think that maybe we can look in four areas.

Isaiah 22:12-14

And in that day the Lord God of hosts Called for weeping and for mourning, For baldness and for girding with sackcloth. But instead, joy and gladness, Slaying oxen and killing sheep, Eating meat and drinking wine: "Let us eat and drink, for tomorrow we die!" Then it was revealed in my hearing by the Lord of hosts, "Surely for this iniquity there will be no atonement for you, Even to your death," says the Lord God of hosts. NKJV

Area number one is Christendom, that area of unholy familiarity where the wheat insist on communing with the chaff, which have gone on to create a God in their own image and a church suited to their own present and sin corrupted culture. The cry of 'Come out from among them and be separate' has, for the most, fallen on the deaf ears of the ecumenically inclined wheat. In this case, though maybe breaking type, I wonder if the compromised wheat will also be uprooted with the tares.

Area number two is 'The optimists,' the revival lookers, (they rarely pray for revival, no, not really, they just talk and look) who have been hoping and predicting for many years that heaven would come and pull them and their nations from under the darkness spreading o'er them. As a testimony to the same, but more as a salve to what they know in their spirit is surely coming, they have danced and sung in their 'celebration worship experiences' of all the glories and victories of their Savior, whilst all the while, Babylon's 'Tartan' army has gathered on their borders. Has this revival hope been faith on their part? Or has this incessant false hope been akin to the prophets of Baal cutting themselves and crying much so that their god would answer by fire, and to make sure he does, they have been lighting their own fires in secret, stirring it up, dumbing it down, cutting themselves and screaming, even celebrating over a multitude if false little fires around the globe? Have the leaders made this madness? Have they deceived their flock? Should the call have gone up instead for shaved heads and weeping, instead of dancing joy, and raised hand smiling, all portraying false hope and manufactured celebration? Has all these been in effect an inner spirit attitude of "eat drink and be merry for tomorrow we die?"

...in all their restructuring and preparing for the day of trouble, they did not really look to the Maker of water, or the keeper of the storehouse of the Lord, and they did not call their people, to weeping and to baldness.

The third area has been the planners and the preparers. These elite stakeholders have seen the dust of marching boots coming towards them. Recent emissaries of financial death have already visited the coffers of their boardrooms and whittled down their mailing lists. Therefore, they have, in secret, planned and made their preparations for survival. They have looked to the reserve armor of the 'House of the Forest;' and restructured their supply sources and gathered together the waters of the lower pool in one central larger reservoir, numbered their possessions and broke down the unnecessary, to build up the broken walls. They have done well. However, in all their restructuring and preparing for the day of trouble, they did not really look to the Maker of water, or the real keepers of the storehouse of the Lord, and they did not call their people, to weeping and to baldness. All the preparation, all the silent restructuring, was done under a false flag of assumed blessing. (Isaiah 22:8-10)

The fourth area are 'the people of the stump.' The despised depressives, who for years have, in disgust, borne their buttocks to the clapping, eyes closed, hand raised and swaying wheat. Like Jeremiah, they have wandered in the wilderness of their own hearts asking if anyone has seen sorrow like their sorrow.

As it is wrong to seek unity where than never be any because Truth never shares a bed with error, so there cannot be rejoicing where God has called for weeping. All planning without God is futile. All saving of resources without acknowledgement of the Giver and His present involvement in present distress is doomed to reserve evaporation and continuing coffer emptying.

I tell you, now is the time for weeping. Now is the time for shaving heads, and for those who can hear, now is the time to bare your buttocks among these three areas of the blind. If not, then there shall be no repentance and no deliverance whatsoever and at last, the fruitful bough of the Lord in this land shall be cut down, and all that shall remain is the Stump. It will be some time for this Stumpy remnant to root, fruit and flower, and in that meantime, all the shade and goodness, which the bough of the lord provided, shall expose our children to the full meaning of life under a dying sun.

Listen: *Then it was revealed in my hearing by the Lord of hosts, "Surely for this iniquity there will be no atonement for you, Even to your death," says the Lord God of hosts. (Isaiah 22:14 NKJV)*

Pray: Father, raise up fearful men, to call Your people out, to gather them into fighting bands. Lord, please, please, please, stay Your hand and help us. Amen and let it be so.

Night-Whisper | **TRUST**

What snake told you that?

Jesus here speaks of two desires. The first desire is to follow Him, to walk behind Him, to place our feet in His footsteps, to go where He is going, to model Him, to do the works of God, to follow Him. Note however, that Jesus also says that if you want to come after Him in His way that there is a double price tag on that privilege.

Matthew 16:24-27

"If anyone desires to come after Me, let him deny himself, and take up his cross, and follow Me. For whoever desires to save his life will lose it, but whoever loses his life for My sake will find it. For what profit is it to a man if he gains the whole world, and loses his own soul? Or what will a man give in exchange for his soul? For the Son of Man will come in the glory of His Father with His angels, and then He will reward each according to his works. NKJV

The first price is that of self-denial. In brief, this denial is in effect a 'triple morning cock crowing, saying, declaring, announcing to the morning madness of all our selfishness that, "Most definitely, absolutely and utterly, you are not your own!" This applied self-denial then acts vehemently toward one's own body, soul and spirit and brings the whole into subjection saying, "I am a servant of the Master and whether loneliness or lack, whether misunderstanding or pain, whether sword or nakedness all become part of God's providential package for me, even so, I shall follow Him." This self-denial then takes up the 'cross' of those decisions, that second price tag, and keeps following on after Christ, no matter what.

Jesus says that such a sold out soul is not only saved but shall find life, even a found and fulfilling life in following hard after Him in self-denying, cross-carrying foolishness.

The second desire, which Jesus talks of, is the desire to save one's own life. That is, to fulfill oneself and to protect oneself, to provide for oneself and to comfort oneself. Such a desire to save one's life, says Jesus, is a but a self-serving doom and an un-regaining and total loss.

A slimy snake once said to me, "If you have not prepared for your own financial future then that's your stupidity and not my responsibility." A brood of vipers later hissed all over the same words and rattled, "No health cover, no life cover, no pension plan, no home, no wages, no temporal inheritance, no wonder you're a mess!" Me, a mess? Yes indeed, I must confess, that the older I get, the more I regret denying myself and following Jesus. Many do. I must confess, the more I compare the life He has given me (or I have chosen, if you wish) with the life I see in settled others, the more I envy them. I do not envy the wicked, no, do not misunderstand me, I envy the saints who have preserved their life in property and pension, in life cover and laid up inheritances. The autumn of old age, which shall all sniff on the Northern wind, approaches us all, you see, but they are prepared. The mortgage is paid, the pension plans are plump, and the winter night may draw in, as it will to do its worst. Meanwhile, that same North wind brings for me, and for most men who leave the Christian ministry in their mid-50's a fear of the future which covers my faith with clouds, and casts a long cold shadow upon my 'following' condition. Maybe I have denied myself too much and in denying myself I have denied others who might rely on me. O sad condition. Has Jesus tricked me? Has He been telling 'porky pies?' Have I taken His words to literally and far too seriously?

> *Yes indeed, I must confess, that the older I get, the more I regret denying myself and following Jesus.*

I wonder if Stephen, that first recorded Christian martyr should have kept his mouth shut. I mean, being so stoned, how could he continue to keep down a good and well-paying job? What parents and siblings did Stephen leave behind, who had to scrape together those unnecessary funeral expenses and then face the future without him? I wonder if the lonely and abandoned felt missionary kid now hates God all the more because of his self-denying parents. Oh, and that imprisoned pastor's wife, clutching that old cold pillow in her half empty bed, does she wish for a little less self-denial on the part of her big mouthed husband? Yes, it seems to me that the self-denial which Jesus speaks of, you know, the one that leads to a cross of death, not only can harm ourselves but even crucify the future of those we love and of those loved ones who maybe now have come to despise our selfish-self-denial of taking up the cross of Christ.

Maybe though, you can have your cake and eat it? Maybe you can make all temporal preparations for preservation of this passing life and then later on, with a safety net of money in the bank, deny yourself? After all, Peter, despite his prolonged absence from earthly, business and nibbling on his upside down cake, probably left a thriving fishing enterprise to his boys (what were their names again?) Ooh and maybe a house to his once accompanying wandering wife and revived mother in law. Whereas Paul, that overt self-denier, left no offspring, no money, no lands, and nothing but the New Testament Church. What good was that to his earthly family? (Who were they again?)

It has been my observation that a few saints who seemingly can have their cake and eat it. A closer look however, shows me that either they are living off an inheritance of their earthly daddies old or stolen goods, have invested and gambled well on the stock market themselves, or, they have simply gotten a good and well-paying job in the religious industry. No, it would appear that Jesus offers no cake to any who follow Him. Just a cross and a cross that gets heavier as the day draws on to its end.

Jesus offers no cake to any who follow Him. Just a cross and a cross that gets heavier as the day draws on to its end.

Now then, some of you reading this will say, "Thank God I am not 'called' to live a life like that!" Moreover, I will say to you, "What snake told you that?" Who lied to you about these Words of Christ being for a select and miserable few? I tell you, if you are not following Christ, you do not belong to Him! Yes, and if you do truly belong to Him, then these words are for you. Deny yourself, take up your cross and follow Him. There is no cake when following Christ! Just a cross.

As for me, though the church should provide for its ministers and double provide for the servants of the Word, I will not lean on that Pharaoh and have his sharp stick pierce my grasping palm. Yes, even though Caesar may have promised to cosset me from cradle to grave, providing I have paid my dues of course, I will not put my hope in that old hag either. Moreover, though my own leapfrog family should be wiser and 'better off' than me, they shall not become the hope and the sustenance of my old age. No, this failing trinity I speak of cannot replace the providence of the Spirit of God. My declaration and covenant to day then is this, "Let God be God and every man a liar! I will follow Him no matter what, daily counting the cost and daily taking up the cross. The God of my youth and of my early vigor shall be the God of my old age and of my shot-small measured jigger." Friends, today this is my covenant and declaration to follow God no matter what. What's yours? Do not step out without counting the cost. Do not draw back, for God takes no pleasure in the soul that draws back.

Listen: *Look! You are trusting in the staff of this broken reed, Egypt, on which if a man leans, it will go into his hand and pierce it. So is Pharaoh king of Egypt to all who trust in him. (Isaiah 36:6 NKJV)*

Pray: Though Wesley, that brand plucked from the burning, would burn down most of the present monstrosities of his denomination, the current Methodist covenant prayer is most profound. Dare you pray it from your heart?

The Methodist Covenant Prayer

I am no longer my own but Yours.
Put me to what you will,
Rank me with whom You will;
Put me to doing, put me to suffering;
Let me be employed for You or laid aside for You,
Exalted for You or brought low for You.
Let me be full, let me be empty,
Let me have all things, let me have nothing.
I freely and wholeheartedly yield all things
To Your pleasure and disposal.
And now, glorious and blessed God,
Father, Son and Holy Spirit,
You are mine and I am yours.
So be it.
And the covenant made on earth,
Let it be ratified in heaven.
Amen.

Night-Whisper | **STRENGTH**

Rebekah, her daughters, and HADEC3

In the late 19th Century the roads in rural Wales were rubbish. Subsequently, a group of wealthy entrepreneurs got together, built new roads, and improved upon the existing ones. This was no philanthropic endeavor however, but a business enterprise. Therefore, to get a great financial return on their investment, 'Toll Houses' were erected at all too many regular intervals to exact money from the Welsh farming road users. For the poor tenant farmers the cost of importing fertilizer by road and then shipping their goods by the same method and paying tolls both ways, in their mind, became nothing but legalized mugging and state extortion. The cost of land rent, forced tithing to the state church and other various taxable Levis, such as those on the building of much hated poor houses, 'pushed' many of the workers over the edge. Consequently, many Welsh men took up the novel disguise of wearing women's clothing and grotesque masks to cover their faces, whilst calling themselves by false women's names in both organization and correspondence with the authorities. Thus, 'Rebekah and her daughters' were birthed!

Genesis 24:60

And they blessed Rebekah and said to her: "Our sister, may you become The mother of thousands of ten thousands; And may your descendants possess The gates of those who hate them." NKJV

Armed with axes and other farming implements, Rebekah and her daughters rose up and destroyed the Toll Gates of those that hated them. As it always does, the rioting eventually got out of hand, resulting in the death of one young woman and indeed, the rioting got so bad that the army was called in. Even so, in just a short time, the rising up and rioting of 'Rebekah's daughters' led to a parliamentary reform of the 'Turnpike Trusts' who were indeed, legally thumb-screwing the poor out of every penny they had.

In Britain, the Highway Agency Digital Enforcement Camera System 3, (HADEC3), is a new 'stealth camera' about to be rolled out across the

Motorway System. Under the guise of creating 'Smart' motorway systems, easing traffic congestion and giving folks a smoother ride on the roads, the HADECS3 cameras will provide no limit to the number of incriminating motorists it can help to prosecute for speeding. Your number plate, date and time stamp are all stored by each HADECS3 speed cameras, and then, if your average speed between the cameras is above the 'ever changing' remote controlled and variable speed limit, you will automatically be issued with a speeding fine. In 2012-13, the Government collected over £284 million in speeding fines alone! This stealth camera system my friends, has nothing to do with curbing speed, increasing safety, or easing travel, it is rather, a fat cash cow of digitally collected indirect taxation, which, when coupled with monies collected from public parking offences will in short time bring in over £1 Billion per annum to the government, local authorities and the Police, who will all then use the money to finance 'other' projects. I tell you, should an organization arise which will physically remove these grey cash cows from the side of our roads, I would be tempted to join them in the tearing down these monstrosities and selling them for scrap!

Are the Greeks now become 'Rebekah's daughters?'

My question tonight then is this, should a Christian become one of 'Rebekah's daughters?' Look now and consider this, for where a nation, a people, a community is being financially 'milked' by either the authorities or businessmen licensed by those authorities, should a Christian rise up and break down those same thumb screw implements of taxation? This is an important question, and the violent answer to this has seen Christian involvement right from the 'Tolpuddle martyrs' to the 'Boston tea party' and maybe, in the second decade of the 21st century, even in humiliated Greece, which is seen now rising up and destroying the financial bondage imposed upon them by that Troika, that Trinity of wealth manipulation, the European Central Bank, the European Union and the International Monetary fund. Are the Greeks now become the current expression of 'Rebekah's daughters?'

Does the Gospel have anything to do with Temporal Liberation Theology? Cromwell and Dietrich both seemed to think so, as did the founding fathers of the USA. From the New Testament however, I cannot directly justify such 'direct and illegal' action. Indirectly, of course, let each man count the cost of resisting the powers and the way in which they are resisted. This, I feel, is a matter of personal conscience. In light of that, the shape of a man's conscience is maybe measured by this question; "Is this law, this action, or command I am subject to and kicking against, evil and contrary to the commands and tenor of the Holy Scriptures?" Soon, in the West, Muslim or otherwise, Sharia law may be imposed upon parts of the nation, or the nation as a whole. Should the Christian resist this 'terror of the Lord?' (For that is what I believe it shall be)" These are important questions for you to consider this night.

The times, they are a changing quickly friends. Therefore, it behooves all Christians then, now in this time of relative calm to do two things: First, by all prayer and within all legal means to actively resist the evil powers that be, whether those powers be secular or religious. Secondly, to prepare for persecution and to consider how you as an individual and we together as an organized Christian community (and we must be organized,) might resist the evils about to come upon us.

Should God's people pay a tax for the privilege of being a Christian in Muslim dominated lands?

Meanwhile, if anyone has a portable plasma cutter out there, I shall see you at Junction 15 on the M25 at Midnight. I shall be wearing a black balaclava and sporting a poker face with goggles and dressed like Lady Gaga. Let Rebekah's daughters ride out once more! "Hiho Sylvia, away!"

Listen: *Let every soul be subject to the governing authorities. For there is no authority except from God, and the authorities that exist are appointed by God. Therefore whoever resists the authority resists the ordinance of God, and those who resist will bring judgment on themselves. For rulers are not a terror to good works, but to evil. Do you want to be unafraid of the authority? Do what is good, and you will have praise from the same. For he is God's minister to you for good. But if you do evil, be afraid; for he does not bear the sword in vain; for he is God's minister, an avenger to execute wrath on him who practices evil. Therefore you must be subject, not only because of wrath but also for conscience' sake. For because of this you also pay taxes, for they are God's ministers attending continually to this very thing. Render therefore to all their due: taxes to whom taxes are due, customs to whom customs, fear to whom fear, honor to whom honor. (Romans 13:1-7 NKJV)*

Pray: Father, should Your people pay a tax for the privilege of being a Christian in Muslim lands? Father, shall the rich get richer and poor get poorer while all the while our pips are made to squeak? Father, incite and ignite Your remnant now to possess the gates of their enemies. Send us into politics, both local and national, that we might fearlessly proclaim and put into place financial and social structures which reflect Your absolute truth and justice. Meanwhile, should we fail to do this and should the sword of Islam or even of corrupt capitalism not be stayed from falling upon us, help us to prepare, mentally, psychologically, physically and spiritually for that which is to come upon us. Lord, please awaken those that presently sleep and fill them with holy zeal to proclaim Your word. Amen and let it be so.

Night-Whisper | **CHARACTER**

What a sight!

What an ending to a most fearful discourse: *"By your patience possess your souls!"* I suppose the corresponding text to the one for our consideration tonight might also be found in Matthew 24:13 where it says: *"But he who endures to the end shall be saved."* These translated English words of 'patience' and 'endures' are of course the same Greek word, however, the difference of tense in each presentation of the word in these two verses might indicate a command in one and a promise in the other. These two phrases then, no doubt, might diverge from one original thought but they most certainly seem to converge on a golden chariot pulled by a pair of paradoxes. Your dignity is the golden chariot of which I speak and 'joy in suffering' and 'life in the midst of death' are the names of the ponies of paradox that pull it. It is your responsibility to lay hold of the reigns of these heart-pounding beasts and pull tight the bit of control into their frothing mouths! You see, your dignity my friend, is your very own to pull together and to steer around this coliseum of racing life, where chariots crash and burn, and eternal fortunes are both won and lost. *"By your patience possess your souls!"*

Luke 21:16-19

You will be betrayed even by parents and brothers, relatives and friends; and they will put some of you to death. And you will be hated by all for My name's sake. But not a hair of your head shall be lost. By your patience possess your souls. NKJV

Toddlers, boys and youths, all care not much for self-control. However, most mature men seek the peace that such patient endurance brings with it. Commenting on these verses, it is Baptist preacher, Alexander Maclaren, who acknowledges the need for such perseverance and self-control when he says, *"For howsoever many days are bright, and howsoever all days are good, yet, on the whole, 'man is a soldier, and life is a fight."*

When our course is never erred from; when no pain or distraction, no deceit or destruction can move us from our destiny; then a man rides in his own golden chariot called 'Dignity.' This is more comfortable than a Porsche, more precious than a Ferrari, and more to be prized than a Lamborghini. Dignity is the outward expression of the inward possession of the soul; it is the grip on who we truly are. Dignity rides onward through the grey fogs of life and in the riding; dignity endures and utilizes both the incurable and the irremovable. Yes, dignity not only endures, but it utilizes for Gods glory and our very own good, all the slings and arrows, which this earthly life might lay upon us. Not only this, but dignity bears up under burdens and bears down on the goal of the Divine will for its life. Dignity is brave, courageous, perseverant, undiverted, unchecked, unhindered, and unheeding to fear, cowardice, temptation and premature rest. The command is: *"Patiently endure the trials and sorrows of this present life, utilize them to the one purpose of God's glory and the victorious end of your race."* The promise is, *"In the so doing, you shall both lay hold of your life and eternally preserve it."*

The command is: "Patiently endure the trials and sorrows of this present life, utilize them to the one purpose of God's glory and the victorious end of your race." The promise is: "You shall both lay hold of your life and eternally preserve it."

The possession of self is found only in yielding to Christ and I cannot better Maclaren in his description of the outworking's of such a yielding when he says: *"such self-control which is the winning of ourselves is, as I believe, thoroughly realized only when, by self-surrender of ourselves to Jesus Christ, we get His help to govern ourselves and so become lords of ourselves. Some little petty Rajah, up in the hills, in a quasi-independent State in India, is troubled by mutineers whom he cannot subdue; what does he do? He sends a message down to Lahore or Calcutta, and up come English troops that consolidate his dominion, and he rules securely, when he has consented to become a feudatory, and recognize his overlord. And so you and I, by continual repetition, in the face of self and sin, of our acts of self-surrender,* **bring Christ into the field;** *and then, when we have said, 'Lord, take me; I live, yet not I, but Christ liveth in me'; and when we daily, in spite of hindrances, stand to the surrender and repeat the consecration, then 'in our perseverance we acquire our souls.'"*

In this present age, a God fearing man is a most unusual sight to behold my friend. Be that beholding sight.

Listen: *For you have need of endurance, so that after you have done the will of God, you may receive the promise: "For yet a little while, And He who is coming will come and will not tarry. Now the just shall live by faith; But if anyone draws back, My soul has no pleasure in him." But we are not of those who draw back to perdition, but of those who believe to the saving of the soul. (Hebrews 10:36-39 NKJV)*

Pray: Father, I yield myself to you. Let that be cured which can be cured, and let that be remedied which can be remedied. However, and in any event, utilize the whole of that which I have t patiently endure, even for Your glory and for my eternal good. I declare then, right now, that all betrayal, loneliness, abandonment, hatred, hurt and harm, shall be but the dogs of war which follow on after my chariot of dignity to aid me in conquering the world the flesh and the devil. Let my enduring then right now, lead to the possession of my soul and life to come. In Jesus name I pray, amen and let it be so.

Night-Whisper | **BECOME**

Of Righteousness and respectability and 'getting over' ourselves

Peer approval is a most terrible thing for it limits unique vocal expression and molds plastic sameness, stiff safeness and silent soundness. The Christian world and all of its fragmented sections are full of peer approval, where righteousness has been replaced with a base and local, culturally Christian respectability. You can feel it, you can touch it, and you can clearly identify it, for it is a foul smell, it is an insidious stench of arms-length Gospel separation and Christendom is full of this offensive odor.

Matthew 5:20

For I say to you, that unless your righteousness exceeds the righteousness of the scribes and Pharisees, you will by no means enter the kingdom of heaven. NKJV

I have observed that doctrinal statements, mission statements, statements of practice, articles of incorporation, board accountability, supporter base comforting and keeping, can all act like 'Chorleywood bread,' continuing to ferment in the bowels of the eater as they all trumpet their position of protectionism. "Ah now, we have to be careful here because…" Look now, all you readers of Night Whispers, you know how I am thankful for separation and in no way seek any false Shangri-La forces of unity, however, there is a felt and smelt spiritual difference between righteous separation and respectable separation and it is this latter monstrosity that makes me kick and gag.

Righteous separation judges the actions and statements of others. It says, "This is contrary to the clear teachings of Scripture. It is damaging to the truth of the Gospel. It does not glorify God. Therefore, we cannot associate with it and so do prayerfully and respectfully ask you to reconsider your position and desist from these practices, actions and statements. If not, then because of your continuing erroneous practice and position, I am afraid we cannot be associated with you." Fair enough.

Respectable separation says, "The way you are doing things is rather embarrassing to us. The manner of your expression we consider trite, silly and offensive to our cultural sensitivities. Your approval rating is low, your Twitter following is minimal, your shame factor is high, your manner is offensive, your bank account is weak and frankly, it's all rather embarrassing. Therefore, for the sake of our own continuing peer credibility, mutual accountability, wise use of donor funds and a thousand other respectable reasons, though we like you, (from a safe distance anyway) we didn't get where we are today by associating with the likes of you. 'Goodbye Reggie!'"

Righteous separation protects the truth of the Word and rightly promotes the one true Gospel. Respectable separation promotes self-righteous sectarianism, superfluous standoffishness, and in the so doing, destroys spiritual unity, like-minded assistance and healthy propagation and promotion of the truth. Peer respectability is a pox on the peace of paradise.

> *Peer respectability is a pox on the peace of paradise.*

I put it to you, that this kind of unholy and self-righteous sectarian respectability will stop you walking the paths of God. I put it to you, that this kind of respectability will foster spiritual separation rather than true spiritual unity. I put it to you, that this kind of peer respectability, would have sidelined Hosea, banished Amos to street preacher status, put Jeremiah in a pit, left John the Baptist in prison, gagged Agabus, sidelined Paul, put Thomas into Theological college, John in Therapy and made Luke the Pope just because he was a Doctor! I put it to you that this kind of respectability crucified Christ and is from the pit of hell!

I have observed that the Lord Jesus deals with such self-righteous peer respectability in two ways: First of all, He allows all the diseased to gather together and then watches them die the slow death of mutual but suspicious ego stroking. Secondly, He greatly humbles those He would save from such a self-curse of cultural respectability, that He might use them.

Once, having been exceptionally prone to peer respectability myself, (many people enter the full time ministry to gain such respectability) I have had to thoroughly investigate how we all might evade both the necessary humbling of the Lord and the terrible slow death of mutual sectarian ego stroking? My remedy is simple, "Get over yourself." Who do you think you are anyway? Who made you better than anyone else?

On a good day, on a great day, what are you but an unprofitable servant simply doing what you were required to do? Yes, my remedy is simple, "Get over yourself."

Listen: *"Two men went up to the temple to pray, one a Pharisee and the other a tax collector. The Pharisee stood and prayed thus with himself, 'God, I thank You that I am not like other men — extortioners, unjust, adulterers, or even as this tax collector. I fast twice a week; I give tithes of all that I possess.' And the tax collector, standing afar off, would not so much as raise his eyes to heaven, but beat his breast, saying, 'God, be merciful to me a sinner!' I tell you, this man went down to his house justified rather than the other; for everyone who exalts himself will be humbled, and he who humbles himself will be exalted." (Luke 18:10-14 NKJV)*

Pray: Father, I would be delivered from this stench of peer resepctability. Lord, change my diaper and talcum powder my behind, for Father, I would be weaned from this. Lord, grant me then, even the meat of a mature outlook. Father, I would grow in understanding and humility. Lord, humble me then under Your mighty hand that I might be both pleasing and useful to You. Help me to just get over myself! Amen and let it be so.

Night-Whisper | **ACTION**

The soon coming 'Wonders of The Lord'

Contrary to the thoughts and prayers and desires of many good people, I do not believe God will revive the church in the West. Frankly, there is nothing left to revive in much of it and worse than that, I do believe the Lord of the church is projectile vomiting the majority of it out of His mouth. Have you noticed how empty church buildings, and there are many in the UK, all look like a pile of pavement vomit, wretched from a high heeled 'ladette' after a Saturday night binge and a cold comfort curry?

Job 14:7-9 NKJV

"For there is hope for a tree, If it is cut down, that it will sprout again, And that its tender shoots will not cease. Though its root may grow old in the earth, And its stump may die in the ground, Yet at the scent of water it will bud And bring forth branches like a plant.

Some bright-eyed professional middle-class brother (they are always middle class) accosted me yet again just the other day regarding my millennial position asking, "Are you pre-millennial? For that would account for your pessimism regarding the influence of the church in this present age?" My response was too simply to ask him, "Are you on heavy anti-depressant medication mate?" Forgive me brethren, but if you are 'Post-mill' or 'A-mill' in your millennial position, then nowadays, not only do I believe your theological conclusions are hermeneutically and historically incorrect, but I think you need psychological counselling! Now that I have offended a large number of you, my medical instructions are even so, by the by, for you see, the real purpose of this particular Night Whisper is to point out the greatly positive aspect of my historical pre-millennial, and present non-revival position. In brief, I want to tell you that I have a growing hope for the immediate future. Why?

Personally, I dislike the Biblical term 'remnant.' For me, in its present Christian cultural usage I find it far too exclusive. It may be a matter of simple semantics, but I much prefer the unusual phrase of 'Holy stump!' The picture of a tree stump, fully rooted, flowering and fruited gets me so excited that I can let the present expressions of church drown in the vomit of her Lord. I can let the closures come, and let the buildings be turned into pubs. Let Mosques occupy what were long time ago now, places of true worship to the one and only Triune God. I can do this because I see Christ is judging the church. THEREFORE, LET THE TRUE FIRE FALL! Let the branch loping begin. Let the leaf-burning make our eyes water and the crackle of dry twigs fill our ears. Let the ground clearance be brought to a speedy conclusion and in it all, let only a holy stump remain. Bring in the bulldozers Lord and let no tears be seen to fall. Yes, let there be no mourning for the dead, for the judgment of the Lord is right; the judgment of the Lord is good, the judgment of the Lord is altogether necessary. When the morning comes, in the clearance of the misty grey, let us see the Holy stump. Solitary, firm, immovable, flowering, fruitful, rooted, ready and waiting. This my friends, is what I am looking for, and I do not think we shall find it in the present expression of the Western church. It has to go.

> *One great sign of their abandonment by God is this, that they only contain rats, willful women and abandoned children.*

Indeed, should God move in a most gracious and unprecedented way in our nations, my deep suspicion is that it will be outside of our present infiltrated and corrupt church systems. These messy and sticky old fungus filled wine skins could never hold the New Wine of God. Therefore, not only do we need to look and pray for a 'move' of God outside of the present church structures, but the Holy people of God need to leave the corrupted structures and preach the Word in the deeps. I believe that when we do this, we shall need other Holy partners to help us pull in the catch. If this is the case my friend, why are you manning dead men's boats? No wonder you have fished all night and caught absolutely nothing. You have been part of the crew of the Marie Celeste, the Baychimo, the Octavius, or of the Flying Dutchman, or even the Titanic! Can these ships of the line ever be repaired? No. Leave them alone. Indeed, one great sign of their abandonment by God is this, that they only contain rats, willful women and abandoned children. I hope that most terrible picture makes you think a little deeper and act a lot more decisively this night.

To remain sane, to remain hopeful, to remain energized, is to leave the rotten hulls of the past, to get in some new boats, then go, and fish in the regions beyond you. Yes, I see it now, it is *"Those who go down to the sea in ships, who do business on great waters, they see the works of the Lord, and His wonders in the deep." (Psalms 107:23-24 NKJV)*

Listen: *Then He got into one of the boats, which was Simon's, and asked him to put out a little from the land. And He sat down and taught the multitudes from the boat. When He had stopped speaking, He said to Simon, "Launch out into the deep and let down your nets for a catch." But Simon answered and said to Him, "Master, we have toiled all night and caught nothing; nevertheless at Your word I will let down the net." And when they had done this, they caught a great number of fish, and their net was breaking. So they signaled to their partners in the other boat to come and help them. And they came and filled both the boats, so that they began to sink. When Simon Peter saw it, he fell down at Jesus' knees, saying, "Depart from me, for I am a sinful man, O Lord!" For he and all who were with him were astonished at the catch of fish which they had taken; and so also were James and John, the sons of Zebedee, who were partners with Simon. And Jesus said to Simon, "Do not be afraid. From now on you will catch men." So when they had brought their boats to land, they forsook all and followed Him. (Luke 5:3-11 NKJV)*

Pray: Deliver us O God our Father, from the prison hulls of our own choosing, from the wrecks of our own making, from the cold rocks and breaking waves of Your very own destructive and righteous. Lord Jesus, these terrible calamities have been whistled downed the wind byYour own sweet lips. Thank you. Now Lord send some men of war, some bright flagged salts from afar to come and pick up the survivors. Then together let us push out into the deeps to see once again 'The Wonders of the Lord.' Amen and let it be so.

| Vol 01 | Q2 | NW00151 | May 30th |

Night-Whisper | **WORD**

How to approach God 'All-Matey'

The band played 'some songs' whilst the congregation lilted in, all clutching their Lattes. The Kids ran amok. The teenagers, still looking cool, hunched their shoulders and reluctantly retired to their positions of 'inconspicuouty.' At the back of the church whilst the smiling congregation still chatted away, awaiting the call to order. The band butted in. In the same manner you would call out the first song at any other gig, the tune took off, and slowly the conversations reluctantly ended as the projector painted the words of 'the song' on the wall. Eventually, the Pastor, kid draped over his right shoulder, shirt slightly out of his pants, left hand in pocket, got to the stage, and read God His rights as he prayerfully praised everyone from the Sunday School team, to the magnificent young people, to the band and to Bert who counted the morning offering and Doris who faithfully made the tea. The service had apparently been officially started.

During the following singing, the kids ran like sugar jacked-up eejits around the front, some twirling ribbons and dancing something like the 'Mashed Potato,' whilst some of older folks, the adults, wandered out and went to the lavatory, or sat down and consulted their phone and their iPad whilst waving their hand occasionally in the air and

Isaiah 6:1-5

.. I saw the Lord sitting on a throne, high and lifted up, and the train of His robe filled the temple. Above it stood seraphim; each one had six wings: with two he covered his face, with two he covered his feet, and with two he flew. And one cried to another and said: "Holy, holy, holy is the Lord of hosts; The whole earth is full of His glory!" And the posts of the door were shaken by the voice of him who cried out, and the house was filled with smoke. So I said: "Woe is me, for I am undone! Because I am a man of unclean lips, And I dwell in the midst of a people of unclean lips; For my eyes have seen the King, The Lord of hosts."

exclaiming, 'Thank you Jesus' and 'Hallelujah!' The God of Christianity is apparently, one very cool, dude!

Meanwhile, down the road multitudes of men only worshippers, together prostrated themselves before falseness, falling down on their faces in unity before their Master, proclaiming his mercy, greatness and majesty. It might be religious ritual, it might be culturally contrived etiquette, but the outward united humility of it all, seemed to mock the long gone majesty now replaced in Christianity with the worship of God All-Matey.

The Sunday morning rugger pitch is full of men pursuing manliness, and the church wives are weeping still whilst these same little absent from church fathered children, once they get to college, will follow the teen girls of today, in soon deserting the God of their mothers in their droves. After all, who gives a rat's about God All-Matey?

The sickest thing in Laodicea is blindness manifest in words without power. The same silly songs, poured out of a plastic throat of swaying emptiness, followed by ten minutes of fumbled spirituality in the back of a car, whilst the practioners of the same, still covered with that unending sense of selfish self-pleasing lacking any real intimacy, tuck their shirts in for another week and walk past the pastoral pimp, shake his hand and hand over their money, whilst still being hungry, thirsty, dissatisfied and empty. Is this what spiritual sexual slavery looks like?

Is this what spiritual sexual slavery looks like?

There is only one way to approach God All-Matey and that is with a hammer. Break that idol all to pieces! Push him over, and snap off his arms like the plaster fly he is. Break his legs, for he never walked in heaven, or offered himself on a cross to pay for your sin. Smash off his nose, fire cannon at his face, and crumble his Egyptian eyeballs in the dust. Will this fix the problem though? No, I am afraid it will not, for it is not until you replace the pimp that the problem will disappear. Prostitution, especially spiritual prostitution, you see, is there to keep the pimps in power and plentitude. Therefore, get rid of the pimps and the worship of false Gods will disappear.

The problem is that the pimps will not go! They, together with the religious machine that keeps on pumping them out, are both institutionalized and embedded. Therefore, in the end, it is you that will have to go. The problem with Laodicea, you see, is not that the tares are among the wheat, but rather, like Lot in Sodom, it is the wheat who are among the tares.

Go find yourself a new vocabulary dude. Go find yourself some new clothes. Wash your mouth out and your mind out and go find yourself some new songs. Sew up your pockets. Get on your knees. Stand to attention when the King addresses you. Make way a Holy highway for entrance to Your Lord. Prepare to meet Your God!

Listen: *See that you do not refuse Him who speaks. For if they did not escape who refused Him who spoke on earth, much more shall we not escape if we turn away from Him who speaks from heaven, whose voice then shook the earth; but now He has promised, saying, "Yet once more I shake not only the earth, but also heaven." Now this, "Yet once more," indicates the removal of those things that are being shaken, as of things that are made, that the things which cannot be shaken may remain. Therefore, since we are receiving a kingdom which cannot be shaken, let us have grace, by which we may serve God acceptably with reverence and godly fear. (Hebrews 12:25-28 NKJV)*

Pray: Give ear to my words, O Lord, Consider my meditation. Give heed to the voice of my cry, My King and my God, For to You I will pray. My voice You shall hear in the morning, O Lord; In the morning I will direct it to You, And I will look up. For You are not a God who takes pleasure in wickedness, Nor shall evil dwell with You. The boastful shall not stand in Your sight; You hate all workers of iniquity. You shall destroy those who speak falsehood; The Lord abhors the bloodthirsty and deceitful man. But as for me, I will come into Your house in the multitude of Your mercy; In fear of You I will worship toward Your holy temple. Amen. (Psalms 5:1-7 NKJV)

| Vol 01 | Q2 | NW00152 | May 31st |

Night-Whisper | **INTEGRITY**

The sentiment of the slashing sword

Someone has told us, a professor maybe, a social and society guru, that postmodern man requires an unpressured journeying choice of non-judgmental spiritual experiences. So, all our church advertising media trots out the same invitational tosh, *"Come and enjoy the sweet spot of God's presence!"* Alternatively. *"We warmly invite your consideration to come to our worship experience."* And God forbid we offend anyone because the bottom line is to keep the punters happy, keep 'em coming and keep 'em giving, cause the mortgage on this church property is heavy and the personnel and programs budget is bigger than any comparable business! Yes sir, all this safe and satisfactory, experiential Christianity, is mighty expensive stuff so we have to keep the golden geese, excuse my mix of metaphor here, for we have to keep them the golden geese, pleased to be fleeced!

Acts 2:37

"Now when they heard this, they were cut to the heart, and said to Peter and the rest of the apostles, 'Men and brethren, what shall we do?'" NKJV

In the same deceitful way, we have been told that postmodern man, especially postmodern Christian man, cannot stomach a message that exceeds more than twenty minutes. Oh, they can watch a football game or maybe Arsenal-v-Manchester United for a couple of hours or more, or a not so decent movie, or stomach a meeting at work which lasts more than a few hours, or...well you get my drift, but for Pete's sake, let's not preach at them, no, let's give them a 10-20 minutes weak insipid talk. The problem is, that someone has told us that a twenty minute message, a talk even, a soft stroking multi-media, person hood affirming and life enhancing, nonjudgmental invitational coaching session, is all we need to make 'em believe. The old fashioned and well fashioned sermon then, like a rust potted old barbers knife, has been folded away and placed in a draw, and the leather strap of sharpening prayer and Bended knee practice has in its turn, been removed from its hook on the wall, rolled up and placed along there with it. The problem is that no one's getting saved now! Oh we get the conversion to cultural Christianity, by no one's getting saved, not really. No, I am afraid; salvation is becoming as rare as rocking horse poop.

The Latin roots of our English word "sermon" means "to stab," or "to thrust through." Certainly, our text for tonight shows Peter's sermon was of soul bloodied spirit cutting and surgical precision. There was no massaging of a message here! There was no soft caressing adjectival prefix to the words delivered from a drip drooled, dancing and effeminate, inoffensive cool dude's little tongue. No, though the listeners had not prepared for surgery, but surgery was what they got and my friends, there was no anesthetic! Yet the sermon not only cut them, it cured them! Imagine that!

> *The Latin roots of our English word "sermon" means "to stab," or "to thrust through."*

So, listen up you leaders, you speakers, and you ear tickling talkers all! Listen up you sissified choirboy, hair combing, cheek squeezing and head patting chumps! For it is time to get the knife back out again. Go on, reach in, right at the back of your study desk drawer and pull out that rusty old, straight razor shaving knife again. Unroll that strop found next to it, hook it on the wall and get to praying and a to practicing once more, for Sunday is surgery time and I tell you right now, if your sermon isn't sharp, if it isn't cutting, if it isn't putting people on the spot of eternal choosing, then you had better pack it in, pack it up and go get yourself a job as a bingo caller or a used car salesman! Go and give talks to the Women's Institute man for it's all your good for now. For I tell you, there is no sentiment in a slashing sword my friend, and each of us teachers, each of us preachers, will give thorough accounting for each sharp slash, and especially the lack thereof! So, stop talking man! Stop tickling ears and patting heads, and start preaching again for goodness sake. Stop listening to all this Post Modern hogwash, which is producing nothing but pale consumers, and commit yourself to let the lion loose once more.

(Oh and by the way, you can always tell when there has been a leak in the devil's massive heavy bottles of his inhalation sedation of nitrous oxide; after all, it is called "laughing gas" for a reason you know.)

Listen: *"For the word of God is living and powerful, and sharper than any two-edged sword, piercing even to the division of soul and spirit, and of joints and marrow, and is a discerner of the thoughts and intents of the heart. And there is no creature hidden from His sight, but all things are*

naked and open to the eyes of Him to whom we must give account."
Hebrews 4:12-13 NKJV

Pray: Lord, may Your Word and Your Spirit both cut me and create me, in Jesus name I ask it, amen.

IT'S TIME TO ORDER YOUR NEXT QUARTER OF....

Night Whispers

& maybe order one for a friend as well!

Check us out at

www.NightWhispers.com

Order at | WWW.TheologyShop.com

---------------------------0---------------------------

NightWhispers is authored by Victor Robert Farrell, produced by WhisperingWord Ltd and licensed for the sole use of:

The 66 Books Ministry

A modern day,

Back to the whole Bible,

Boots on The Ground,

Proclamation Movement.

www.66Books.tv

Night-Whisper | **CONSIDER**

The problem of Prometheus and the preparation for death

Pastors who imitate the preaching and the moral action of the prophets without also imitating the prophets' deep praying and worship so evident in the Psalms are an embarrassment to the faith and an encumbrance to the church. *(Eugene Peterson – Working The Angles: The Shape of Pastoral Integrity)*

Ecclesiastes 7:2
"Better to go to the house of mourning than to go to the house of feasting, for that is the end of all men; and the living will take it to heart." NKJV

I neither want to be an embarrassment nor an encumbrance, but I am afraid, that my natural tendency is to be so, for I have seen what Promethean fire and its resultant adrenalin-led activity can do in raising the dancing blue flames of man-made hope, both seen flickering and realized in books like "Your best life now." Yes, I've seen what those flames of so called prophetic doing can achieve, what they can get done and boy do we need to get things done! For a when I look around, oh friends, when I look around, there is so much to be done, and frankly so much that we can do now and yet, there is oh so very little time to do it in. The needs are so great and our ability to meet those needs are now so possible, that I just want to get on down and go buy that excavator. Yeah! Stoke that fire and lay hold of that yellow hot, JCB, earth-moving machine and flip that mountain on its back; build that tunnel, ford that stream, make a way through that mighty river, 'cause I've got, "high in the sky, apple pie.... hopes" that we can move that rubber tree plant! Yes sirree, move it wherever we so well please. We can do it! Let's shake that thing, yes, let's shape this thing called our destinies, this thing called our possibilities, yes, let's get up, let's get down, let's get with it and let's just do it baby, cause we are preparing people for life! Preparing people for change, preparing people to better themselves, to better society and to better the nations of the world! Hallelujah and chaaaaaaaaarge! Have you not heard, "We can do it! Yes, we can." (Actually, that didn't turn out so well did it?)

Peterson (in the book I mentioned previously) points out how the present generation of church (I believe the Laodicean Church) has bought into the Promethean myth in such a way that, *"We have let ourselves be co-opted in the struggle against limits, committed to raising the standard of living: bigger machines, cheaper chicken...uncritically using the means offered by the world...so uncritically applauded and so readily at hand.......we have joined in the struggle to make life better for everyone with any available means.....the problem is that Prometheus does not pray, there is too much to do and there is little time to do it."* Did you get that? Prometheus does not pray!

Do remember that in the legend, Prometheus redeemed humanity from the tyranny of mortality, by causing mortals to cease foreseeing their personal doom, by placing in them blind hopes and lastly, by stealing fire from the gods and giving it to humanity, for their pleasure, for their profit and for their continual and technological advancement. Does that sound familiar?

Peterson is right in his statement about proclaiming prophets and their lack of prayer, for if there are two things that characterizes both the present pastorate and the postmodern community of the saints, it is first, a distinct lack of prayer and secondly, a lack of preparation for a good death. In less than a century, over 8 billion people will die on this planet. Surely, this is something we should prepare for and in the so doing, that preparation for death should turn our so short lives into journeys that are baptized in the warm and wet, ever running river of prayer? This is not miserable thinking but it is Biblical thinking! There is so much to do and so little time to do it in, that we really must pray, and then pray even more. Yet the doing, the blind man-made doing, has squeezed out all our praying.

Tell me, do you have a Promethean fire in your own personal boiler tonight? After all, just where are you getting your central heating from? What is raising the power of your personal steam, your church's steam, your mission's steam? Have you numbered your days? Have you and do you consider your mortality? Is your life, lived in its ever-lengthening shadow? If you find the thought of that last question maybe to be defeatist, or even repugnant, then I can virtually guarantee pastor, brother, sister, friend and mate, that you've got some strange Promethean fire in your boiler, and I tell you, it needs putting out! For if you don't put it out, it sure as hell will burn you out! Mark my words here. Mark my words.

Yes, the two best things and most Biblical things you can do is pray and in praying, prepare for your ultimate demise. Think about that tonight.

Listen: *"And Nadab and Abihu, the sons of Aaron, took either of them his censer, and put fire therein, and put incense thereon, and offered strange fire before the Lord, which he commanded them not. And there went out fire from the Lord, and devoured them, and they died before the Lord." Leviticus 10:1-2 KJV.*

Pray: Lord teach me to pray. Lord teach me to number my days. For Lord, I love this strange Promethean power. I just love it Lord! I do not wish to be a Luddite Lord, but I do ask You to put the false fire out and then my Lord, send the Holy fire from Your throne, in Jesus name I ask it, amen.

| Vol 01 | Q2 | NW00154 | June 02nd |

Night-Whisper | **SEE**

From the beak of the eagle

As the British Empire began to close up shop, today in 1953, it would appear that the last of the well-loved, most recently respected and most dignified of British monarchs, was crowned the Queen of the peoples of the United Kingdom of Great Britain and Northern Ireland, Canada, Australia, New Zealand, the Union of South Africa, Pakistan and Ceylon, and other Possessions and Territories of the falling Empire. The Coronation of Her Majesty Queen Elizabeth II took place today in the Abbey Church of St Peter, Westminster.

Psalms 141:2

"Let my prayer be set before You as incense, the lifting up of my hands as the evening sacrifice."
NKJV

The form and order of service for that ceremony is as awesome as was her Royal Majesty on that day. From that right Royal ceremonial text, much can be drawn for our edification. However, it is from part 7 of the service, entitled "The Anointing," from which tonight we ourselves can get some instruction and unction from heaven. I say from heaven, because the very vessel, the golden eagle from whose beak is dripped the oil for the anointing of monarchs, the Ampulla, as it is called, had apparently been delivered from heaven, via the hands of The Virgin Mary, to Thomas a Becket himself. Upon the delivery, whilst getting Becket's signature for said same heavenly package, Mary also declared that all Kings anointed with said oil should become "champions of the Church."

The Ampulla, hidden and then lost in France for a couple of centuries, was eventually "rediscovered" through a dream given to a holy man. Its subsequent propaganda use, for the reclamation of lands then lost in that fair land of France, made its ceremonial coronation use, of inestimable value to any British monarch seeking the justification of heaven for the temporal conquests of any piece of earth, especially French earth!

The importance of the Ampulla became evident, when in its first use in the Coronation of Henry II, it is was given its very own chariot in his

Coronation procession. Indeed, whilst being covered with a damask cloth, it was carried by no less an important figure than the sacristan of the Abbey of Marmoutier himself, the Ampulla being drawn to the Abbey of Westminster, by a milk-white steed.

Legend and propaganda apart, it is to this same Ampulla, to this same oil dripping beak of the golden eagle which we now turn attention. For in the ceremony of the anointing of Elizabeth, the Archbishop with one hand on the Ampulla and another on the consecrated Queen says:

Strengthen her, O Lord, with the Holy Ghost the Comforter;
Confirm and stablish her with thy free and princely Spirit,
The Spirit of wisdom and government,
The Spirit of counsel and ghostly strength,
The Spirit of knowledge and true godliness,
And fill her, O Lord, with the Spirit of thy holy fear,
Now and for ever;
Through Jesus Christ our Lord. Amen.

"Arising from her devotions, disrobed, assisted, uncovered, going supported before the altar." I tell you tonight, that there is no better way, probably no other right way, that either a Prince or a pauper, can be begin to set upon any work for which they are commissioned by heaven to do.

Now we come to the important bit, the instructive bit, the apple of burning gold set in a frame of shining silver, for just before the Archbishop shall anoint her hands, her breast and her head with the sign of the cross made with the heavenly anointing oil, something of vast and vital importance is done. It is written in the liturgical order of service for the day as follows,

In the meantime, the Queen rising from her devotions, having been disrobed of her crimson robe by the Lord Great Chamberlain, assisted by the Mistress of the Robes, and being uncovered, shall go before the Altar, supported and attended as before.

"Arising from her devotions, disrobed, assisted, uncovered, going supported before the altar." I tell you tonight, that there is no better way, probably no other right way, that either a Prince or a pauper, can be begin to set upon any work for which they are commissioned by heaven to do.

Do you see this? Have you thought about this? Have you begun to be devoted to God's will in this? Attentive to His voice, ready to receive His great commission for you? Have you laid aside your crimson robe yet and approached the altar of all Heaven's sovereign power, naked, supported, aided, needy? If you haven't, if all you have done is gripped a bunch of bright colored paper, university degrees and smiled with glee at flashing photographs, whilst looking up at the tumbling black, academic mortarboards falling down from a blue thrown into sky, then may God help you, and may God have mercy upon any congregation to which men have sent you to shepherd and rule over, for you shall always be a chump in the church and never a true "champion of The Church."

> *God have mercy upon any congregation to which men have sent you to shepherd and rule over, for you shall always be a chump in the church and never a true "champion of The Church."*

You see, public humbleness and expressed and naked need before the alter of the Lord, always precedes the dripping of the oil form the beak of the eagle, always precedes a successful rule, yes, and I mean always. Without it, you shall never know, neither shall you assume, your rightful and powerful, authoritative presence in the church of Jesus Christ.

Listen: *"Then Zadok the priest took a horn of oil from the tabernacle and anointed Solomon. And they blew the horn, and all the people said, 'Long live King Solomon!' And all the people went up after him; and the people played the flutes and rejoiced with great joy, so that the earth seemed to split with their sound." 1 Kings 1:39-40 NKJV*

Pray: Lord send the eagle of Your heavenly commissioning and may we feel its sharp talons, like a crown of thorns, pierce our cranial flesh, break our skulls, and stab our minds and then O our King, when we gaze to Your heaven for relief, drip from its screaming beak, the oil of Your commissioning upon our desperate and heavenward gazing heads. In Jesus name we pray, amen.

| Vol 01 | Q2 | NW00155 | June 03ʳᵈ |

Night-Whisper | **DANGER**

The prophets and the profiteers

Having weathered several hurricanes in South Florida and lived through their aftermath, it was there as a Brit, that I first heard and of the term "gauging" and saw it put into unscrupulous practice.

Nehemiah 5:1-7

"A great protest was mounted by the people, including the wives, against their fellow Jews. Some said, 'We have big families, and we need food just to survive.' Others said, 'We're having to mortgage our fields and vineyards and homes to get enough grain to keep from starving.' And others said, 'We're having to borrow money to pay the royal tax on our fields and vineyards. Look: We're the same flesh and blood as our brothers here; our children are just as good as theirs. Yet here we are having to sell our children off as slaves — some of our daughters have already been sold — and we can't do anything about it because our fields and vineyards are owned by somebody else.' I got really angry when I heard their protest and complaints. After thinking it over, I called the nobles and officials on the carpet. I said, 'Each one of you is gouging his brother.'"
(from THE MESSAGE: by Eugene H. Peterson.)

Price gauging is the pricing of products, often way above the market price, when no alternative retailing source is available. In England, we call this profiteering. Governments of course and especially local authorities, frown on this practice and are very much against it, even bringing the full weight of the law against the practicing profiteers. That is, unless they or their often larger and more powerful corporate buddies are doing it themselves.

All of us seek succor, safety, satisfaction and power in having more than enough. However, if you are government or big business, then a "much, much more than enough" position is a seeming very safe and powerful place to be in, even if it is at the expense of others. Yes, I am afraid to say that often the very worst offenders in price gauging and profiteering in times of peace especially are our very own Governments and large national corporate bodies.

It was no different in Nehemiah's days. The exiles had returned from Babylon to physically rebuild the capital city and its entire supportive economic infrastructure. This redemption of land, this redemption of society, this redemption of people, was a massive, a costly and most sacrificial job. Guess what? The rich Israelites were price gauging the poor workers. Guess what? The rich rulers were profiteering from the plight of the poor workers and by their self-indulgent pocket lining, the rich and ruling classes were keeping themselves economically safe and economically powerful to ensure their continued economic selfishness into the future and all at the terrible expense of their poorer brethren, who were hungry, mortgaged up to the hilt and selling their children into economic slavery. If we think about it, most of us in the world are in the same poor position even today.

> *The rich rulers were profiteering from the plight of the poor workers and by their self-indulgent pocket lining, the rich and ruling classes were keeping themselves economically safe and economically powerful.*

The answer to this in Nehemiah's day was not so much a fair trade policy, but rather a merciful policy. The answer was not communism, neither was it consumerism, no, the beginning of the answer to this disgusting usury, this plundering profiteering, this pernicious price gauging, was naming, shaming, shocking, and the shaking and all of whom were involved! This was done in terms of a very powerful and prophetic, condemnation, comparison, command and cursing! We need the same today. Shame on us the church, for it would appear that even a 'sold out' Fleet Street has more courageous folks with the spirit of prophecy upon them, than we do. Let us call usury a disgrace. Let us call usury sin. True prophets address socioeconomic situations, ethical and technical and also geopolitical ones, as well as personal and national sin. The Scaredy cat and settled, middle class and professionally ruled church has a long way to go to try to reclaim our prophetic voice. No wonder the world is not listening to us, for in our personal disengagement and silence, we are grossly compliant with the sins of our nation.

Listen: *"What you're doing is wrong. Is there no fear of God left in you? Don't you care what the nations around here, our enemies, think of you? 'I and my brothers and the people working for me have also loaned them money. But this gouging them with interest has to stop. Give them back their foreclosed fields, vineyards, olive groves, and homes right now. And forgive your claims on their money, grain, new wine, and olive oil.' They said, 'We'll give it all back. We won't make any more demands on them. We'll do everything you say.' Then I called the priests together and made them promise to keep their word. Then I emptied my pockets, turning them inside out, and said, 'So may God empty the pockets and house of everyone who doesn't keep this promise — turned inside out and emptied.' Everyone gave a wholehearted 'Yes, we'll do it!' and praised God. And the people did what they promised." (from THE MESSAGE by Eugene H. Peterson. Nehemiah 5:9-13)*

Pray: Lord, send us some Christian politicians anointed with the powerfully prophetic and then Lord, send them into the board rooms and the cabinet rooms, send them into the wine cellars and the dinner parties, send them into the gated and armed communities, send them with commands and cursings, that people may be most thoroughly delivered from economic bondage, that spiritual freedom would quickly follow. In Jesus name we ask it, amen and let it be so.

Night-Whisper | **CHANGE**

Mystery slappers

Recently, I hired the services of a mystery shopper. Via a Christian organization, I paid a non-Christian to go into a local church and report on a set of criteria ranging from welcome to worship, the accuracy of notice board facts and even friendliness. The report back was very instructive and as a side issue, the church in question appeared to fair very well. In our text for tonight, a mystery slapper visits the apostle Paul. However, the report back, is maybe not so good. Even so, I reckon we are all in need of a visit from some mystery slappers and it would appear that God in His outrageous goodness, sends them along quite regularly!

Acts 23:1-3

"Paul surveyed the members of the council with a steady gaze, and then said his piece: 'Friends, I've lived with a clear conscience before God all my life, up to this very moment.' That set the Chief Priest Ananias off. He ordered his aides to slap Paul in the face. Paul shot back, 'God will slap you down! What a fake you are! You sit there and judge me by the Law and then break the Law by ordering me slapped around!'" (THE MESSAGE by Eugene H. Peterson.)

Observing and reporting on the apostle Paul's reaction to this mystery slapper, both here and later in the passage, does gives me some hope as to my own humanity. Not excuse for sin mind you, no, but hope as to the imperfect kind of vessel God still deems to use. Later, just a few verses down from this, Paul's political machinations are going to open a whole can of trouble for him! But here, please note that the slap in the face, is followed by an instantaneous fight response from Paul in the form of a strong verbal threat and then a swift following curse in the shape of a desire for of God's largest of hands to be sent slapping across the face of the seeming source of his present humiliation and pain, that being, the High priest himself. It has always been the best test of a man's sanctification to first falsely accuse him and then publicly slap him. Our response to such treatment, will always reveal how far we have gone, how far we have left to go in our own sanctification.

If you know someone who exhibits an "holier than thou, I have arrived and have much to teach you" kind of attitude, may I invite you please, to just walk up to him and slap him around the face a bit. Just once mind you! If he is wise, then he shall find his response to such treatment most instructive to himself. I wonder if most Pastoral selection committees should employ mystery slappers and then following employment, they should be recruited to go slap the pastor on at least a bi-annual basis. I think it's a thought worthy of further consideration, especially if the pastor has not been thoroughly weaned from seminary yet.

I wonder if most Pastoral selection committees should employ mystery slappers?

If you have been around long enough, you will undoubtedly have had one of those condemning conversations, maybe one of those spiritually castrating letters even, which question your heart, question your morals, question your calling, question your integrity? If you haven't had yours yet, well just wait a while, its coming! Maybe the following instruction will be of help to you when the face slapping arrives.

I spoke with a man who had this happen to him, and he told me that after his initial Pauline response to the slap in the face, a good walk to both talk with God and to work off the adrenalin had brought to him a quiet revelation, which was followed on by almost a fit of giggles! For he realized in full, that what had been said about him was in fact nowhere near the truth of just how bad he really was! He certainly was not fit. In and of himself, to be in any holy calling, indeed, he was there only by the grace of God. More than that though, if what was in his heart had been manifest much more externally than it had been, then he would by now be the only person still locked up on Alcatraz. "If they knew how bad I really was," he said, "They wouldn't come anywhere near me." The fact that he was much worse than the mystery slapper had said, and that God still loved and used him, simply made him giggle! Don't get me wrong here, he was not engaging in any secret external sin, but rather, his sinful heart was often rife with wicked inclination. In the same way, I think Paul knew he was better than those who had slapped him around. However, Paul also knew that he was as bad as and if not worse than they were.

If the boiler of your reactions, if the rudder of your choices, if the aiming ballista of your own fiery tongue, yes, if your heart itself is to be called into question by others, then in all possibility, every accusation will stand true....and then some! Once you see that the ridiculous response of self-protection to such a small slap in the face from a mystery slapper, is of slight regard in comparison to the unseen and hidden, raging drives and actions of your heart, then I can see how such a realization, how such a revelation, can lead to fits of giggles. I am sure, each one of us are all far, far worse, than anyone else could ever realize. If you don't think you are, then my friend, then I prophesy that a slappin' is a comin! Watch out now.

> *I am sure, each one of us are all far, far worse, than anyone else could ever realize. If you don't think you are, then my friend, then I prophesy that a slappin' is a comin!*

Listen: *"The power of sin within me keeps sabotaging my best intentions, I obviously need help! I realise that I don't have what it takes. I can will it, but I can't do it. I decide to do good, but I don't really do it; I decide not to do bad, but then I do it anyway. My decisions, such as they are, don't result in actions. Something has gone wrong deep within me and gets the better of me every time. It happens so regularly that it's predictable. The moment I decide to do good, sin is there to trip me up. I truly delight in God's commands, but it's pretty obvious that not all of me joins in that delight. Parts of me covertly rebel, and just when I least expect it, they take charge. I've tried everything and nothing helps. I'm at the end of my rope. Is there no one who can do anything for me? Isn't that the real question? The answer, thank God, is that Jesus Christ can and does. He acted to set things right in this life of contradictions where I want to serve God with all my heart and mind, but am pulled by the influence of sin to do something totally different." (Romans 7:17b-25 from THE MESSAGE: The Bible in Contemporary Language © 2002 by Eugene H. Peterson.)*

Pray: Lord, thank You for the gift of the mystery slappers. Help me to take note of the white spittled mess slapped from the bowels of my soul, that I later will find lain across my bright red, stinging cheek. Amen.

Night-Whisper | **CONSIDER**

What's your monument?

Moses was alone with God when his spirit passed from his body into the spiritual realms. Before the demonic equivalent of Burke and Hare, like a pair of old hunting dogs, howled to get hold of the left behind corpse, it was Michael the Archangel, following the nod of God, who swooped down and laid the old corpse of the man of God across his own powerful right shoulder, and began to move in the direction of the appointed place, the secret place of burial. However, it was not long before his speedy obedience was halted by Lucifer himself, who, seizing the dangling right arm of the corpse, pulled Michael round into his angry red face whilst shouting, "And just where the hell do you think you're going with that me old mucker?"

Jude 9

"Yet Michael the archangel, in contending with the devil, when he disputed about the body of Moses, dared not bring against him a reviling accusation, but said, 'The Lord rebuke you!'" NKJV

This attempted cadaver kidnap, resulted in a fierce dispute between these two most powerful beings and in the heat of that disputation, it was Michael who called on the storm stopping rebuke of God Himself to halt the devil, back him up and bind him in situ whilst Michael slipped away, armed with his silver shovel, to rid fickle Israel of the remains of a possible idolatry that would most certainly rise, Mecca-like, Stalin-red-square-like amidst the masses, even as a rampant replacement for God Himself! In the same weird way, it is possible that any corpse, especially the dead bodies of the once powerful and influential, could become an object of subtle idolatry.

It was James Douglas, 4th Earl of Morton and newly elected regent of Scotland, who, mourning over the body of John Knox in the graveyard of St Giles, testified rightly that, *"Here lies one who neither flattered nor feared any flesh."* Now of course, if you were to go and find this same wept over grave of tears and astonishing accolades, yes, if you were to look for the grave of John Knox, this "Ruffian of the Reformation," then you might not see the wee plaque laid in the tarmac indicating its actual location, as it will probably be covered by a motor vehicle left in parking space 44 adjacent to St Giles Cathedral. Yes, there is no grave marker for the greatest Scot who ever lived as it is hidden under a parking lot! Scotland, you see, has no national monument for Knox. Or is there?

Now, you might think the absence of a great monument acknowledging the gravesite of this great Scot is outrageous but remember that it was Dr. Charles D Brokenshire who apparently wrote of Knox saying, *"Scotland has erected no monument on the grave of John Knox, for Scotland is his monument."* Imagine that tonight. Imagine having a nation as a monument to you. Just imagine that! The monument of Moses is Israel! The monument of Knox is Scotland! What's your monument tonight then? What are you aiming to leave behind you as a remembrance and as a glory to God Most High? Might it be maybe a generation true to God? A nation glorifying God, now, that's a great monument to aim to have don't you think? Therefore, if you think you are a real history maker, not a singing one, we have far too many of those, but a real one, then allow me to ask you once more will you: "What's your monument 'gonna' be?" What are you building tonight that might scratch the sky after your departure?

> *What are you building tonight that might scratch the sky after your departure?*

Listen: *"Ask of Me, and I will give You the nations for Your inheritance, and the ends of the earth for Your possession." Psalms 2:6 NKJV*

Pray: Oh God, grant me a bigger vision, one far greater than any slab of marble could ever be. In Jesus name I ask it, amen and let it be so!

| Vol 01 | Q2 | NW00158 | June 06th |

Night-Whisper | **PREPARE**

Getting rid of your secret prayer language

Part of my basic training as a young sailor was the learning of naval slang. The fact is, that there was so much of it, from Dhoby (washing) to Rabbits (presents – legitimate or otherwise,) and that it's use was so prolific in the Royal Navy, that it meant that unless you knew the local lingo, you wouldn't have much of a clue what other sailors were saying to you! An enclosed world, leads to a very specific and enclosed language. Do you see that?

Luke 18:1

"Then He spoke a parable to them, that men always ought to pray and not lose heart." NKJV

The prayer life of Christians can so easily become that same old enclosed world and frankly, the language, especially the prayer language of such closed worlds is rather boring, limiting, disconnected and lifeless. Indeed, if I were God, (immediate prayer of thanks from you that I am not!) then I would be AWOL from many a Christian prayer meeting, or to put it another way, if I were God, I would rather go "on the trot," or rather "do a runner," than turn up at a prayer meeting. The problem is that often our language is both like our hearts and our subject matter, in that they have become nothing but pitiful expressions of enclosed, tired, predictable and boring Christian colloquialisms. Well, somebody had to say it, for the mould of our boring "blah blah blah, blah blah" communication needs breaking and the only way to do this, is to marry a more expansive personal reality with the rawness of the Scriptures.

Most Christian groups have a 'secret' prayer language, that is, a language they use when they are gathered together to pray which is disconnected from both the reality of their regular lives and the people around them and the language of Scripture. It is pure local Christian community colloquialism, or as I prefer to call it, boring drivel! Prayer limiting, non-descriptive, stuttering, "justing," boring drivel. ("Lord we just want to, I just want to, we just, will you just, I just...." good grief!) This kind of secret prayer language of the group enclosure is often not the real language of our lives and so is of necessity, thoroughly disconnected from who we truly are. If this language IS the language of your lives, and for some it is, then brethren, you need to get out of the chicken coup a little more, or watch more TV! (I never thought I would actually say that, but there you go.) When you speak, be who you are in 'real life.' When you pray, be who you are in real life, yes, ditch the local C.C.C. the Christian Community Colloquialisms.

Most Christians refuse to use the language of the Scriptures when they pray. One of the reasons has been the insistent and continued the use of the King James Version of the Bible. A translation that despite all its majesty and beauty was nevertheless made for the Royal court of ancient English Kings. It was disconnected then from the common vernacular and how much more so several hundred years later. I am from the county of Derbyshire and as a youngster I spoke much in thee's and tha's and thou's and subsequently feel somewhat more comfortable with that King James translation but even I use the New King James version and also heavily supplement it with several other translations. We need to take an understandable version of the Scriptures, especially the Psalms and start praying them aloud. We need to take the text from the page and make it live on the expression of our own verbal reality. Pray the Psalms aloud but for your own soul's sake, please make sure to get a translation that is nearer your own common language, get something you connect with. The language of your day, in all its constructions and explanation and expression, is the very language in which you should pray. Let's get rid of the C.C.C. that dreaded secret prayer language and inject the Word of God into our everyday prayer live.

> *We need to take an understandable version of the Scriptures, especially the Psalms and start praying them aloud.*

Listen: *"It's your heart, not the dictionary, that gives meaning to your words. A good person produces good deeds and words season after season. An evil person is a blight on the orchard. Let me tell you something: Every one of these careless words is going to come back to haunt you. There will be a time of Reckoning. Words are powerful; take them seriously. Words can be your salvation. Words can also be your damnation." Matthew 12:34-37 (from THE MESSAGE:by Eugene H. Peterson.)*

Pray: God's glory is on tour in the skies, God-craft on exhibit across the horizon. Madame Day holds classes every morning, Professor Night lectures each evening. Their words aren't heard, their voices aren't recorded, But their silence fills the earth: unspoken truth is spoken everywhere. God makes a huge dome for the sun — a superdome! The morning sun is a new husband leaping from his honeymoon bed. The day breaking sun is an athlete racing to the tape. That's how God's Word vaults across the skies from sunrise to sunset, Melting ice, scorching deserts, warming hearts to faith. The revelation of God is whole and pulls our lives together. The signposts of God are clear and point out the right road. The life-maps of God are right, showing the way to joy. The directions of God are plain and easy on the eyes. God's reputation is twenty-four-carat gold, with a lifetime guarantee. The decisions of God are accurate down to the nth degree. God's Word is better than a diamond, better than a diamond set between emeralds. You'll like it better than strawberries in spring, better than red, ripe strawberries. There's more: God's Word warns us of danger and directs us to hidden treasure. Otherwise, how will we find our way? Or know when we play the fool? Clean the slate, God, so we can start the day fresh! Keep me from stupid sins, from thinking I can take over your work; Then I can start this day sun-washed, scrubbed clean of the grime of sin. These are the words in my mouth; these are what I chew on and pray. Accept them when I place them on the morning altar, O God, my Altar-Rock, God, Priest-of-My-Altar. (Psalms 19 from THE MESSAGE: The Bible in Contemporary Language © 2002 by Eugene H. Peterson. All rights reserved.)

Night-Whisper | **CHOOSE**

Another woman – another well

You will agree that our text for tonight runs in some respects in parallel with the story of Rahab in the book of Joshua. Two of the well-known runners of David the King are spotted by his civil war enemy, take refuge in an unnamed house, and are hidden and protected by an unnamed woman. When asked a direct question by the soldiers of 'Absalom the usurper' she lies, she deceives them and then diverts them away from their quarry. Make no mistake about it, this unnamed woman, drawn unwillingly onto center stage of this civil war conflict, saves the men, saves the day and saves King David and his Kingdom. Some might extrapolate further in saying that this unnamed woman saved the messianic line, thus making way for the coming Messiah, the Savior of the world. It is only in nice middle class front rooms and respectable religious pulpits where such "lying" is hissed at. David's men praised her for these lies! Absalom's men cursed her for them, and died.

2 Samuel 17:17-20

"Now Jonathan and Ahimaaz stayed at En Rogel, for they dared not be seen coming into the city; so a female servant would come and tell them, and they would go and tell King David. Nevertheless a lad saw them, and told Absalom. But both of them went away quickly and came to a man's house in Bahurim, who had a well in his court; and they went down into it. Then the woman took and spread a covering over the well's mouth, and spread ground grain on it; and the thing was not known. And when Absalom's servants came to the woman at the house, they said, 'Where are Ahimaaz and Jonathan?' So the woman said to them, 'They have gone over the water brook.' And when they had searched and could not find them, they returned to Jerusalem."

Life is messy. Living righteously is messy, costly, and bloody. Decisions we have to make, many of which are thrust upon us, many we wish we did not have to make, have enormous consequences attached to them. That unknown woman got up that morning to make some flour, to bake some bread and ended up saving Israel before she went to bed. Life is like that.

We live this Christian life in an already running reel, a story that flickers wildly on the walls of eternity, each frame scratched and grazed, browned by the sin of a fallen humanity and always containing the dark shadow of the black topped hat, waxed moustache villain of Satan himself. Our biggest surprise whilst watching this story play itself out, is all of a sudden to find ourselves in the scene, cast center stage, the whole plot seemingly pinned upon just what we shall do next? Now that's frightening!

We live this Christian life in an already running reel, a story that flickers wildly on the walls of eternity, each frame scratched and grazed, browned by the sin of a fallen humanity and always containing the dark shadow of the black topped hat, waxed moustache villain of Satan himself.

Maybe tomorrow you too shall be called onto center stage to play your part? When that happens, whatever you choose to do next, despite the mess, despite the machinations of your heart, despite the ridiculous inconvenience, always choose for King Jesus! Moreover, may you choose to hide, provide for, and protect His Royal runners.

Listen: *"Now it came to pass, after they had departed, that they came up out of the well and went and told King David, and said to David, 'Arise and cross over the water quickly. For thus has Ahithophel advised against you.' So David and all the people who were with him arose and crossed over the Jordan. By morning light not one of them was left who had not gone over the Jordan." 2 Samuel 17:17-20 NKJV*

Pray: Lord, when I am center stage, saving the Kings runners and all the Kings men, grant me a poker face and good lies. In Jesus name I ask it, amen.

Night-Whisper | **RESCUE**

Below bastards – the position of the pariah people

Joshua 9:22-27

"Then Joshua called for them, and he spoke to them, saying, 'Why have you deceived us, saying, "We are very far from you," when you dwell near us? Now therefore, you are cursed, and none of you shall be freed from being slaves — woodcutters and water carriers for the house of my God.' So they answered Joshua and said, 'Because your servants were clearly told that the Lord your God commanded His servant Moses to give you all the land, and to destroy all the inhabitants of the land from before you; therefore we were very much afraid for our lives because of you, and have done this thing. And now, here we are, in your hands; do with us as it seems good and right to do to us.' So he did to them, and delivered them out of the hand of the children of Israel, so that they did not kill them. And that day Joshua made them woodcutters and water carriers for the congregation and for the altar of the Lord, in the place which He would choose, even to this day." NKJV

So, Israel in not seeking the counsel of God, have been duped into an unwanted protectorate alliance with the Gibeonites. The Gibeonites were kept alive, but they and their descendants were cursed with a perpetual and menial servitude. They were a protected class but to all of Israel they were a pariah class. Indeed, they were the untouchables within Israel, eventually living in the suburbs of the temple and in the Levitical cities. It was the Gibeonites who were also culled and killed by Doeg the Edomite under the direction of mad King Saul and so consequently, it was later King David, who, wanting to avert the disaster of the judgement of God upon Israel for carrying out these particular murders, also handed the seven remaining sons of Saul over to the Gibeonites for summary disposal. Obviously, the outcome of this Saulish massacre was a diminishing in the Pariah class and so it was King David who later supplemented their ranks with captured enemy soldiers. These new soldiers of current capture combined with of the old Gibeonites and together became known as the "The Nethinim" or, "The Given Ones," their tasks and duties being totally at the behest and discretion of the Levites.

The later whoring of Israel in chasing after foreign Gods led to among other things, the worship of Astarte, a demon of lust embodied in female form and linked with the so-called sacred prostitution of fertility worship. This Astarte worship actually took place in the temple and in all probability, the Nethinim females were active participants in all its sexual practices, so much so, that their subsequent descendants could not trace their fatherhood at all. Probably because of this, the Talmud lists these "social outcasts in sacred service," as well below bastards and foundlings! Nethinim then, could never marry Israelites. They were perpetually cursed and excluded. Nevertheless, their eventual disappearance after the post-exilic return to the land seems to indicate that they were eventually absorbed into general Israelite society. The sect and the sin went underground you see, lying like a viral infection waiting for its ignition point. May I present you with but a small handful of thoughts gleaned from the history of this circumcised caste tonight.

> *Astarte was a demon of lust embodied in female form and linked with the so-called sacred prostitution of fertility worship.*

First. That sin absorbed, will eventually reveal itself in time.

Second. That God allowed the social outcast into a sacred service for Him.

Third. That like it or not, and I don't like it, the Lord allowed the perpetuation of a pariah class as a continual reminder as to what the people of God had been saved from.

Fourth. That these pariah people were "given ones" and were made both vital and integral to the function of the temple.

Fifth and finally, for those with true spiritual sight, even this degrading position of continual menial servitude was nevertheless far, far more desirable then dwelling in the damned tents of the wicked.

Think about that tonight; ponder this blessed curse of the pariah people. Now, remember your exalted position in Jesus and your privilege of being Royal sons, a Holy priesthood who are honored to be able to offer spiritual sacrifices to God most high. You are not below bastards, you are above the angels, and you are the adopted sons of God.

Listen: *"I would rather be a doorkeeper in the house of my God than dwell in the tents of wickedness." Psalms 84:10,b & c..*

Pray: Lord help me to appreciate the blessedness of my position in Jesus Christ my Lord, for in Him, having been raised from the position of a pariah, having been moved from being listed below even a foundling and a bastard, I am now found at the top of the list, yes, I am now even adopted by You and possess the full rights and inheritance of a Son of God. Thank you for this O my Great Father, in Jesus magnificent name, amen.

| Vol 01 | Q2 | NW00161 | June 09th |

Night-Whisper | **CHANGE**

Rizpah and the hanging of red meat

Oxygen in the blood produces lactic acid. It is the work of this meat tenderizing acid in game that has been hung for some time, that makes the meat more concentrate and full of flavor. The longer the meat is hung, the more tender and tasty the eating.

2 Samuel 21:11-14

"And David was told what Rizpah the daughter of Aiah, the concubine of Saul, had done. Then David went and took the bones of Saul, and the bones of Jonathan his son, from the men of Jabesh Gilead who had stolen them from the street of Beth Shan, where the Philistines had hung them up, after the Philistines had struck down Saul in Gilboa. So he brought up the bones of Saul and the bones of Jonathan his son from there; and they gathered the bones of those who had been hanged. They buried the bones of Saul and Jonathan his son in the country of Benjamin in Zelah, in the tomb of Kish his father. So they performed all that the king commanded. And after that God heeded the prayer for the land." NKJV

It is English poet Wordsworth whose poem "Rizpah" tells the story of a mother, mad with obsession concerning the bones of her dead son, Willy, who was sentenced and cursed to be hung on the gallows for simply robbing the mail. Eventually, she secretly buries the bones in a shallow grave on consecrated ground next to the church and in the poem she recounts her actions to a genteel lady sat at her side in the final hour of her life, saying,

Do you think I was scar'd by the bones? I kiss'd 'em, I buried 'em all
I can't dig deep, I am old—in the night by the churchyard wall.
My Willy 'ill rise up whole when the trumpet of judgment 'ill sound,
But I charge you never to say that I laid him in holy ground. They would
scratch him up—they would hang him again on the cursed tree.
Sin? O, yes, we are sinners, I know—let all that be,

And read me a Bible verse of the Lord's goodwill toward men—
"Full of compassion and mercy, the Lord"—let me hear it again;
"Full of compassion and mercy—long-suffering." Yes, O, yes!
For the lawyer is born but to murder—the Savior lives but to bless.

In our text for tonight, we are presented with the summary of one of the most sorriest of scenes ever recorded in Scripture. Rizpah, that grief consumed woman of old, has for five months been watching over seven hanging corpses, each one made black by the wind, dried in the sun, rotted all to a jerk chicken scarecrow consistency, two of which, were her own dear sons. By day Rizpah has kept away the birds and by the night the hungry jackals. Rizpah had five sorry months of the attendant care of corpses, with time to contemplate some well-hung meat.

> *Rizpah had five sorry months of the attendant care of corpses, with time to contemplate some well hung meat.*

A three-year famine in the land had brought King David to seek the reason why, and it had been revealed to him, that it was because of Saul's unlawful attempted genocide of the Gibeonites that this curse had come upon the nation. The surviving Gibeonites were then consulted and refusing all bloody money, demanded seven of Saul's sons, got them, killed them and hung them up for all to see. Now the law was very clear concerning capital crimes, in that the bodies should be buried at even time. These seven corpses however, no doubt under the command of David, were hung in the face of God, waiting for the curse to be lifted and the rain to come. Five months of well-hung meat and still there was no rain, just the pain of a mother looking endlessly on the rotting corpses of her two dead sons.

Rizpah's daily ritual, led eventually to make King David likewise "honor" the dead. So, sending for the remains of dead King Saul and Jonathan his son, he gathered them together with the bones of the seven corpses and interned them with dignity in the family grave. It was after this that God heeded the prayer for the land. It was after this I say. Selah.

Two thousand years ago, the Son of the King of the whole earth was hung on a tree, His mother looking on endlessly, her heart pierced through with a sword. Like a deep cut and tenderized scarecrow, He bled out is life down the wood of His cross for all the world to see, and there He was made a curse for you and there He was made a curse for me. God ate His own Son up in judgement on that most scandalous of crosses and as often as we eat that bread and drink that cup, we too remember the tenderness and tastiness of hanging meat, in that most terrible of sacrifices. The law of sin and death in the hands of lawyers can lead only to cursing and condemnation. The most merciful God however, made His son a curse for you, and only He can most truly set you free from the condemnation and judgement, which now rests upon you. There is a reason that your land is parched. There is a reason for your thirst.

Listen: *"The plain fact is that bull and goat blood can't get rid of sin. That is what is meant by this prophecy, put in the mouth of Christ: You don't want sacrifices and offerings year after year; you've prepared a body for me for a sacrifice. It's not fragrance and smoke from the altar that whet your appetite. So I said, 'I'm here to do it your way, O God, the way it's described in your Book.' When he said, 'You don't want sacrifices and offerings,' he was referring to practices according to the old plan. When he added, 'I'm here to do it your way,' he set aside the first in order to enact the new plan - God's way - by which we are made fit for God by the once-for-all sacrifice of Jesus. Every priest goes to work at the altar each day, offers the same old sacrifices year in, year out, and never makes a dent in the sin problem. As a priest, Christ made a single sacrifice for sins, and that was it! Then he sat down right beside God and waited for his enemies to cave in. It was a perfect sacrifice by a perfect person to perfect some very imperfect people. By that single offering, he did everything that needed to be done for everyone who takes part in the purifying process."* (Hebrews 10:4-14 from The Message, by Eugene H. Peterson.)

Pray: Tell me the story slowly, that I may take it in, that wonderful redemption, God's remedy for sin. Tell me the story often, for I forget so soon; the early dew of morning has passed away at noon. Tell me the story softly, with earnest tones and grave; remember I'm the sinner whom Jesus came to save. Tell me the story always, if you would really be, in any time of trouble, a comforter to me. Tell me the same old story when You have cause to fear that this world's empty glory is costing me too dear. Yes, and when this world's glory is dawning on my soul, tell me the old, old story: "Christ Jesus makes thee whole." (From Katherine Hankey's The Old, Old Story)

Night-Whisper | **INTEGRITY**

Baby got Babylon

In 2008 whilst walking down the cool streets of little London, full of sashaying women with Sacral Chakra tattoos curled on their flesh in Celtic-Klingon style, all with bared browned mid-rift, and pierced belly buttons touting silver studded birth stones, highlighting their hipsters, all hanging precariously just above their pubic mound, it caught my attention regarding the vast number of them that also seemed to be wearing leather belts with the words "Jesus loves you" emblazoned on them in studded silver! Upon investigation, it seems that London's Spitalfields "All Saints" fashion designers had given Jesus some popular "street cred" amongst folks who neither knew anything about Him nor cared! All they had hanging from their anorexic hips was an anorexic religious phrase, whose only value was a fashion titter that even Tetzel would have refused to utilize! The statement was to them, something meaningless, something quaint, and something from a bygone age. While looking at this, (the belts I mean) it got me thinking just how good a job the devil had done in reducing the message of the Gospel to the equivalent of a smelly little low level flatulent emission, and how dastardly complicit the church had been in helping him.

Revelation 17:1-2

"Then one of the seven angels who had the seven bowls came and talked with me, saying to me, 'Come, I will show you the judgement of the great harlot who sits on many waters, with whom the kings of the earth committed fornication, and the inhabitants of the earth were made drunk with the wine of her fornication.'" NKJV

If I was thinking positively tonight I would probably, comment on the wonderful opportunity we have in walking up to said ladies, blokes and those who aren't quite gender sure and saying, "Hey, Jesus does love you! Let me tell you how!" However, I think in this day and age, you could get maced, thumped, arrested for sexual harassment, or picked up by a "tranny." If you tried that evangelistic approach. Yes, you need wisdom when you're evangelizing in the early twenty first century, that's for sure.

When the church has so devalued the central core of the Gospel, the love of God in Christ Jesus, that a company called All Saints can take it and market it as a fashion accessory, then my oh my, I reckon all the bodies of the old saints will be turning in their graves! Yet, we have only ourselves to blame, for even now we are offering Christ as a life fashion accessory, a daily supplement to make you feel good, a way to achieve your dreams, the means to discover God's great plan for your best life now! (Prosperity guaranteed for sure.) Good grief my friends, even as I write, I know of at least two hip postmodern youth endeavors coming out with their own brand of Gospel clothing! Of course, in sarcastic answer to such crass Christian marketing, the secular made "What Would Jesus Do" thong is already available on line and let's not scowl at it, for it is we, the church, who have brought the Gospel down to this crass level of consumerism, for we have created a religious industry with more junk and shallowness than the world would ever stoop to. New Testa-Mint candy and Christian Coffee Mugs emblazoned with our current heroes of clay, all on sale in failing Christian bookshops along with all the other tut! I mean for goodness sake!

> *Even now we are offering Christ as a life fashion accessory, a daily supplement to make you feel good, a way to achieve your dreams, the means to discover God's great plan for your best life now!*

If you need a lapel pin to proclaim the Gospel, a rubber bracelet to bind you to His cross, New Testa-mints to make your breath smell nice and a whole bunch of other crap to keep you on track, then my friend, get the hell out of Christianity and get out fast, because all you have done is bought into the religious industry and the 1st church of Ichabod that empowers the whole great Laodicean machine. I tell you, you are probably still lost and getting more lost by the minute, because all this whore will do is take your 10% as a down payment, then fleece you for the rest of your days. Strong words, but true words. Strong words, but necessary ones, for hundreds of thousands are being converted to Christian culture instead of being converted to Christ and every day as a Pastor, I deal with the aftermath of the returned goods of disappointed buyers.

Christ, His forgiveness. Christ, His presence. Christ, His power. Have you got Him? Have you got those? Nothing else matters.

Listen: *"So he carried me away in the Spirit into the wilderness. And I saw a woman sitting on a scarlet beast which was full of names of blasphemy, having seven heads and ten horns. The woman was arrayed in purple and scarlet, and adorned with gold and precious stones and pearls, having in her hand a golden cup full of abominations and the filthiness of her fornication. And on her forehead a name was written: mystery, babylon the great, the mother of harlots and of the abominations of the earth. I saw the woman, drunk with the blood of the saints and with the blood of the martyrs of Jesus. And when I saw her, I marveled with great amazement."* NKJV

Pray: Lord, strip me bare! Take away all my accessories to the Gospel and just give me the real deal. In Jesus name I ask it, because I believe He loves me. Amen!

| Vol 01 | Q2 | NW00163 | June 11th |

Night-Whisper | **CARE**

The "physog's" of three women at a window

Zwinglian reformed minister, pastor and "first preacher" of St Peter's church in Zurich, was none other than Johann Kaspar Lavater, (1741-1801.) Theologian, Swiss nationalist, writer, politician, preacher, poet and scientist, he is also credited with being the father of 19th Century physiognomy which, in brief, is the discernment of inner qualities by the outward examination of set facial features.

2 Samuel 6:16

"Now as the ark of the Lord came into the City of David, Michal, Saul's daughter, looked through a window and saw King David leaping and whirling before the Lord; and she despised him in her heart." NKJV

Lavater's works on physiognomy were so successful that they continued to influence descriptive novelist's way after his death, the facially descriptive works of Charles Dickens being a prominent example. Nowadays of course, the whole Greek rooted work is considered as pseudo-scientific nonsense. Nevertheless, we all know that the eyes are indeed the windows of the soul and more often than not, our unfeigned features, our steady state countenance almost always proves to be a true witness of our soulish state.

The Bible speaks of three women seen looking out of a window and surely, there is no better place for the fixed and stable features of a face to be truly observed. There are no mirrors; there are no onlookers, only the face at the window. Through the intimation of the Biblical text, I believe we can glance at the windows of the soul, through those same facial frames set in solid silver for all the world to see. Maybe Pastor Lavater was right after all?

The three women at the window in the Bible are respectively: The mother of Sisera, Michal the daughter of Saul and the wife of the wild dancing King David, and finally, Jezebel. (See Judges 5:28-30, 2 Samuel 6:16 and 2 Kings 9:30-31) Together, these three friezes of fallen female royalty all combine to present a picture of dire disappointment, seduction and despising destruction. They carry in their faces nothing short of a fetal fatality, for the child of their destruction is already birthed upon their cheeks, because they have forsaken the one true God, despised His purpose, seduced His people and killed His prophets.

There is no misogyny in my observations, no, they are indeed just that, observations. Tonight consider that maybe and I say maybe, some of our inner world can be captured in our outer shadow. Sometimes a good stare then at our steady state appearance can be a truer diagnostic to our real condition than any words offered by any earthly man.

Maybe tonight, if you dare, it's time to take a good look in the mirror and then with God's help, take some corrective action, for often times, our physog tells us much, much more than we ever care to know. Go take a good long look at that man in the mirror.

> *They carry in their faces nothing short of a fetal fatality, for the child of their destruction is already birthed upon their cheeks, because they have forsaken the one true God, despised His purpose, seduced His people and killed His prophets.*

Listen: *"The mother of Sisera looked through the window, and cried out through the lattice, 'Why is his chariot so long in coming? Why tarries the clatter of his chariots?' Her wisest ladies answered her, Yes, she answered herself, 'are they not finding and dividing the spoil: To every man a girl or two; for Sisera, plunder of dyed garments, plunder of garments embroidered and dyed, two pieces of dyed embroidery for the neck of the looter?'" Judges 5:28-30 NKJV*

Pray: Lord, help me rightly examine myself, in Jesus name I pray, amen and let it be so.

| Vol 01 | Q2 | NW00164 | June 12th |

Night-Whisper | **BELIEVE**

Frankly, she was wrong

In 1942, a young girl aged just thirteen wrote expectantly in her new red checked diary, saying, *"I hope I will be able to confide everything to you, as I have never been able to confide in anyone, and I hope you will be a great source of comfort and support."* In Amsterdam, she would soon go into hiding, spending the next two years of her life recording her experiences, thought, ideas and dreams, before being caught by the Nazis and shipped to Bergen Belsen, where she would later die of tuberculosis, just one month before the end of World War II. Today is Anne Frank Day, a good day for the life of this remarkable and very young woman to be remembered.

Romans 7:18-19

"For I know that in me (that is, in my flesh) nothing good dwells; for to will is present with me, but how to perform what is good I do not find." NKJV

On July 21st in 1944, despite Anne's continual confinement and fears, she writes in a most remarkable and hopeful way saying, *"It's difficult in times like these; ideals, dreams and cherished hopes rise within us, only to be crushed by grim reality. It's a wonder I haven't abandoned all my ideals, they seem so absurd and impractical. Yet I cling to them because I believe, in spite of everything, that people are truly good at heart."* Unfortunately, in her observation of humanity as a whole and of individuals within it, Anne was so very, very wrong.

One of the major differences between Christianity, secular humanism and many world religions, is it's one damnable conclusion that the fountain of man, that the root of man, that the heart of man, is essentially not good, no, it is un-good, bad, even evil! This Biblical truth runs contrary to every fiber within our being, and that is despite the volcanic evil which like refluxial acid burns its way like hot lava, trenching its way up our throat to more often than not, explode from our devouring mouths. Even so, humanity declares to us repeatedly, that age-old lie, that in truth, we are good, yes in truth, we are intrinsically loving and good, we just need a chance to shine, we just need the opportunity to let the goodness of humanity, the goodness of ourselves, to freely flow out from us. This is a beautiful dream but remains a timeless lie, despite it being pushed down our throat repeatedly by anything and everything that Gene Roddenberry ever touched or touched upon.

The purpose of such a Biblical and damnable observation of humanity, even of you in particular, is to bring you on your knees to Jesus. The purpose of such a Biblical and damnable observation of humanity, of even you, is to make you Christ centered instead of self-centered.

This is a beautiful dream but remains a timeless lie, despite it being pushed down our throat repeatedly by anything and everything that Gene Roddenberry ever touched or touched upon.

Modern man, proud and undaunted in his hiding ignorance of his own true heart, will never the less hate you and seek to hurt you should you ever dare to point out to him the truth of God's word regarding their true nature and state. Even so, only sick sinners can come to Christ because the blind and self-taught healthy don't even want to hear His word. Do not be fooled my fellow sinful friend, you are corrupt at your core.

Coming to Christ, abiding in Christ and having Him in the person of the Holy Spirit abide in you, gives you a new nature to grow into, and an ever fresh and present power source to do so.

Listen: *"The Pharisee stood and prayed thus with himself, 'God, I thank You that I am not like other men — extortioners, unjust, adulterers, or even as this tax collector. I fast twice a week; I give tithes of all that I possess.' And the tax collector, standing afar off, would not so much as raise his eyes to heaven, but beat his breast, saying, 'God, be merciful to me a sinner!' I tell you, this man went down to his house justified rather than the other; for everyone who exalts himself will be humbled, and he who humbles himself will be exalted." Luke 18:11-14 NKJV*

Pray: Lord, this is a hard thing to believe. The older I live the more I see the truth of it in others, yet Lord, the less I am willing believe it fully about myself. What fierce and subtle perversion Lord, what adeceitful and damnable heresy I seem to always believe about the so called intrinsic goodness in me. Jesus, be my center, be my goodness, then this night and on the morrow and forever more I pray, help me to abide in You. Amen and let it be so.

Night-Whisper | **PREPARE**

Wonder down the wire

It was at the beginning of the 21st century that American based company Verizon Wireless came up with several catchy phrases to boost its already substantial market share. Those two major catchphrases were "Can you hear me now?" and "It's the Network." The former catchphrase was placed in the mouth of a horn rimmed spectacled, everyman type of guy who represented the thousands of Verizon employees travelling North America verifying the Network's signal strength. The latter phrase, clothed itself in the same horn rimmed spectacled Network Test Man but this time, he was visually backed by a vast crowd of other support employees, all dressed in various work outfits and posing in different support situations but all, I say all, attentive to the but one customer, making the but one important call, on the one ad only Verizon network. Well, so what?

Matthew 6:6

"But you, when you pray, go into your room, and when you have shut your door, pray to your Father who is in the secret place; and your Father who sees in secret will reward you openly." NKJV

Prayer for most of us is a very lonely endeavor. Yet still, for safety's sake, for authenticity's sake, for fellowship's sake, Jesus instructed us to move into a solitary place with the Father. Yet once all the excuses for not being able to get alone with God are rightly placed in the garbage, our fearfulness of being alone with ourselves and of being alone with God are still one of the most profound hindrances to private prayer. Maybe my following observations will cast some interesting light on this fallacy of our being alone with both God and ourselves?

Rightly or wrongly, my practice when praying has been to ask God for privacy between us. At the times when I do get alone with God, I often then ask to be alone with God, just Him and me. No, you didn't misread that. Indeed, I often ask for a booth with smoked glass reflective windows, thoroughly insulated walls and a private line to boot, for what I am about to say, is just between me and Him alone. Yes, within the secret place, I go even further in asking this especial request of privacy with God, and so for a couple of reasons.

The first reason for my request for privacy is that, like the Verizon Wireless Network ad suggests, we are never alone with God. Attendant angels, attacking demons, the choir of similar saints moved by the Holy Spirit to pray in the same way, righteously voyeuristic angels who continually observe the works of God in His church, as well as that maybe great crowd of heavenly onlookers, all looking on, many maybe kneeling and praying with me, are, I am sure, right there with me. That's why, when I am alone with God, I am often quite conscious of far from being alone. The spiritual world is a busy and noisy place.

> *When I am alone with God, I am often quite conscious of far from being alone. The spiritual world is a busy and noisy place.*

The second reason is that there are some things I do not want the enemy to hear. I need a "data scrambled" prayer line, if you will. My enemy knows too much already. The challenge is that I am not sure his ear muffling is automatic? No, I wonder if the accuser of the brethren, like some guilty playground bully has already ran to the headmaster to tell lies on the beaten, bruised and broken little boy coming running, weeping with his complaint, knocking on now on God's kind and understanding study door? Yes, the devil often goes before us, and he being there upon our arrival is ready to pick up some more ready ammunition to throw back on us and on God so, I therefore often ask for the devil to be removed, together with all his ugly lackeys, so I can be truly alone with God. Well, without the devil anyway.

Remember tonight then, that Christ has commanded you to pray and when you do so, to get alone with God.

Remember tonight though, that when you get alone with God, you are rarely alone with God and sometimes, often times, you need to ask for privacy. Think about that and be sure ask for a private line. It's worth thinking about!

Listen: *"Then I heard a loud voice saying in heaven, 'Now salvation, and strength, and the kingdom of our God, and the power of His Christ have come, for the accuser of our brethren, who accused them before our God day and night, has been cast down. And they overcame him by the blood* *of the Lamb and by the word of their testimony, and they did not love their lives to the death. Therefore rejoice, O heavens, and you who dwell in them! Woe to the inhabitants of the earth and the sea! For the devil has come down to you, having great wrath, because he knows that he has a short time.'" Revelation 12:10-12 NKJV*

Pray: Lord in the many private places placed before me tomorrow, grant me a private line, a clear connection and wonder down the wire, in Jesus name I pray, amen.

Night-Whisper | **RESPECT**

'Oh Aberystwyth! Bring back the old, old thing ' or, 'the singing of meat'

I wish God would stop doing new things! What with Toronto, Brownsville, Lakeland, Brompton, Cwbran and many other unnamed places, God seems to never tire of doing 'new things.' Surely, if Christ does not yet return, then in the future, together with no doubt many other new locations, the ever growing and even now, monumental list of "God doing new things," will have grown substantially. Yes, I wish God would stop doing new things and start doing some of the old ones again, actually just one old thing. I wish He would save and sanctify people like He used to do in all the days gone by.

Jeremiah 6:16

"Thus says the Lord: 'Stand in the ways and see, and ask for the old paths, where the good way is, and walk in it; then you will find rest for your souls.' But they said, 'We will not walk in it.'" NKJV

June is the traditional time for the trooping of the color. I watched it today and Horse Guards Parade in London was again decked in magnificence! It was very moving to observe the five foot-guard regiments troop the chosen regimental colors of the year, past Her Majesty Queen Elizabeth II, each guardsman having his chest puffed out, bags of swank, eyes peering directly into the eyes of the monarch, with the mounted cavalry bands changing the tune of the quick march to match those songs long associated with each regiment then passing in front of the watching Royalty. All rousing tunes they were as well, tunes such as, "The British Grenadiers," "Milanollo," "Hielan Laddie," "St Patrick's Day" and "The Rising of The Lark."

It was during the rest of the preparatory slow and quick marches that my heart was arrested by two pieces of music in particular: Les Huguenots and Aberystwyth, those two magnificent tunes, the former a Waltz, musically inter-dispersed with "A Mighty Fortress is our God" and the latter, the tune to which the old hymn, "Jesus Lover of My Soul" used to be sung. I remember a time when the musical connectivity of such tunes would bring the associated words into a national remembrance, for they were tunes that would bring with them an awe, a thankfulness toward God, a testimony of His grace toward us and of our dependence upon Him. Now they are just forgotten and disconnected tunes. Even in the church now, they are mostly just forgotten and disconnected tunes.

> *My God! We need a musical renaissance and a noteworthy revival!*

My God! We need a musical renaissance and a noteworthy revival! With some old tunes, or better still, some new tunes with an old theme of people saved from sin and sanctified to Him singing them! I tell you, not even the Stump will root, fruit and flower without a return to the singing of meat.

In the coming days, the old church, which will arise once again, decked in New Testament clothes, will need to have known and memorized spiritual songs at the head of its vanguard around the walls of this rebuilt Jericho, this rebellious city of self-cursing. It is the spirit that needs lifting, not the soul, and only meaty words can do that. We have no use for worship leaders in the New Testament church, just singing prophets, poets who have seen God in His glory. We need words that are worthy of remembrance.

Yes, I wish tonight with all my heart that God would troop His color stop doing new things and do His old thing once again.

Listen:

> *A mighty Fortress is our God, a Bulwark never failing;*
> *Our Helper He amid the flood of mortal ills prevailing:*
> *For still our ancient foe doth seek to work us woe;*
> *His craft and power are great, and, armed with cruel hate,*
> *On earth is not his equal.*
>
> *Did we in our own strength confide, our striving would be losing;*
> *Were not the right Man on our side, the Man of God's own choosing:*
> *Dost ask who that may be? Christ Jesus, it is He;*
> *Lord Sabaoth His Name, from age to age the same,*
> *And He must win the battle.*
>
> *And though this world, with devils filled, should threaten to undo us,*
> *We will not fear, for God hath willed His truth to triumph through us:*

The Prince of Darkness grim, we tremble not for him;
His rage we can endure, for lo! his doom is sure,
One little word shall fell him.

That word above all earthly powers, no thanks to them, abideth;
The Spirit and the gifts are ours through Him who with us sideth:
Let goods and kindred go, this mortal life also;
The body they may kill: God's truth abideth still,
His Kingdom is forever.

(Martin Luther)

Pray:

Jesus, lover of my soul, let me to Thy bosom fly,
While the nearer waters roll, while the tempest still is high.
Hide me, O my Savior, hide, till the storm of life is past;
Safe into the haven guide; O receive my soul at last.

Other refuge have I none, hangs my helpless soul on Thee;
Leave, ah! leave me not alone, still support and comfort me.
All my trust on Thee is stayed, all my help from Thee I bring;
Cover my defenseless head with the shadow of Thy wing.

Wilt Thou not regard my call? Wilt Thou not accept my prayer?
Lo! I sink, I faint, I fall—Lo! on Thee I cast my care;
Reach me out Thy gracious hand! While I of Thy strength receive,
Hoping against hope I stand, dying, and behold, I live.

Thou, O Christ, art all I want, more than all in Thee I find;
Raise the fallen, cheer the faint, heal the sick, and lead the blind.
Just and holy is Thy Name, I am all unrighteousness;
False and full of sin I am; Thou art full of truth and grace.

Plenteous grace with Thee is found, grace to cover all my sin;
Let the healing streams abound; make and keep me pure within.
Thou of life the fountain art, freely let me take of Thee;
Spring Thou up within my heart; rise to all eternity.

(Charles Wesley)

| Vol 01 | Q2 | NW00167 | June 15th |

Night-Whisper | **OBEY**

The correct use of cotton buds and spiritual direction

It was reported earlier this year of my writing that a boy who had been partially deaf for nine years was suddenly cured, when a cotton wool bud popped out of his ear. Apparently aged two years of age, unbeknown to his parents, he mightily stuffed one of these right up into his right ear and broke off the end. Up until age, 11 there followed some nine years of earache, partial deafness leading to some behavioral difficulties and exclusion and not doing so well at school. In addition to this were the many visits to doctors and specialists, all who had somehow missed the now wax coated cotton bud. The boy's growing body, over the years had eventually ejected the alien intruder and BAM! A miracle of healing had now begun to transform his life.

James 3:1-2

"My brethren, let not many of you become teachers, knowing that we shall receive a stricter judgment."
NKJV

Being a mentor, being a spiritual director, trying if you will, to be a meta-physician, a curer of souls, carries with it a most awesome responsibility. Mostly dealing in the spiritual and the ethereal, even dealing with the majesty of the secret and inner places of the heart, the possibility of misdiagnosis and of consequent spiritual deafness and subsequent stunted or twisted growth you might cause in others is of a far greater possibility than with any standard medical practitioner. Yet, we still send tens of thousands of young inexperienced consultants, full of information but still wet behind the ears out onto the wards of our churches each and every year, and my oh my, how great is the carnage that cometh forth! Spiritual misdirection and the subsequent production of profound spiritual deafness and the bitter twistedness of most people in our churches are testimony to the fact that they are often times being fooled by their denominations and failed by their shepherds. Good grief even the far too early deployed shepherds, those spiritual curer's of souls, are themselves leaving their posts in their droves, never to return!

In terms of spiritual discipleship, in terms of good friendship we all become the spiritual directors of someone, somewhere, sometime. May I offer then, some guidelines tonight for each us to follow in the days to come.

First, listen. Be slow to speak; slow to construct a response in your own mind, even whilst the other is speaking. Make the phrases, "I don't know,' 'I'm not sure,' and 'I wonder if," your own very best of friends. Use them much, for they are true and a whole lot more certain than much of the conclusions you might wish to hurry out of your mouth. Listen.

Second, suggest. Suggestions are always investigative rather than declarative. The advantage of applied suggestions is a personal discovery of the problem. This personal discovery after following suggestions is far more powerful than any declaration you could make. Make the phrases, "I don't know, but... "I'm not sure, however..." and "I wonder if," your very best of friends. Suggest.

> *Listen. Suggest. Seek. Watch. Pray. Put them in the Son and then, Stick with them.*

Third, seek. Suggestions are mere signposts. They are clues. To go on a search following clues demands attention, demands application and most of all requires support and supply. Help people seek out the roots of their issues. Seek.

Fourth, watch. People of suggestive searches often sit down, slack off in the searching, wander off in the wrong direction, find themselves lost in deep woods wandering in vast disorienting wastelands. People need watching in terms of their pursued sanctification. Watch.

Fifth, pray. This cannot be underestimated. Prayer is the "walkie talkie" connection with base. Prayer is direct contact with headquarters. Prayer is contact with the three persons who are sure to help us. God The Father, God The Son, and God The Holy Spirit. Pray.

Sixth, put them in the Son. Plants and people only grow in the Son. Ask for His light to shine. Pray light upon the seeker, pray light upon the searcher, and throw light upon their path. Put them in the Son.

Seventh, stick with them. Oh the relief we feel when all our problem people leave. Oh how we are so thankful when the difficulties depart. Oh how we are relieved that we do not have to stick with them. True discipleship, however, true shepherding is mostly marked by stickability. Therefore, stick with them.

It goes almost without saying, that a Chief Executive Officer Senior Pastor cannot do this. Jesus had twelve disciples. We do not consider anyone worth following or listening to unless they have 12,000! With this strange and most unbiblical ratio, I wonder if any healing, wholeness and true holiness, can never ever come. I say, it can never come. Many people go missing in the mega. Remember that.

Listen: *"For we all stumble in many things. If anyone does not stumble in word, he is a perfect man, able also to bridle the whole body."* James 3:2 NKJV

Pray: Oh Lord, keep back Your servant also from presumptuous sins; let them not have dominion over me. Then I shall be blameless, and I shall be innocent of great transgression. Let the words of my mouth and the meditation of my heart be acceptable in Your sight, O Lord, my strength and my Redeemer." (Psalms 19:13-14 NKJV)

Night-Whisper | **COST**

Of Betty Crocker brioche and tired sweaty bakers

It is the infamous Marie Antoinette, Archduchess of Austria and Queen of France and Navarre, who when confronted with the poverty and starvation of her people through lack of bread, is reputed to have replied, "Qu'ils mangent de la brioche" or, "let them eat cake!" I find this a most resonant statement, for in these strange days, one of the reasons I go to many churches is for the indulgence of eating cake. For other people it is good coffee or sweet overly iced donuts, but for me, it is cake! Chocolate cake, gooey cake, angel cake (always best served at charismatic churches,) fruit cake, (if you're going to get some of the latest new thing that God is supposedly doing now, especially in North America) millionaire shortcake, (for the prosperity minded among us,) indeed, any kind and combination of cake will do for me! Especially, yes especially if there is no bread! Are you listening now? There is rarely any bread.

Nehemiah 9:15

"You gave them bread from heaven for their hunger, and brought them water out of the rock for their thirst, and told them to go in to possess the land which You had sworn to give them." NKJV

I am always amazed at what substandard fodder we Christians can become satisfied with. So much grotty grey gruel, each Sunday, simply slopped down on our empty and not so white, waiting plates. Yes, thank God for cake, because it's the only thing that keeps me going back to church!

I am perpetually pleased though, at seeing the onset of wide eyes and open mouths on the faces of malnourished Christians when first encountering real bread, for when gruel fed saints eventually get a taste of some real bread, some heavenly brioche, burgeoning fat with the goodness of God, they'll change restaurants, yes, they'll start a revolution and chop of the heads of all the lazy French chefs who gave them grey gruel and Betty Crocker, quick served cake as a substitute for hard earned study bread.

Whenever I take on a Pastorate, I am always a little perplexed at the known workload that is about to come upon me once again, for I desire to be a good baker, and with good bakers that make the best of breads, there are no short cuts, yes, despite me being only 5' 6 there are no short cooks. For me, this means rising earlier than most, to light my oven. It means maintaining my yeast at just the right temperature, and much more than this, it means finding the right fertilizer for my soil, it means digging, ploughing, sowing, reaping, milling, and God help me, it means a lot of unseen sweat, shed in lonely fields. Preparing bread is the hardest work I have ever done.

For me, this means rising earlier than most, to light my oven. It means maintaining my yeast at just the right temperature, and much more than this, it means finding the right fertilizer for my soil, it means digging, ploughing, sowing, reaping, milling, and God help me, it means a lot of unseen sweat, shed in lonely fields. Preparing bread is the hardest work I have ever done.

Preacher, if your folks are going to church mostly for the cake, then you're a lazy slob and a disgrace to your baker race. You're a Betty Crocker crook, serving up sugary rubbish that isn't even your own and frankly, you needs must get out of the kitchen. Friend, if you are a member of a congregation and all you are going to church for is some of that gooey cake, then eventually, your teeth are going to fall out, and your paunch will grow lopping belt fat, and cover any reproductive organs you might have had. You'll die of spiritual diabetes.

Preachers need to work and the vast majority of that work must take place in the study and be well practiced in front of the solitary mirror. Pastor, your people need bread and it is your job to prepare it for them. It is only silly queens that cry, "Let them eat cake!" Remember that. Selah.

Listen: *"In the sweat of your face you shall eat bread." (Genesis 3:19 NKJV)*

Pray: Lord, we pray for our bakers, that they would rise early to their tasks, labor long on their production, and serve us well with the bread from heaven. Lord send us workers and not shirkers, we Your hungry people pray, amen.

Night-Whisper | **OBEY**

The newer colossus of true love amidst a lost liberty

Today in 1885, the Statue of Liberty, that most famous gift from France to the USA, arrived in New York harbor onboard the French frigate, Isere. It was Poet Emma Lazarus, a forerunner of Zionism who also argued for the creation of a Jewish homeland, who, in an aid to raising money for the pedestal that the statue would rise upon, wrote the sonnet, "The New Colossus." This same poem, which in 1903 was placed on a bronze tablet to the interior wall of the pedestal, intertwined itself with the spirit of Lady Liberty and has been united to her ever since. It reads,

Deuteronomy 28:15 & 43

"But it shall come to pass, if you do not obey the voice of the Lord your God, to observe carefully all His commandments and His statutes which I command you today, that all these curses will come upon you and overtake you. The alien who is among you shall rise higher and higher above you, and you shall come down lower and lower. He shall lend to you, but you shall not lend to him; he shall be the head, and you shall be the tail."
NKJV

> *Not like the brazen giant of Greek fame, With conquering limbs astride from land to land; Here at our sea-washed, sunset gates shall stand A mighty woman with a torch, whose flame is the imprisoned lightning, and her name Mother of Exiles. From her beacon-hand glows world-wide welcome; her mild eyes command the air-bridged harbor that twin cities frame. "Keep, ancient lands, your storied pomp!" cries she with silent lips. "Give me your tired, your poor, your huddled masses yearning to breathe free, the wretched refuse of your teeming shore. Send these, the homeless, tempest-tossed to me, I lift my lamp beside the golden door!"*

And so she did. Yet not today.

The high idealism and the melting pot phenomenon that was the United States is now bubbling hot and boiling over. Britain is no different, for we, the center of the Commonwealth opened our doors long since this day I write and most recently, Europe, gripped with Berlin Wall falling fever, has dropped its borders and like a half cut drunken cook, has taken the frying pan by the handle and shaken the five bean chili into one obnoxious mess. It is not economics, color or race that ferments our countries stewing conflict, but rather, the clash of cultures and their deep religious roots, for a man's belief system shapes everything he touches, from artefacts to architecture, from politics to paintings and from recipes to relationships, yes, even from table top to tongue! When the inviting culture is swamped and swallowed up, when the cuckoo in the nest becomes the reigning king, then it will always kill the hatchlings and steel the worm from the mother's mouth.

> *When the inviting culture is swamped and swallowed up, when the cuckoo in the nest becomes the reigning king, then it will always kill the hatchlings and steel the worm from the mother's mouth.*

I wonder if the principles drawn from the nation poisoning spittle, of the great cursing's of mount Ebal, might be applied to Britain, Europe and North America today. Have we been grossly disobedient to His known commandments and statutes, failing to serve Him with joy, gladness and thankfulness of heart, for our once golden doors of hope, have most obviously now become the broken gates of multi-cultural invasion.

It is not only the rising recruitment of hate crime officers to hundreds of hate crime units around the country that makes the future look bleak for us Bible believing Christians, but in 2008, respected statistical projections for church attendees in Britain in just 40 years' time is less than 900,000 people. Attendees that is not born again Christians but overall attendees! Unless God visits us with true conviction of sin and real conversion to Christ the King, then I wonder if everything else that is going on in the church at present, will be considered by the future remnant to be nothing but a circus sideshow, a silly distraction and even the deception of a dancing devil. I wonder. The church is dying.

For my brethren in Britain, I must inform you that now is the time to decide how you will live in not only a Post-Christian country but also an ever-increasing anti-Christian one. Concerning the nation and our church, all our gates are broken down. We are over-run, swamped, swallowed, pitiful, poor blind and naked. The church of the living God refuses to remove its sphincter shrouded head from its own seemingly safe intestines and have its eyes washed out with eye salve. This 'rectum oblivion,' is nothing short of demonic. Our leaders have nothing to offer but tickets for seats at a three ring circus where howling Christians buzz like fat flies, all lying on their backs whilst kicking their legs in the air and the invitation to the ever diminishing youth of our increasingly small church nation is to form band and make an MP3. Our foundations are fractured beyond repair. Our family silver I almost spent. The church as we know it will fail and fall and a complete rebuild will be required. Tell me, what part will you have in that?

Make no mistake about it, the church of Jesus Christ can no longer maintain its ministers and modern state and structures. It will contract and collapse. Have you thought about this? Have you considered this? Have you asked God what you must do in the coming rebuild? Prayer, proclamation, and the practice of sacrificial love must become once again the concrete base for the starry pedestal upon which we heavenly Zionists, erect the statue of true liberty, "Jerusalem above," which is free! Maybe if we do that, we can rightly say to all those within our broken gates:

> *The church of the living God refuses to remove its sphincter shrouded head from its own seemingly safe intestines and have its eyes washed out with eye salve. This 'rectum oblivion,' is nothing short of demonic.*

"Come all you tired, you pitiful you poor, You huddled and burdened Masses, yearning to breathe free. Come all ye wretched refuse upon this teeming shore, Heaven-less and homeless, tempest-tossed before The gates of hell, See Christ lift His light, before His open, golden door!"

Listen: *"Moreover all these curses shall come upon you and pursue and overtake you, until you are destroyed, because you did not obey the voice of the Lord your God, to keep His commandments and His statutes which He commanded you. And they shall be upon you for a sign and a wonder, and on your descendants forever. 'Because you did not serve the Lord your God with joy and gladness of heart, for the abundance of everything, therefore you shall serve your enemies, whom the Lord will send against you, in hunger, in thirst, in nakedness, and in need of everything; and He will put a yoke of iron on your neck until He has destroyed you.'" Deuteronomy 28:45-49 NKJV*

Pray: Jesus, please wake Your people. Then Lord, help us to love our neighbors in passionate prayer, in truthful proclamation and in powerful practice, in Jesus name we pray, amen.

Night-Whisper | **GOODNESS**

Holy helicopters! Or, slipping the snares of surrounding sorrows

The distress of waves, floods, surrounding sorrows and confronting snares, were, according to the personal biography of David the King in the summary of his own life, the common waters of his dire distress.

2 Samuel 22:5-7

"When the waves of death surrounded me, the floods of ungodliness made me afraid. The sorrows of Sheol surrounded me; the snares of death confronted me. In my distress I called upon the Lord, and cried out to my God; He heard my voice from His temple, and my cry entered His ears." NKJV

In Psalm 18 and the following verses of tonight's text, found just beyond 2 Samuel 22:8, David depicts himself as a man washed out to sea, lost at sea even, isolated, alone, weighed down, with miles of sucking water below and ten thousand miles of empty sea's around him, having nothing to cling to, his cold legs pumped to exhaustion, struggling to keep his neck and nose above the cold and pounding waves which continually raise themselves up, to loom like mountains above his struggling head, always ready to fall upon him with all their pent up fury! Alone and drowning in a vast unfriendly sea, David can do nothing, I mean absolutely nothing but desperately tread water, hold his nostrils above the waves, look to heaven and open his mouth when he can in desperate cries of "God help me please!"

What follows from this simplest and purest of pleading prayers is nothing short of describing a North Sea coastguard helicopter rescue! David says that his "come - save my sorry ass" pleas to God, were heard in the rescue control room of the temple of God and in being heard, salvation was immediately dispatched to rescue him from these same dark consuming waters. David justified his holy helicopter rescue, because of his own clean hands. He was on the right side of God you see, therefore, this is why mercy came a running towards his desperate plea.

There is no better place to be than on the right side of God. Even when the flood of dark waters comes in upon us, it is still a strong and standing side to be found upon, a side of full expectancy. Yes in times of flood, being on the right side of God, is a very good place to be. Surely, if you keep yourself on the right side of God then you can surely always expect a rescue.

In times of flood, being on the right side of God, is a very good place to be.

In all your tomorrows, in conviction, confession, contrition and close communion, do keep on the right side of God, so that when the dark floods come upon you, as they most surely will, then amidst the waters you can call and look with confidence for the holy helicopter of His swift and sure deliverance.

Listen: *"He sent from above, He took me, He drew me out of many waters." 2 Samuel 22:17 NKJV*

Pray: I will love You, O Lord, my strength. The Lord is my rock and my fortress and my deliverer; My God, my strength, in whom I will trust; My shield and the horn of my salvation, my stronghold. I will call upon the Lord, who is worthy to be praised; so shall I be saved from my enemies." Psalms 18:1-3 NKJV

Night-Whisper | **COST**

An open heart, an open house and an open wallet

Nehemiah the Jew, cupbearer to the King of Babylon was on a good ticket. Wily, wealthy, healthy and settled, there was no reason he should be moved from his sumptuous and most prosperous position. Except that he was a practical man, a patriotic man and above all a prayerful man and friends, any spiritual mathematician will tell you, that the product of prayerfulness and practical patriotism, will always produce problems in the heart in which that equation unfolds itself. Go ask Cromwell.

So one day, Nehemiah receives some Jews from Jerusalem, his own home capital city, and hears the lamentable tale of the sorry state that both it and its people are in. The equation starts to unfold, and moved by this Divine and mathematical injunction, Nehemiah has the courage to gain the permission of his earthly potentate, to return home for a time (a well thought out and planned for time by the way) for the sole purpose of restoring the people of God and their capital city, to a place of protection for them, a place of prayer for them and a place of prosperity for them. The personal cost to Nehemiah was substantial. From the superb heights of Babylonian safety, Nehemiah was returning to a blitzed city, a city of broken walls and a city of broken spirits. He was returning under a cloud of suspicion both from his own people and his enemies, even under attack, from his enemies and his own people, yet, he was bringing to their beleaguered table, his wisdom, his

Nehemiah 5:14,15

"From the time King Artaxerxes appointed me as their governor in the land of Judah - from the twentieth to the thirty-second year of his reign, twelve years - neither I nor my brothers used the governor's food allowance. Governors who had preceded me had oppressed the people by taxing them forty shekels of silver (about a pound) a day for food and wine while their underlings bullied the people unmercifully. But out of fear of God I did none of that." (from The Message: by Eugene H. Peterson.)

wiliness and his wealth. It is the latter I wish to talk about this evening. Nehemiah's wealth.

Nehemiah was not backward in coming forward in laying out the personal cost to himself of such a radical restoration and I am glad of it, for be sure, such radical restoration is exceptionally costly. Following Nehemiah's own practicality then, let us do the same and highlight that for twelve years, he did not take what was rightfully his. On the contrary, from his own substantial pockets, he financed and fed a multitude of projects and people. This was not an unplanned, frittering away of personal resources but rather, a well-led example of sacrifice for focused rebuilding. Every penny was both well spent and accounted for. I think that we might consider installing Nehemiah permanently in No11 Downing Street!

> *This was not an unplanned, frittering away of personal resources but rather, a well-led example of sacrifice for the purpose of focused rebuilding.*

The time has come in my own country of Britain to have a purposeful and focused rebuilding of the church of the living God, for all its walls are broken and breached, and for all the talk of fire, the only fire of any effect is that which has burned down all our gates. Indeed, the enemy has their storehouses in our very temple courts and the two assassins of Sanballat and Tobiah, have already unsheathed their swords among us. Today, right now, we need a multitude of Nehemiah's, all consumed with zealously, who shall, at great personal cost, give their lives in the form of their relocation, their leadership, their expertise and most practically and most especially, their wallets. Without them, Jerusalem shall not be built again in this most green and pleasant land. Are you a Nehemiah?

Listen: *"I had work to do; I worked on this wall. All my men were on the job to do the work. We didn't have time to line our own pockets. I fed one hundred and fifty Jews and officials at my table in addition to those who showed up from the surrounding nations. One ox, six choice sheep, and some chickens were prepared for me daily, and every ten days a large supply of wine was delivered. Even so, I didn't use the food allowance provided for the governor - the people had it hard enough as it was. Remember in my favour, O my God, everything I've done for these people." (from Nehemiah 5:16-19, The Message: by Eugene H. Peterson.)*

Pray: Work out Your equations in the hearts of them that can do Jerusalem good O Lord. In Jesus name we ask it, amen.

Night-Whisper | **CONFIDENCE**

The mark of the lion

After an almost complete collapse in the sale of eggs in 1956, the British Egg Marketing Board was set up to promote this most natural of food sources by purchasing all the eggs produced in the UK, grading them to a national standard and then stamping them with a Lion Logo as a testimony to that high quality which would be seen by the customer, and communicate to them, that this egg was safe, that this egg was disease free, that this egg was even above the expected legal standards! Yes, this egg was approved!

1 Thessalonians 2:4

"But as we have been approved by God to be entrusted with the Gospel, even so we speak, not as pleasing men, but God who tests our hearts." NKJV

In our text for tonight, Paul says that he and his team are lion stamped approved eggs. The face of their sky has been seen and discerned, yes, even like five new oxen; they have been yoked and driven, pushed and pulled, and found to still plough a straight line! They have been thoroughly examined under the grading microscope of God and being found free of falseness, free of disease and free of self-seeking guile, have thus been retained in His service as an excellent product. Indeed, after His preparation of them, God so believed in them, that He entrusted the Gospel to them.

In God's economy, before any apostolic entrusting, there comes a trying, a testing, a grading and a stamping. Much of what we see today (and it's not new) of those people who count themselves as apostles, as folk entrusted with special knowledge, even Divine favor, fire, gifts and new spiritual insight, are nothing short of rotten eggs! They are not graded, and upon examination bear no mark of the Lion they say they represent, but rather, they bear the odor of a deceptive and pocket lining guile.

God's school colors are black and blue, look for those colors. God graduates don't give two hoots for the favor of men and the backing of other great names. Look for that. All of God's approved men bear the mark of being with the Lion, so, look for the claw marks, the punctured flesh, especially around the back of the neck, the limp, indeed, look for any evidence of the heavenly damage if you will. Finally, and this is important, all of God's approved men have been taught by heaven just how to roar. Listen for that roar in their powerful proclamation.

> *Finally, and this is important, all of God's approved men have been taught by heaven just how to roar. Listen for that roar in their powerful proclamation.*

Meanwhile, if you come across any egg not bearing the stamp of the Lion, avoid it like the plague! For in the end it will be found tasteless, yokeless, smelly and poisonous, even pungent with Sulphur. These are dark days therefore watch out for yourselves.

Listen: *"We never used words to butter you up. No one knows that better than you. And God knows we never used words as a smoke screen to take advantage of you. Even though we had some standing as Christ's apostles, we never threw our weight around or tried to come across as important, with you or anyone else. We weren't aloof with you. We took you just as you were. We were never patronising, never condescending, but we cared for you the way a mother cares for her children. We loved you dearly. Not content to just pass on the Message, we wanted to give you our hearts. And we did. You remember us in those days, friends, working our fingers to the bone, up half the night, moonlighting so you wouldn't have the burden of supporting us while we proclaimed God's Message to you. You saw with your own eyes how discreet and courteous we were among you, with keen sensitivity to you as fellow believers. And God knows we weren't freeloaders! You experienced it all firsthand. With each of you we were like a father with his child, holding your hand, whispering encouragement, showing you step-by-step how to live well before God, who called us into his own kingdom, into this delightful life."*
(1 Thessalonians 2:5-12 - from The Message: by Eugene H. Peterson.)

Pray: Lord, give me a nose for bad eggs, even before they are cracked open. Lord, help me to discern the mark of the Lion on those You have approved and entrusted with Your good news. In Jesus name I pray, amen.

Night-Whisper | **DANGER**

Dealing with the seven dwarfs of a much diminished Christianity

In present day Christianity dwarfism in on the rise. Like some Disneyland Mickey Mouse theme park ride, the Seven Dwarfs of "desperate, dopy, dumb, duped, deceived, demonized and destroyed" are roaming the world selling the largest silver foiled covered roast turkey legs you can imagine and can you believe it, the whole world of Christianity is seemingly buying their airplane tickets, putting on their big ole' mouse ears and silly sad tiaras and lining up like lemons to have their pips squeaked and a few more drops squeezed from their wallets. Even the elect!

Matthew 24:23-25

"Then if anyone says to you, 'Look, here is the Christ!' or 'There!' do not believe it. For false christs and false prophets will rise and show great signs and wonders to deceive, if possible, even the elect. See, I have told you beforehand." NKJV

If you are being sucked into the sad money factory, if these seven dwarves are pulling you down to their level, if their fatheaded big mouths have infected you with this curse of dreadful dwarfism, then may I recommend a course of antibiotics for you tonight? Yes? Well, here they are: Take some time, just a long weekend maybe, grab some popcorn, plug in the DVD player and let 'er rip. Make sure you have some extra rolls of toilet tissue available though, cause this stuff I'm giving you will purge you, and great will be the cleansing thereof. Here we go then.

On Friday, settle down and open up Ian Murray's most marvelous book, *Revival and Revivalism, The Making and Marring of American Evangelicism 1750-1858*. In my opinion, there is no greater book to lay some concrete foundations in your mind and heart for what we have seen birthed on the American Scene and exported abroad. This should take you until lunchtime Saturday. Now, take the rest of the afternoon and the night to plough through the following films:

The Night of The Hunter, starring Robert Mitchum.

Elmer Gantry, starring Burt Lancaster.

Marjo, starring Marjo Gortner

Leap of Faith, starring Steve Martin.

Now on Sunday, get thee hence to a good church. Somewhere that has a good welcome, good worship and a good word. I don't mean a talk either, I don't mean a twenty-minute recruitment infomercial, I mean a message from a man that takes his time to unpack the Word of God before you in both fear and trembling. A man of Godly hesitation, a man who has one foot on the balances of judgement and another in the fire of hell! A chef of extraordinary care who knows he's pulled some fugu fish from the Sea of Galilee and you are there to eat his prepared delicacy. It tastes good doesn't it? You want more don't you? It's interesting that good preaching will either have your tongue hanging out for more, or have you up on your feet with your fingers stuck deep into your ears begging him to stop the serving of such hot and steamy, illuminating Linguini!

> *A man of Godly hesitation, a man who has one foot on the balances of judgement and another in the fire of hell!*

I tell you, this short, long weekend course of antibiotics will stop your dwarfism in its tracks. However, such a cathartic release will have messed up your spiritual GI tract like never before. Don't worry though, because this will pass. Rest up; grab some good audio sermons from Dr. J Vernon McGee, AW Tozer, Paris Reidhead, Leonard Ravenhill, and indeed, anyone else whose knees audibly knock together when they preach. Do this and thou shalt recover? Oh and may I challenge you good folks affected by such dwarfism to do just one more hard thing tonight? Brace yourselves now, for here it is: "More than anything guys, please just grow up!"

(PS: No actual dwarfs were harmed in the constructing of this message, though many of you have been. For the better.)

Listen: *"But there were also lying prophets among the people then, just as there will be lying religious teachers among you. They'll smuggle in destructive divisions, pitting you against each other - biting the hand of the One who gave them a chance to have their lives back! They've put* *themselves on a fast downhill slide to destruction, 2 but not before they recruit a crowd of mixed-up followers who can't tell right from wrong. They give the way of truth a bad name." (2 Peter 2:1-3 from The Message: by Eugene H. Peterson. All rights reserved.)*

Pray: Lord, help us not to believe everything we hear, but carefully weigh and examine what people tell us. Help us to quickly spot those lying preachers let loose in the world, in Jesus name we pray, amen.

Night-Whisper | **PREPARE**

Chiseled

I've always wanted to be chiseled. You know, tough, muscular, sculptured, less than five percent body fat, a lean mean fighting machine. However, spending most of my time seated, bent over and bashing at the keys, has meant that the plastic bits holding my six-pack together, burst open a long time ago and I now have a small keg instead. Chiseled indeed! Ha! The older I get, the more I resemble Winnie the Pooh and no doubt, I shall probably end up eventually smelling like him as well.

1 Kings 6:7

"And the temple, when it was being built, was built with stone finished at the quarry, so that no hammer or chisel or any iron tool was heard in the temple while it was being built." NKJV

This body of mine seems to take up an increasing amount of time with respect to daily maintenance and the more I care about it, the less my God seems to, for the terrible Kray twins of time and gravity, are slowly taking over all parts of my parish and their demands for protection money increase with every year.

Today, Spurgeon wonderfully comments on our text for tonight by saying,

As in the building of Solomon's temple, "there was neither hammer, nor axe, nor any tool of iron, heard in the house," because all was brought perfectly ready for the exact spot it was to occupy - so is it with the temple which Jesus builds; the making ready is all done on earth. When we reach heaven, there will be no sanctifying us there, no squaring us with affliction, no planning us with suffering. No, we must be made meet here - all that Christ will do beforehand; and when He has done it, we shall be ferried by a loving hand across the stream of death, and brought to the heavenly Jerusalem, to abide as eternal pillars in the temple of our Lord.

"Beneath His eye and care,
The edifice shall rise,

Majestic, strong, and fair,
And shine above the skies."

How wonderful. Friends, God want us be chiseled saints as well but in a way, which is completely contrary to our desires. God is not dealing with the Kray twins today. The gangsters are not yet locked up but rather, roam all our towns terrorizing and slashing, ever threatening and always following through. Now listen, for God's love for us means that sometimes He takes care of our bodies in the healing of them. Yes, sometimes He answers our many, our oh so many prayers, for healing with a "Let it be so!" However, most of the time, He doesn't! No, most of the time, He seems to disdain our present distress, He seems to, most of the time, never even turn His face toward our broken down bodies. We answer this seeming offensive disdain with conclusions such as, "lack of faith," "out of season," "lack of gifting," "lack of anointing," "unbelief," and so on and so forth. Sometimes, some of these conclusions may be applicable but most of the time, most of the time I say, the Master Mason never even raises His eyes, nor turns His head towards the physical brokenness we bring to Him.

> *God's love for us means that sometimes He takes care of our bodies in the healing of them. Yes, sometimes He answers our many, our oh so many prayers, for healing with a "Let it be so!" However, most of the time, He doesn't!*

In terms of priorities, may I suggest to you that these failing edifices of ours, these flesh covered tents, all falling to pieces before our very eyes, are presently some way down His bride's "honeydo" list. Yet, despite our ailments and even because of them, every day, God chisels away at us, forming our hearts, molding our spirits, expanding our souls, and making us ready for the everlasting Kingdom, which all creation groans for to be revealed. I wonder if this present work of chiseling sanctification is so thorough, so precise, so exacting, that the Master Mason refuses to be distracted from His work in progress, His Masterpiece which is you! It's not that he does not care about. He just has more important things to do with you.

No doubt, like me, you shall still pester Him to come and fix a lesser work, to come and patch up a failing form and sometimes, because he loves us, He shall do this. However, most of the time, He evidently doesn't and this is because He is involved in a far greater work in this quarry of His world.

This present and walking ruin of our bodies is unfit to house His Masterpiece. To that end then, He has prepared for us a new body, a resurrected one, a chiseled Masterpiece to beautifully house His present preparation. By all means then, pray for healing. Above all though, be patient and have faith that all the pain has purpose. Have faith in this my friends, and with the help of the Holy Spirit, turn your pain to hope.

Listen: *"Therefore, leaving the discussion of the elementary principles of Christ, let us go on to perfection, not laying again the foundation of repentance from dead works and of faith toward God, of the doctrine of baptisms, of laying on of hands, of resurrection of the dead, and of eternal judgment. And this we will do if God permits." Hebrews 6:1-3 NKJV*

Pray: I believe in God, the Father Almighty, the Creator of heaven and earth, and in Jesus Christ, His only Son, our Lord: Who was conceived of the Holy Spirit, born of the Virgin Mary, suffered under Pontius Pilate, was crucified, died, and was buried. He descended into hell. The third day He arose again from the dead. He ascended into heaven and sits at the right hand of God the Father Almighty, whence He shall come to judge the living and the dead. I believe in the Holy Spirit, the holy Catholic Church, the communion of saints, the forgiveness of sins, the resurrection of the body, and life everlasting. Amen. (The Apostles Creed)

Night-Whisper | **RESCUE**

Removing the leper's squint

The Parish church of St Peter's, in the small village of Twineham sits nested amongst the green trees of England, not far from the base of the South Downs of East Sussex. The first incumbent Rector is listed in the 13th Century and the stone font dates to that same period. Apart from the overgrown area of the graveyard rented by non-conformist Quakers for a peppercorn rent of a few pennies and the last of the wooden bedstead headboards, used as a grave marker instead of a stone, (a practice apparently only seen in Sussex) out of all the other fascinating features of this church I found two holes in the walls of the church to be the most intriguing artefacts of them all. The churchwarden showing me around told me that at these points, and through these holes, the local lepers would receive the Eucharist and on occasion, through grated bars would be allowed to watch the priestly practice of the Mass.

For medieval man, the Latin incanted magic of the Eucharist, performed by well-robed priests, was a mystery not to be missed! Indeed, magic coupled with superstition was so rife in those days that even the 13th century font, still standing tall and cold at St Peter's Twineham still bore the marks of having a lock put on the lid, to stop the "Holy Water" being stolen for use in rites of local witchcraft! Even so, with all these passing pictures of lives long gone, yet still set and seen in wood and stone, it is the image of a gnarled and excluded, dirty and stinking

Luke 5:12-15

"One day in one of the villages there was a man covered with leprosy. When he saw Jesus he fell down before him in prayer and said, 'If you want to, you can cleanse me.' Jesus put out his hand, touched him, and said, 'I want to. Be clean.' Then and there his skin was smooth, the leprosy gone. Jesus instructed him, 'Don't talk about this all over town. Just quietly present your healed self to the priest, along with the offering ordered by Moses. Your cleansed and obedient life, not your words, will bear witness to what I have done.'" (The Message: by Eugene H. Peterson.)

leper, standing outside in the cold and the wet, stealing a squint at the magic through and oblique angled holes in the wall and receiving the Eucharist of life through the same, which sticks with me most this night. This small hole in the wall, this only place of access to the unwanted, is known as a "leper's squint."

> *This small hole in the wall, this only place of access to the unwanted, is known as a "leper's squint."*

Some folks, famous sinners all, gangsters, gang leaders, drug dealers, football players, boxers, pop stars and politicians, when they "come through for Christ" (what an odious and self-exalting phrase) are placed by us on pedestals for the entire world to see. Indeed, we put these redeemed and famous sinners up there for all the world to see and then shout out to all the gazing, awestruck Christians, "Come see this stinking sinner, now washed, made whole, made free! Free that is, apart from his CD, DVD, book and biography, all of which are yours for just $14.99, on sale in the lobby after he's sung and we've taken up a love offering." Yup, we love them famous sinners, coming through for Christ! Yup, get 'em in, get 'em up and get 'em on the circuit of sinners since redeemed. Yes, put them up the for all the world to see, for isn't Jesus most powerful and magnificent, to save such a famous wretch as thee?

I say this mockingly tonight for the sole purpose of contrast, for it is only this dark contrast that will allow us to see the white and staring eyes of all the leper's peering through our squints. Yes, I am afraid to say that in our churches of today, we still have a multitude of squinting lepers. Who are they? Why are they there? How did we allow this to happen?

These folks, this most leprous lot are the once forgiven people who have fallen whilst in harness. Their sin, whatever it was, has become to the Christian community, dastardly inexcusable, abuse-able and totally unusable to the "once saved and serving, never dare put one foot wrong again" kind of Gospel we conservatives have been preaching. These modern day lepers are growing in number and surely are some of the saddest folks I have ever seen. They have become to us, ugly, odorous, shunned, separated, excluded, never to be trusted, shut up, cast out in the cold and wet, to be left peering at the magic through a leper's squint. Moreover, good riddance to them as well, because they let me down, they let our side down, and beyond all of that, they cast a shadow on the keeping power of Christ. Yes, above all, in their bad decision, they moved Christ from being the most desirous in their life, to being the least desirous of all! That's what we hate the most, the fact that their sin, their deceitful sin, has cast doubt on the efficacy of the message we proclaim and for Christ to keep us, as well as casting a most terrible light on the some of the same snakes of doubt and ungodly desires, slithering around in the dark of our own dear lives. Think about that. Be honest with yourselves.

Let us remember tonight though, that the greatest story of redemption left to us by our Lord Jesus Christ, is not of a famous stranger finally "coming through to Jesus," and still making a few bob on the side, but rather of a profligate, a prodigal, a known but long lost son finally coming home! Yes, the greatest story of redemption is of a son finally coming home and still ripe with the smell of pig shit on him and when that happened, yes, when the longed for family member finally returned, he wasn't stepped down, he wasn't dressed down, he wasn't hosed down, and he wasn't made to go out in the cold and peer at the magic he once so loved through a cold, low, leper's squint. No, rather was clothed upon, ringed up, taken in, embraced and given a party hoe down. It's shocking isn't it? I reckon Jesus intended it to be so, for grace is nothing short of being just that, absolutely shocking! Especially to returning sons who have messed up.

> *The greatest story of redemption left to us by our Lord Jesus Christ, is not of a famous stranger finally "coming through to Jesus," and still making a few bob on the side, but rather of a profligate, a prodigal, a known but long lost son finally coming home!*

It's going to be very tough, yet until we get rid of every lepers squint, and welcome home the wounded and stinking prodigals, our communities, though quite respectable, shall never truly bear, the Maker's mark of grace.

Listen: *"Don't pick on people, jump on their failures, criticise their faults - unless, of course, you want the same treatment. That critical spirit has a way of boomeranging. It's easy to see a smudge on your neighbour's face and be oblivious to the ugly sneer on your own. Do you have the nerve to say, 'Let me wash your face for you,' when your own face is distorted by contempt? It's this whole travelling road-show mentality all over again, playing a holier-than-thou part instead of just living your part. Wipe that ugly sneer off your own face, and you might be fit to offer a washcloth to your neighbour." (Matthew 7:1-5 The Message by Eugene H. Peterson.)*

Pray: Lord, Surely, every sin against You by a redeemed child is a spit in Your face, and a rape of Your grace. I have to tell Lord that I feel really let down by those former leades who have messed up, they should have known better. But Lord, we should have known better as well. Yet upn his return to you, I remember You said to St Peter, that cursing and cowardly denier, "Feed my lambs." We are sorry for our sins O Lord and the sins of our leaders. Now then, will You release the rapists of Your grace and restore us all the cursing St Peter's by re commissioning again those You have most astonishingly redeemed, that they might to speak once more of Your most outrageous grace. Amen and let it be so.

Night-Whisper | **CONSIDER**

Sticking around to taste the vintage

The age of a bottle of wine has an important bearing on its character, that is, its taste, its color and its bouquet, all of which in turn I find manifest their impact on my tongue in terms of beauty, balance and my bank account! I say my bank account because I have tasted older and sweeter wines that have cost enormous amounts of money, and frankly, they don't taste as good as some much cheaper varieties. This is not only a subjective observation but also a proved and objective reality. Material cost, does not make an older wine taste better, no it is much, much more than age, which goes into making a great vintage wine.

Song of Solomon 4:10

"How fair is your love, my sister, my spouse! How much better than wine is your love, and the scent of your perfumes than all spices!" NKJV

Not all wines of course improve with age, only a comparatively few wines seem to have the capacity to morph into a mature flavor whilst maintaining an inner, tip of the tongue, dancing vigor. You can't always tell which wines these will be but providing the harvest was good, it is the combination of time, temperature and the right kind of environmental tools which will allow the Master winemaker the opportunity to soften any harsh wine characteristic into something, smooth, something soft and something velvet on the tongue. To taste it though, listen now, to taste it and enjoy it, you really have to stick around.

You need to know tonight that I do not know a great deal about wine, however, I do know a little about people. In this gained and increasing knowledge which I have accrued over the years, I have observed that when a man has finally begun to drink of a great bottle of wine, then his face bears a subtle and shining, well-oiled gladness and that all in his life and all in his limbs seem to bounce, with re-sprung sinew-ed strength. I tell you, if you're sure of the roots, sure of the fruits and sure of the sunshine of God's grace, then it's well worth sticking around to see God finally uncork His vintage!

I wonder if the Scriptures might suggest that there is nothing better for a bitter old man than some sweet decanter full, of rich red, vintage wine. Let me speak clearly here this night. Stick with your spouse, for if the Master winemaker has His way, the best is yet to come.

Listen: *"Give strong drink to him who is perishing, and wine to those who are bitter of heart." Proverbs 31:6 NKJV*

"And wine that maketh glad the heart of man, and oil to make his face to shine, and bread which strengtheneth man's heart." Psalms 104:15 KJV.

Pray: Lord, if there is one thing needed in our life, it is the removal of stupidity and the infusion of stickability. Give us faith, courage and tenacity today and in all the years to come, to stick around and taste the uncorked vintage. In Jesus name we pray, amen.

Night-Whisper | **HOPE**

Dealing with "Die Falscher"

Former award winning *Times* correspondent, Lawrence Malkin, brought out a book in 2006 called *Krueger's Men,* the true story of Operation Bernhard. Very quickly, the book was turned into a compelling film that competed at the Berlin Film Festival in 2007. The film was called *Die Falsher* or, *The Counterfeiters*.

3 John 4

"I have no greater joy than to hear that my children walk in truth."
NKJV

Major Bernhard Krueger, a conspicuously correct SS engineer, ran a production line of Jewish prisoners in Sachsenhausen concentration camp near Berlin. Operation Bernhard was named after him and the intent of the Nazi operation was to destabilize the British economy by flooding the country with counterfeit Bank of England, £5, £10, £20, and £50 notes! From 1942 to 1945, the Nazi's forged more pound notes than all the reserves in the vaults of the Bank of England, some 132 million pounds equivalent in 2015 to over £3.5 billion! The plan was that the German air force would drop the money over Britain but in the end, it was used to finance the failing war machine, pay off many of its spies, bail out its fleeing war criminals and finance their flight to other countries. Much of it eventually ended up in the bottom of Lake Toplitz but Malkin also suggests that some of it was used by the Israeli underground to finance the founding of Israel in terms of its military, its infrastructure and the return of the Jewish Diaspora.

Despite the German air force being almost destroyed and therefore not being able to drop the counterfeit notes over Britain, the use of them abroad by the Nazis was rife and rampant, so much so, that the Bank of England and Britain, in order to prevent the counterfeits from infecting the economy, imposed a wartime blockade on bringing notes of £5 and above, into the country! There is of course a methodology of attack here and also a principle of protection for us to take note of.

I hope the method of spiritual attack is clear. If you want to disrupt and destroy a spiritual economy then flood the market with counterfeits, fraudulent goods of such high copycat quality, that they themselves even believe they are the "real deal." This has always happened, this is happening today and I believe, will happen all the more as we approach the end of days.

> *If you want to disrupt and destroy a spiritual economy then flood the market with counterfeits, fraudulent goods of such high copycat quality, that they themselves even believe they are the "real deal."*

There is little you can do to stop such a greedy and lying counterfeit invasion, save to thoroughly examine the source and quality of the goods on offer. This can only be done by blockading the export of such spiritual destructive weevils and discouraging the importing of the same. Please! Don't go bringing that destructive counterfeit rubbish back here!

The church is not a totalitarian regime, neither is it a government agency with emergency powers to block and to quarantine! However, the leaders of the church do have the authority, do have the necessity, do have the holy duty even, to both exclude and examine any teaching from the pulpit, which might destroy the general economy of the local church, which is fed and nourished, guided and directed through the preached Word. The pulpit needs to be protected and saved from such insidious and fatal infections.

Let's not be deceived. The devil is out to destroy our spiritual economy. So far, he's doing a damn good job of it as well. Leaders! You must rise up and protect the pulpit before it is all too late.

Listen: *"But there were also lying prophets among the people then, just as there will be lying religious teachers among you. They'll smuggle in destructive divisions, pitting you against each other - biting the hand of the One who gave them a chance to have their lives back! They've put themselves on a fast downhill slide to destruction, but not before they recruit a crowd of mixed-up followers who can't tell right from wrong. They give the way of truth a bad name. They're only out for themselves. They'll say anything, anything, that sounds good to exploit you. They won't, of course, get by with it. They'll come to a bad end, for God has never just stood by and let that kind of thing go on. God didn't let the* *rebel angels off the hook, but jailed them in hell till Judgement Day." (2 Peter 2:1-5 from The Message by Eugene H. Peterson)*

Pray: Lord, help us be aware of all the tactics of total war and then let us be astute and wise in dealing with Die Fascher, in Jesus name we ask it, amen!

Night-Whisper | **PREPARE**

Jecholia of Jerusalem

The ancient patronymic naming system of Welsh offspring eventually led to a good number of people all bearing the same name and all living in the same locale, though being totally unrelated by blood! In an aid to distinguish one another, they were later identified by both their name and their occupation. So, Dai the local train driver might have been called, "Dai the Steam," where as his neighbor the undertaker might have been called "Dai the Box" the baker, "Dai the Bread," and so on and so forth. We can surmise from our text tonight that Jecholia was a common name, and persons were distinguished not so much by their occupation but by their locale. Enter stage left then, "Jecholia of Jerusalem."

2 Kings 15:1, 2

"In the twenty-seventh year of Jeroboam king of Israel, Azariah the son of Amaziah, king of Judah, became king. He was sixteen years old when he became king, and he reigned fifty-two years in Jerusalem. His mother's name was Jecholiah of Jerusalem." NKJV

The Bible says very little about this woman, indeed she is only mentioned because of her relation to her most famous husband and her even more famous son. However, I would suggest that her name bears the marks of Royalty and I wonder if it reflected both her demeanor, destiny and her progeny? After all, surely to be called "Jecholia of Jerusalem" was a great honor, for you are named not only after the city of the great King, but your name means the "power and perfection of the Lord!" Now how would you like a name like that to live up to?

Jecholia of Jerusalem survived her husband and was a great mother to the young King Uzziah. Some have suggested that Uzziah may not have been the first born of Amaziah, yet the people took him and made him King. If this is the case, then Jecholia of Jerusalem had groomed him good, for this King ruled well for 52 years and no doubt the prayers and advice of Jecholia of Jerusalem were always available to him. Therefore,

Uzziah, son of Jecholia of Jerusalem, pupil of Zechariah, had his guided prosperity walk hand in hand with his personal piety and all were truly blessed. Uzziah became a great general, a wow of a warrior, a fantastic farmer, a brilliant builder, a fellow of great fortifications and of even greater fame! In the end, it seemed nothing could be greater; nothing could be higher, than the maybe rippling muscled torso and square-jawed highly successful King Uzziah.

Now I wonder, and that's all it is, I wonder if before the great smiting of this great king, that Jecholia of Jerusalem had died? I don't know at all, but I wouldn't be surprised, for behind every great man, not only is there a surprised woman, but usually a loving one, a long suffering one and a praying one, and oh my friends, when a prayer warrior of love departs the field of grace, it can be a most precarious time indeed, for those who have previously trod on serpents, were able to do so because those serpents had previously been substantially subdued by prayer. Oh! How I long for the persistent prayer of old ladies that can move mountains over a cup of tea.

> *When a prayer warrior of love departs the field of grace, it can be a most precarious time indeed, for those who have previously trod on serpents, were able to do so because those serpents had previously been substantially subdued by prayer.*

In any event, Uzziah got a big head. It would appear there was no one left around, with the loving authority to give him the slap he needed. So, he sinned against the Lord by entering the sanctuary of the His Holy Temple and personally burning incense on the incense altar. Azariah, the high priest, went in after him with eighty other priests of the Lord, all brave men, confronted Uzziah saying, *"It is not for you, Uzziah, to burn incense to the Lord. That is the work of the priests alone, the descendants of Aaron who are set apart for this work. Get out of the sanctuary, for you have sinned. The Lord God will not honor you for this!"* However, Uzziah, who was holding an incense burner, became furious! Moreover, as he was standing there raging at the priests, leprosy, like a raging flesh eating acne, suddenly broke out on his forehead. When Azariah the high priest and all the other priests saw the leprosy, they rushed Uzziah out of the temple. As you can imagine, Uzziah himself was eager to get out as well because the Lord had slapped him. Yup, the Lord had slapped him bad. So, King Uzziah ended up with leprosy until the day he died, living in isolation, excluded from the temple, dying alone and even being buried not with his ancestors, but adjacent to them in a field nearby.

I wonder if the prayers and advice of Jecholia of Jerusalem brought him to the throne, sustained him there and prospered him there as well? I wonder if she gave him a good slap now and again? I wonder if her absence, her lack or prayers and loving slapping, led to the swelling of his head and the subsequent blindness of his eyes and the poisoning of his heart. I wonder.

To all the Jecholias' of Jerusalem I say "Live up to your name and keep praying for your sons." Oh, and while you are praying for them, please remember me.

Listen: *"Pride goes before destruction, and a haughty spirit before a fall." Proverbs 16:18 NKJV*

Pray: Lord, fill our lives with Jecholia's! In Jesus name we pray, amen and let it be so.

Night-Whisper | **DANGER**

The pantomimic caricatures of the wonderful word of God

The Scriptures are very clear concerning the blind stupidity of men, especially when it comes to the desire for sex. Our text for tonight is couched in the context of a warning against the results of adultery. The wise sayings of the book of Proverbs, touch on this particular subject not a few times and paint in words that can only be described as a clear but metaphorical caricature, the whole process of dissatisfaction, illicit desire, enticement, fulfilment, change, realization, loss and regret, in full color and panoramic pantomimic proportion! Yes, the warning passages against adultery call the reader into the participation of active warning, into joining in with the shouting and cheering, weeping and wailing, booing and hissing against the presented characters. Let's have a quick look at these pantomimic caricatures.

Proverbs 6:22

"When you roam, they will lead you; when you sleep, they will keep you; and when you awake, they will speak with you." NKJV

The wife. Quiet, tired, little, even a little worn, a little worn out even. Busy with kids, managing the household, her brow marked by time and worry, her thighs and belly stretch marked by their offspring. What she wants most at night is sleep. However, she has to stay up sewing.

The seductress. Buxom, beautiful, a honey red lipped pouting smooth operator, a lady of the red cord district, sashaying her "come up and see me sometime" invitation everywhere she goes. Exciting, inviting, and caressing you with her eyes, undressing herself before you. What she wants most at night is sex.

The young man or the older husband. "Oddie" like in the display of his hung out tongue and hung out mind. Led by his loins, blinded by his throbbing desire, sucked into the darkness of his fantasies, ready to rock and roll and play roulette with the buxom "lady in red," longing for Las Vegas and the chance to play, forgetting the one great truth, that the house always wins in the end. What he wants most at night is to play and be played upon and he thinks S.T.D. is an abbreviation for 'Standard.' He is an idiot of infinite proportion.

The pantomime with its characters all play themselves out in the book of Proverbs not so much with the action between the sheets but with the reaction of the young man or the older husband when they eventually wake from their stupor, thirsty, naked, tied to a cactus in the desert, with no credit left on their plastic and no way home.

The warnings are pantomimic in proportion; because God paints them in the largest of letters that they might be seen over the big boil of blind stupidity that often grows between men's eyes. It needs to be seen and for those that do see it, the book of Proverbs is layered and littered with strips of hazard tape all shouting out one little phrase, "Don't go there stupid!"

The book of Proverbs is layered and littered with strips of hazard tape all shouting out one little phrase, "Don't go there stupid!"

The take home of our text for tonight is that each day, we need to be lead, kept and spoken to. It is the Word of God and His great commandments therein that will do this, and quite specifically, His great commandments delivered to us from the mouth of our mother! The Bible is fantastically brilliant in that it encourages the replacement of the pictures of buxom beauties in the minds of the tempted man, with pictures of his frowning mom! Now, is that hilarious or what?! Yet it is so thoroughly practical. "Guys whenever you're thinking about that kind of stuff," *says* God, "Think about your mother and remember what she told you. Think about her words, listen to her loving scolding's and warnings, feel her slapping hand, right up the side of your head! Hold her words in your heart; let them be a protective amulet hanging round your neck against this destructive power of seduction, for "My son," says your mum, "The product of her seduction and your stupidity is disaster of every kind. Wake up! Run away!"

For sure, we need some straight talking Godly mothers to rise up in our midst to imbibe our kids with Godly instruction, even if it is "right up the side of the head!" Let us buy a ticket tonight and get involved in the pantomime of the book of proverbs. Let us remember our mothers and their warnings and let us mark out our path between the black and yellow, bumblebee warning hazard tape of the pantomimic caricatures of the wonderful word of God.

Listen: *"My son, keep your father's command, and do not forsake the law of your mother. Bind them continually upon your heart; tie them around your neck. When you roam, they will lead you; when you sleep, they will keep you; and when you awake, they will speak with you. For the commandment is a lamp, and the law a light; reproofs of instruction are the way of life, to keep you from the evil woman, from the flattering tongue of a seductress. Do not lust after her beauty in your heart, nor let her allure you with her eyelids. For by means of a harlot a man is reduced to a crust of bread; and an adulteress will prey upon his precious life. Can a man take fire to his bosom, and his clothes not be burned? Can one walk on hot coals, and his feet not be seared? So is he who goes in to his neighbour's wife; whoever touches her shall not be innocent." Proverbs 6:20-29 NKJV*

Pray: Lord, help me to fall in love with Your instruction, yes; help to make the best of friends of correction and to listen to the wise voice of my mother and the strong command of my father that I might be delivered from total ruin. So grant me my own cistern with running water, a well with a bucket, an enraptured fountain, valleys of invitation and the soft-sided hills of a loving wife, in Jesus name I pray, amen!

Night-Whisper | **CONSIDER**

The monosodium glutamate of the mind

Chilean winemaker, Aurelio Montes, actually plays Gregorian chants to his maturing wines! Believing that the "gentle" vibrations improve both the quality and the energy of the wine, Montes has even had a Feng-Shui designed barrel room built in the form of an amphitheater, thus allowing each barrel of wine the optimum, good vibrational exposure! Now I reckon that kind of experimentation does not provide you with best of scientific data to either ratify or deny the practice. However, Montes also teamed up with Professor Adrian North, of Edinburgh's Herriot Watt University, to determine how music effects our taste perception of the wines, which we might imbibe. The results of this scientific testing are fascinating, as the Watt University study found that people rated the change in the taste of their wine by up to 60% depending on the type of music they were listening to! Yes, 60%! Now, apart from the basic fact that retailers can now scientifically suggest and sell music recommendations on their wine bottles, this research also raises the question, as to why music makes wine taste up to 60% better! The answers the scientists give us to this question is a, "cognitive primary theory," where the music sets up the brain to respond to the wine in a much more receptive way by the music somehow turning itself into the mono sodium glutamate of the mind! Fascinating, but so what?

Joel 3:18a

"And it will come to pass in that day that the mountains shall drip with new wine." NKJV

Well, imagine you're driving down the road and the church sign you see is bright, welcoming and inviting. You pull into the parking lot and there is plenty of space to park. Nice! The maybe long walk to the campus, is cancelled and improved upon by the shade covered golf cart, which drives you lazily to the front of the sanctuary and the drop off at the large chandelier filled, smoke glassed entranceway, which is both intriguing and attractive, as are the warm handshakes of the well-dressed greeters. Just lovely, and my oh my, the gentle sounds of the indoor fountain and the crisp smell of fair trade Columbian coffee, or better still, the very overpriced but very cool Starbucks brew, which draws you along tippy toed and by the aroma held nostrils, to the iced donut table, where you can grab a Krispy Kreme and then sit down to peruse the glossy and colorful, tactile and hip, sweet spot of a service order, is just delightful! In the distance, the pleasant sound of worship music, surfs the undulating atmosphere as the electronic countdown display on the triple jumbo-tron, beats the "prepare to have your desires met" drum into a rising and pulsating expectation. To top it all, you have heard that the leaders speaking today, praying today, preaching today, have just returned from the latest tributary of the river from the very throne of God Almighty, and are all blessed up and blasted all to pieces and popping with an anointing power from on high! Hallelujah and Oh my goodness, they've probably, hopefully, brought back the blessing with them, or at least that is what you expect they've done because the local Christian radio station and those famous Christian TV channels, have all been reporting on the "revival" all day, every day, for weeks now. So, when you're finally together with a whole bunch of other expectant folks and the praise band kicks in and the smiling preacher recounts the rumors of revival as fun frolicking facts of the Father's blessing, delivered from streets

it's not long before that cognitive priming trigger is pulled and boom!

of gold, imprinted with the footprints of angelic visitation, well, it's not long before that cognitive priming trigger is pulled and boom! You're on the floor. Boom! You're wallets in the bucket. Boom! You've bowed your heads and closed your eyes! Boom! You've slipped your hand up, slipped out of your seat, slipped down the front, "repeated after me," signed the card, moved from the prospect list, to the 101 discipleship class, and oh my gosh, in the seeming twinkling of an eye, you've gotten saved, gotten sanctified, got set free and got signed up for membership and the club dues of 10% and all of this, I say and all of this, without one hint of conviction of sin and true repentance for a lifetime of sinning against a Holy God and I tell you what, even so, despite all that, the expected and delicious, dew drop dripping wine of pop culture Christianity, tasted better than you ever expected. I mean ever expected!

It's only a theory of course, but I wonder if much of the circus we sometimes witness and expect, even long for and enjoy, is nothing more than the outworking of cognitive priming theory? I mean, wouldn't the results of crowds of disappointed people later leaving the back door of the church in those coming colder months, suggest the use of this monosodium glutamate of the mind? After all, we all know that such a well sprinkled Chinese meal might satisfy you now, but in fact it will only satiate the titillated hunger pangs a wee bit, before in just a short, short time, you're feeling starving hungry again and go looking for a fix of another kind. For the initial meal, consumed in all its tastiness didn't in fact contain one ounce of nutritious value at all, indeed, it was a false meal, an emotional filler, a fat, heart stopping killer of a meal.

> *Indeed, it was a false meal, an emotional filler, a fat, heart stopping killer of a meal.*

It has been my experience, that there is only one thing that can be guaranteed to be authentic and that is, a Word and Spirit convicted heart, confessing its sins of sinning against a Holy and wholly justifiable, very angry God. However, this I am afraid, in our present day, has become as rare as rocking horse poop.

Are all of those Sunday meeting, mega church preparations mentioned in the previous paragraphs, made for the people of God to simply gather together and then via their consumerist ways to inadvertently sin? Are these mega methods of attraction merely mental manipulation maybe? No! They are nice and culturally appropriate things. Yes, they might be even the correct use of right things. However, the enemy, to deceive even the very elect, has used these culturally appropriate and right things, to greatly deceive people! It would appear, in my opinion, that we have been deceived and left childlike, and are not man enough and mature enough to know the difference between the manipulation of the mind and soul, and the deep conviction of the Holy Spirit and the Word of God. Maybe, until we grow up and learn this, the use and so thorough application of this learned and inductive mega methodology will be nothing short of a false Gospel!

Let us allow the river within us, to bubble up and flow out from us. Let us make sure that the Word of Christ dwells in us richly. Let us be filled with the Spirit. Let us pray for a personal Holy Ghost revival and most importantly, let us ask our God to turn His face towards us once more and be merciful to us. For surely, when the plutonium power of the Word and the Spirit are brought together in our praying hands, the sun like spark and effulgent flash of irradiation, will x-ray even the densest of beings, showing them clearly who they are before an Holy and an angry God. Now that's conviction of sin, righteousness and judgement and that's what I call "enmity to the natural man!" Bring it on!

Listen: *"For those who live according to the flesh set their minds on the things of the flesh, but those who live according to the Spirit, the things of the Spirit. For to be carnally minded is death, but to be spiritually minded is life and peace. Because the carnal mind is enmity against God; for it is not subject to the law of God, nor indeed can be. So then, those who are in the flesh cannot please God." Romans 8:5-8 NKJV*

Pray: But we are not in the flesh but in the Spirit! You, the Spirit of God dwells in us and we are alive because of righteousness. Give life then to our bodies, minds, soul and spirit and then lead us as Your children, from bondage bound fear, to open exultation and proclamation of our relationship with You, our dearest and most lovely, most Holy heavenly Father! Holy Spirit, come bear witness with our spirit that we are children of God, and comfort us in all our sufferings and assure us and help us to rightly and abundantly live off and live in, that great inheritance which is in Your Son and our Savior, Jesus Christ the Lord. Amen!

| Vol 01 | Q2 | NW00181 | June 29th |

Night-Whisper | **SEE**

Reflective donkeys

It's true! "A British-based donkey welfare group has started a campaign to put reflective tags on Namibia's donkeys. The idea is to make the animals easier to see at night, and thus to avoid collisions on main roads." Namibia, even at the beginning of the 21st Century has over 150,000 donkeys in its Northern region alone, with each householder owning at least five! The phrase "as common as a Namibian donkey" is obviously well used in the vernacular of North Africa! This makes me giggle profusely!

John 12:14-15

"Then Jesus, when He had found a young donkey, sat on it; as it is written: 'Fear not, daughter of Zion; behold, your King is coming, sitting on a donkey's colt.'"

You see, the problem is that donkeys are and have always been figures of mirth and even figures of dumb stupidity! Certainly, on the south coast of England, being referred to as "a right donkey" is no compliment.

So, here in our text for tonight, the King of Kings rides into His earthly capital on a figure of dumb stupidity. No State coach, no snarling Alexandrian Bucephalus, punching the skies with its strident hooves, nope, just the dope of a donkey quietly carrying the Eternal King of ages. It is a weak and stupid picture and me thinks it is purposefully so, for here the King of Kings comes slowly, steadily, surely, humbly, approachably, easy to be touched, easy to be tagged, and easy to be taken.

I wonder if even today Christian, your King has approached you in the same manner and you have failed to recognize Him, for you expected a right royal, spotless white unnamed steed, to pound its own way across your waiting horizon in purposeful prepared and glorious redemption, charging down your enemies and trampling the devil under foot! Oh, that particular riding magnificence is coming, one day, make no mistake about it, yes and amen, the tattoo thighed Savior is coming to stomp His authority over the heads of the devil and all who follow him but it wasn't today! No, today, Jesus was still riding on donkey and maybe you missed Him because of it?

The truth is, O thought to be forgotten friend, Jesus still rides on donkeys. Think about that and from tomorrow, whenever you smell that damp offensive odor, common to all dismal drudging donkeys who have been ridden hard and put away wet, take a better look at the rider, because Jesus might just be smiling right back on at you. He who has ears to hear, let him hear. Especially if they are long and furry goofy looking ones! Singing: "Hey ho, away we go, donkey riding, donkey riding, hey ho, away we go, riding on a donkey!"

> *He who has ears to hear, let him hear. Especially if they are long and furry goofy looking ones!*

Listen: *"Then the King will say to those on His right hand, 'Come, you blessed of My Father, inherit the kingdom prepared for you from the foundation of the world: for I was hungry and you gave Me food; I was thirsty and you gave Me drink; I was a stranger and you took Me in; I was naked and you clothed Me; I was sick and you visited Me; I was in prison and you came to Me.' Then the righteous will answer Him, saying, 'Lord, when did we see You hungry and feed You, or thirsty and give You drink? When did we see You a stranger and take You in, or naked and clothe You? Or when did we see You sick, or in prison, and come to You?' And the King will answer and say to them, 'Assuredly, I say to you, in as much as you did it to one of the least of these My brethren, you did it to Me.'" Matthew 25:34-40*

Pray: Holy Spirit please do me a favor tomorrow will you? Could you put some reflective tags and number plates on all the donkeys that Jesus shall be riding into my life because the truth is, I am often as a blind as a bat and dumber than a mule. Indeed, give me ears as big as a donkey, that I may hear Your voice. Eee-aww, amen, Hallelujah and goodnight.

Night-Whisper | **INTEGRITY**

Let the juice----loose! Serve it like sushi

I remember performing some poetry for about forty very rough, 'rough sleeping' homeless folks in the city of Brighton. It was surprisingly well received. Afterward a very well spoken, silver-faced, Einstein-like figure came over to me and said, "I just wanted to say how much I appreciated your poetry and especially your delivery. You know of course, that you are following in the footsteps of the great Englishman, Chaucer, who also communicated so well in the vernacular of his day." I was really pleased with this. Sure, he was raving tooting bonkers, but I was really pleased with his comments. So, when I arrived home I immediately shared my grand comparison with the proud bubble burster of my home, my wife, who simply said, "Hmmm, yes, Chaucer. He was crude as well." Typical. What does she know anyways?

Mark 12:37b

"And the common people heard Him gladly."
NKJV

Unfortunately, we have upwardly diminished the power of the Bible in making it palace worthy rather than pavement worthy, making it a book for the studious instead of a book for the sidewalk. The common people heard Jesus gladly and I can guarantee you, He was not received in the majestic language of the King James Version. The common people. They heard Him. They received Him. Gladly! I am not talking about dumbing down here either, but rather about tooling up with the words of the day.

We need to regain some street credibility in the delivery of the Scriptures. Before that happens however, we need to let loose the so long now muzzled, powerful jaws of that Lion of God's word and allow it to roar once more. I wonder if the hidden and diluted Word of God we are peddling from our pulpits now, which over the years we have also so tightly dressed up like a gay and mincing, little white and pink padded poodle-ette, is quite frankly too embarrassed to be taken out doors? For our misuse of it in this way, and that is what the diluting of the Word of

God is, a gross misuse of it, has robbed it of its awesome power and thoroughly embarrassed it. God help us please! For this Word in its undiluted form is the very life giving juice dripped from the leaves of the squeezed out tree of life! So, yes indeed, we need to let the juice loose even if it does cause so many letters to be written by 'disgusted of Tunbridge Wells!' I say again, "Let the juice loose"!

We have so tightly dressed up like a gay and mincing, little white and pink padded poodle-ette, is quite frankly too embarrassed to be taken out doors?

However, before we can let this juice loose once more, I wonder if we need to let loose most of the Christians who read the juicy book and especially those frightened little folk we have sent to seminary dentistry, where they have had their teeth removed and the rough and ready garments of the prophet replaced by a smart and casual respectability. Lord God! (and that's a calling prayer) I hate respectability. With a vengeance! You see, I reckon that nice speaking polite little Christians have done more damage to the Kingdom of God than the devil could ever do.

I have two things to leave with you tonight.

First an equation and frankly, maybe it's just me, but I do find that in my life, that the more righteous I experientially and practically become, the less outwardly, pretentiously respectable I both appear and act. How's your life adding up in terms of middle class, middle England respectability tonight? Are you above all things, nice?

Secondly, that when a clawed and sharp beaked, sharp-eyed hawk even gently glides past the settled nests of the starling colonies, the little birds attack it. Prophet. Jesus street preacher. Watch out for the darling, little starlings for they are not as sweet as you might think and I tell you, they do not want their nice little nest much ruffled, especially if their religion gets in a state. If you are not nice, they will peck you to death.

Even so then and never the less, do remember to drink the Bible in its undiluted form dear friends, yes remember to simply let the juice loose and always preacher, I mean always serve it like sushi. Raw!

Listen: *"Then they secretly induced men to say, "We have heard him speak blasphemous words against Moses and God." Acts 6:11-12 NKJV*

Pray: Deliver us O God, from all the darling, darting starlings and all the 'Disgusted's of Tunbridge Wells', yes deliver us from all the pale pulpit pansies planted in graveyard flower pots and placed neatly in old varnished pulpits, who hate to be disturbed and loathe to disturb others. Don't give us gold fillings O Lord! No, You can keep all that useless rubbish Lord, but rather, please grow us a new set of sharp canines and grant us that deep and guttural, testosterone filled roar of the prophets of old. Lord set the juice loose and give us some "street cred" once again, in Jesus name we ask it, amen and let it be so!

DID YOU REMEMBER?

DON'T FORGET TO ORDER YOUR NEXT QUARTER OF NIGHT WHISPERS.

Check us out more at WWW.NightWhispers.com

Buy at WWW.TheologyShop.com

THE MISSION STATEMENT OF THE 66 BOOKS MINISTRY

WWW.66Books.tv | Our Mission is:

1. "To proclaim Jesus, the Savior of the whole world, from the whole Bible, because He is wonderful!"

2. Indeed, we are constrained by the love of God, to communicate the rawness of the Bible to real people, in real ways, and our driving and major project of '66Cities' shall take us to the 66 most influential cities of the 250 nations of the world in the next 25 years. That's 16,500 cities!

3. We are aiming to build relationships with grass roots, real people, that is, ordinary people, who, in their own countries and cities, want to do extraordinary things for Jesus and the Kingdom of God, to bring a Biblical Gospel message that is relevant to now, in a world that has come to believe that Jesus is irrelevant to their lives.

If you would like to partner with us in this great task. Then we want to hear from you! Contact me today on vr@66books.tv

MORE ABOUT 'THE 66 BOOKS MINISTRY'

WWW.66Cities.com | By the year 2047, by the grace of God and according to His will and favor, The 66 Books Ministry shall be preaching consecutively from each of the 66 Books of the Holy Bible, the Gospel of the Lord Jesus Christ in 16,500 of the most influential cities of the world on an annual and ongoing basis!

We do not underestimate the quality teams of trained people that this will take, together with the need for vast amount of materials and finances which will also have to be raised. However, as most futurists indicate that the growing global population will be gathered mostly in major world cities in the coming years, there is a necessity laid upon the church to present and proclaim the God of the whole Bible, through the primacy of preaching in these cities. We are convinced that this is a paramount and pressing concern.

"For since, in the wisdom of God, the world through wisdom did not know God, it pleased God through the foolishness of the message preached to save those who believe" 1 Corinthians 1:21NKJV

"Preach the Word! Be ready in season and out of season. Convince, rebuke, exhort, with all longsuffering and teaching." 2 Timothy 4:2NKJV

The church is looking for a revival. The 66 Books Ministry, however, is trying to start a revolution of a return to the preached Word, from the whole of the Bible as a precursor to any and all coming revival.

For "whoever calls on the name of the Lord shall be saved." How then shall they call on Him in whom they have not believed? And how shall they believe in Him of whom they have not heard? And how shall they hear without a preacher? And how shall they preach unless they are sent? As it is written: "How beautiful are the feet of those who preach the gospel of peace, Who bring glad tidings of good things!" Romans 10:13-15 NKJV

We are unashamedly looking for and seeking to foster a massive, huge, releasing, transformative, and exceptionally disruptive reversal and revolutionary change, both within the church and then in the world. We are not just another mission trying to do the same as every other mission. We are intent on revolution!

To this revolutionary end, we have no fear of seeming failure and will cultivate that audacious atmosphere within our ministry. We want to attract grass roots people who are people of faith risk takers, for we believe it is people of such life hazarding attitudes that are used by God to make breakthroughs in the world for the Kingdom of God. Hanging back for fear of seeming failure, hanging back and waiting for the trained professionals, both wastes the time of the church time and kills the spirit of victory.

In that spirit then, we therefore are believing that this task can be accomplished by such people within the time frame we have given ourselves.

Fully assured then, that we are in full obedience with the great commission of our great God and Savior Jesus Christ, we do, with great confidence in Him, turn ourselves happily to this so great a task in the hope that, like a happy hound straining at the leash to be let loose, we believe that many other people will smile along with us and be part of this brand new grass roots 21st Century Global City Mission.

If you want to know more and want to be part of what we are doing then go to www.The66BooksMinistry.com or call us in the USA on **855 662 6657**, or email V.R. directly on vr@66Books.TV

AUTHOR BIO | PURPLE ROBERT

It won't take too much investigation for you to find out that Purple Robert is in fact, Victor Robert Farrell (Born 1960 and alive until now and still kicking) was born in Chesterfield England to Scottish parents with Irish grandparents, which is an obvious recipe both for writing and emotional disaster if ever there was one!

He grew up a culturally excluded Roman Catholic (his parents were divorced,) which is one of the reasons why he hates religion with a passion, and that's an interesting enough fact by itself, because he is also an ordained protestant minister to boot.

Purple Robert. became a Christian whilst serving on board a Polaris Submarine at the end of the cold war. He has gone on to do many things, including being a broadcaster, App developer, performance poet, and the long-time author of 'Night Whispers,' which is read in over 100 counties and is also translated into Spanish (see www.Night Whispers.com)

Currently, Purple Robert is also President of The 66 Books Ministry: a grass roots global city mission endeavor. I suppose it is this concoction of background and experience which means Purple Robert's communication is always raw and emotive. After all, and as he says, *"If Christianity can be relevant on a Monday morning, several hundred feet underneath an unknown ocean, in a pornographic sewer pipe carrying enough nuclear weapons to destroy a continent whilst hiding from the Russians, then it can be relevant anywhere and everywhere!"*

Purple Robert sees himself as a servant of the 'Word of the Lord' to tasked communicate the God of the whole Bible. His proclamation of the same is done in very raw terms to very real people, is both his burden and his passion.

| May 26th | Reading 147 of 366 |

MORNING → | HISTORICAL BOOKS

BOOK 11 of 66 → | 1 KINGS 16,17

Signpost Words → | "AN ANSWER"

Highlight Verses → | 1 Kings 16:31-34

And it came to pass, as though it had been a trivial thing for him to walk in the sins of Jeroboam the son of Nebat, that he took as wife Jezebel the daughter of Ethbaal, king of the Sidonians; and he went and served Baal and worshiped him. Then he set up an altar for Baal in the temple of Baal, which he had built in Samaria. And Ahab made a wooden image. Ahab did more to provoke the Lord God of Israel to anger than all the kings of Israel who were before him. In his days Hiel of Bethel built Jericho. He laid its foundation with Abiram his firstborn, and with his youngest son Segub he set up its gates, according to the word of the Lord, which He had spoken through Joshua the son of Nun. NKJV

Some Observations → |

This is nothing but an extended killing time, and it is God who is slaughtering His wayward nation. Decade after decade the decadent mobster kings steer the people more and more out of the way of the Lord. Dogs lick up the blood from slaughtered corpses, birds peck the watery eyeballs out of the maggot eaten heads. Death and destruction stalk the land, yet still the people rise up to pray to an idle and engage in sexual sin. The mercy of God is seen on two legs and heard from one mouth, even the prophets of the Lord. Now, dropped from heaven, out of nowhere, in answer to the madness of Ahab the loon, a prophet like no other arrives on the scene. Elijah the Tishbite!

A Call To Action → |

Fine pulpits and finer churches, are rarely the abode of the prophet.

EVENING → | PAULINE EPISTLES

BOOK 46 of 66 → | 1 CORINTHIANS 15

Signpost Words → | "ASSURANCE OF SALVATION"

Highlight Verses → | 1 Corinthians 15:1-11

Moreover, brethren, I declare to you the gospel which I preached to you, which also you received and in which you stand, by which also you are saved, if you hold fast that word which I preached to you — unless you believed in vain. For I delivered to you first of all that which I also received: that Christ died for our sins according to the Scriptures, and that He was buried, and that He rose again the third day according to the Scriptures, and that He was seen by Cephas, then by the twelve. After that He was seen by over five hundred brethren at once, of whom the greater part remain to the present, but some have fallen asleep. After that He was seen by James, then by all the apostles. Then last of all He was seen by me also, as by one born out of due time. For I am the least of the apostles, who am not worthy to be called an apostle, because I persecuted the church of God. But by the grace of God I am what I am, and His grace toward me was not in vain; but I labored more abundantly than they all, yet not I, but the grace of God which was with me.... NKJV

Some Observations → |

The two 'wee' words we Evangelicals dislike to discourse upon are 'if' and 'unless.' I believe that once we are saved we are always saved, 'IF' we continue on receiving, believing and standing. I believe that once we are saved we are always saved, 'UNLESS' we prove ourselves to be unfaithful and reprobate in forsaking the Christ of the Scriptures. Paul did not believe he was saved by our works, yet by grace he worked his little heine off!

A Call To Action → |

Continuance in the work of grace is the key to your own assurance.

JOIN THE FELLOWSHIP OF THE BOOK

WWW.TheFellowShipofTheBook.com

The Fellowship of The Book is a Daily Bible Reading Fellowship. It is a morning and evening devotional of four books available each quarter of the year. It includes

Signpost Words
Highlight Verses
Some Observations
Call To Action

Consecutively, Chronologically and in many other ways, Read The Bible Thru in 1 just one year, with both Morning and Evening reading to keep your mind focused on the Lord of the Word and the Word of The Lord. Buy this and several other ways to 'Read the Bible Thru in a Year Books' at www.whisperingword.com

ANOTHER BOOK BY THE AUTHOR, VR

Habakkuk A Prophecy For Our Time

As the Church in the West is found to be mostly dead and covered with Laodicean lukewarm vomit, as The Lord, slips the dead things silently over the side of the storm tossed ship into the dark oblivion of the waves of secular humanism and rising Islam, what remains will need to be fortified with steel to live in a quickly changing anti-Christian world of persecution. There is no better prophecy more equipped to speak to such a remnant who shall be so very besieged. Welcome to Habakkuk, 35 of 66, a prophecy for our time.

Buy at www.whisperingword.com

ANOTHER BOOK BY THE AUTHOR, VR

The 66-Minute Bible

I am told that there are 788,258 words in the King James Bible and of these 14,565 are unique. That's a lot of words! I have been reading the Bible for nearly forty years on an almost daily basis. It still remains to me the most exciting book on the planet, however, it never gets any easier. Bible reading is a spiritual discipline and for me the emphasis is on discipline. I created this resource to aid you in your Bible reading, it gives your brain a sixty second overview of the Bible, a loose enclosure to herd the narrative of the book into something that can be seen as a whole. It was never created to be a substitute, but an aid. Just saying…… Friends, welcome to the most exciting book on the planet! V.R.

Buy at www.whisperingword.com

AN INTRODUCTION TO 'PURPLE ROBERT'

Some Dangerously Different Devotionals!

Now, before I go any further, this guy comes with warning shots! The opening parts of his currently seven volumes pf poetic works says quite clearly, *"If you are easily offended by low level expletives...**Go no further. Do not read this book!** If you are prudish in any way ...**Go no further. Do not read this book!** If you do not want to be challenged...**Go no further. Do not read this book!** If you want to be stroked into unchanging sleep and into the stupor of remaining as you are...**Go no further. Do not read this book!** If you hide under the respectable covers of a comfortable religion...**Go no further. Do not read this book!** If you are frail in faith and dishonest about life under this sun...**Go no further.** If you have no real integrity regarding the state of your own heart,* **then do not read this book!** *If however, you are grown up, honest and have a basic human integrity, ENJOY!"* So, there you go, you have been warned!

Purple Robert is a Performance Poet and a Metaphysical Biblical Realist. If you want to hear some of his work and get hold of the 66 Poems each of the Seven volumes contain, then go to www.PurpleRobert.com and purchase them today.

Also Buy at Buy at www.TheologyShop.com

www.ingramcontent.com/pod-product-compliance
Lightning Source LLC
Chambersburg PA
CBHW031613160426
43196CB00006B/122